Infield Fly Rule
Is in Effect

Infield Fly Rule Is in Effect

The History and Strategy of Baseball's Most (In)Famous Rule

HOWARD M. WASSERMAN

McFarland & Company, Inc., Publishers
Jefferson, North Carolina

Library of Congress Cataloguing-in-Publication Data

Names: Wasserman, Howard M., author.
Title: Infield fly rule is in effect : the history and strategy of baseball's most (in)famous rule / Howard M. Wasserman.
Description: Jefferson, North Carolina : McFarland & Company, Inc., Publishers, 2019 | Includes bibliographical references and index.
Identifiers: LCCN 2018048497 | ISBN 9781476667157 (softcover : acid free paper) ♾
Subjects: LCSH: Baseball—Rules. | Fielding (Baseball)
Classification: LCC GV877 .W37 2019 | DDC 796.35724—dc23
LC record available at https://lccn.loc.gov/2018048497

British Library cataloguing data are available

ISBN (print) 978-1-4766-6715-7
ISBN (ebook) 978-1-4766-3428-9

Front cover: Derek Jeter settles under a pop-up, which the umpire declares an infield fly, July 30, 2014, © 2019 JamesBond/Flickr; *background*: baseball diamond © 2019 gigello/iStock

Printed in the United States of America

McFarland & Company, Inc., Publishers
Box 611, Jefferson, North Carolina 28640
www.mcfarlandpub.com

To Jen, who is perfect
and does understand the Infield Fly Rule,
and to Lily, who is learning it
at just the right age

Table of Contents

Acknowledgments

This book would not have happened without the many legal scholars who preceded me in the study of the Infield Fly Rule and made it an issue of legal-academic inquiry. Special mention to the late William Stevens, who in 1975 wrote the article that inspired generations of law professors and legal scholars to think and write about the Rule.

Thanks to Spencer Weber Waller, Alex Pearl, Steve Treder, and Mitchell Berman for reading and commenting on early drafts of this book as well as earlier iterations of these arguments. Special thanks to the Honorable Andrew Guilford, baseball fan and United States district judge, for comments on early drafts, for provocative email exchanges, and for serving as scholarly interlocutor on the Infield Fly Rule and other baseball subjects.

I published several early versions of the arguments that form this book. Significant publications include *Just a Bit Aside: Perverse Incentives, Cost-Benefit Imbalances, and the Infield Fly Rule*, 164 U. PENN. L. REV. ONLINE 145 (2016); *An Empirical Analysis of the Infield Fly Rule*, 4 J.L. (3 J. LEGAL METRICS) 127 (2014); *Football and the Infield Fly Rule*, 61 UCLA L. REV. DISCOURSE 272 (2014); *The Economics of the Infield Fly Rule*, UTAH L. REV. 479 (2013); and *In Defense of Baseball's Infield Fly Rule*, THE ATLANTIC (2012). I also have written countless posts on the Infield Fly Rule and other sports rules at my blogging homes, PrawfsBlawg (http://prawfsblawg.blogs.com/) and Sports Law Blog (http://sports-law.blogspot.com/). I thank the many readers whose comments on early posts inspired this broader project and who have helped me to sharpen what became the analytical framework for explaining and defending the Infield Fly Rule and expanding it to other sports. I presented several early papers on these ideas at the annual Cooperstown Symposium on Baseball and American Culture and the annual NINE Spring Training Conference; thanks to participants of both conferences for their input.

Thanks to Jim Evans, Rich Marazzi, and Brent Rice for sitting for telephone and email interviews and for sharing their thoughts and experiences with the Rule as umpires, teachers, and rules commentators.

Chapter 5 would not have been possible without the team of current and former students of FIU College of Law who helped with the empirical portion of the study; several have told me this was the most fun they had in law school and that it made great interview fodder. From the Class of 2014: Brittany Tarazona. From the Class of 2015: Mark Erdman, Megan Gil, Sara Gordils, Daniel Horton, Alejandro Leiva, and Ryan Maguire. From the Class of 2017: Ashley Allison, Sebastian Bohorquez, Rachel Gonzalez, Andrew Gordon, Astrid Menendez, Erica Weintraub, and Robert Young. From the Class of 2018: Tucker Pryor. From the Class of 2019: Alanah Drennan, Angelique Gulla, Megan Labgold, and David Martellino. Kristian True provided additional assistance. Veronica Torres organized the charts, graphs, and images.

The advent of advanced metrics has led to numerous online sources that record and calculate statistics and metrics, data that I applied to measure the empirics of the Rule. In calculating Run Expectancy, I used the *Custom Statistics Report: Run Expectation*, available at http://www.baseballpros pectus.com/sortable/index.php?cid=975409. In calculating Win Expectancy, I used the win expectancy calculator from gregstoll.com, https://gregstoll. dyndns.org/~gregstoll/baseball/stats.html#V.0.1.0.1. In identifying statistics for non-infield-fly comparators, I relied on Baseball Reference's Play Index/ Batting Events, https://www.baseball-reference.com/play-index/event_ finder.cgi?type=b. I found game reports and play-by-plays at RetroSheet, http://www.retrosheet.org/ and at Baseball Reference, http://www.baseball-reference.com/.

For editing and proofreading assistance on the manuscript, thanks to Josefine Blick, Shannon Crosby, Tal Knight, Tucker Pryor, and Cori Varsallone, all FIU College of Law Class of 2018.

Thanks to Gary Mitchem and everyone at McFarland & Company for supporting me in this project.

Thanks to the Honorable R. Alexander Acosta, former dean of FIU College of Law, who did not need much convincing that the Infield Fly Rule was an appropriate subject for legal scholarship. Thanks to Tawia Ansah, former interim dean of FIU College of Law and Antony Page, current dean of FIU College of Law, for supporting me through the final stages of the project.

Lawrence Wasserman[Z"L] taught me the Infield Fly Rule more than 40 years ago, so this project would not have been possible without him. Thanks to Iris Wasserman, for making me a baseball fan.

Preface

This book begins with an obvious question—why? Why an entire book about the Infield Fly Rule and only that Rule? Why an entire book about a single rule known by name to all baseball fans; understood by only some of those baseball fans (and almost certainly fewer of those fans than believe they understand it[1]); criticized by many baseball fans from its inception[2] and more so in recent years[3]; and perceived by non-baseball fans as complicated to the point of incomprehensibility? As journalist and baseball fan John Dickerson put it, the "Catholic Church has no papal decree so complicated and misapplied as the infield fly rule."[4]

And if the Infield Fly Rule is worthy of an entire book, why would a legal academic write it?

The moment I learned the Rule remains one of my clearest and most distinct childhood memories. I was about eight or nine years old in the late 1970s, a newly minted baseball fan living in New Jersey and enjoying the New York Yankees of Reggie Jackson and Thurman Munson that won five division titles, four American League pennants, and two World Series in six years.[5] (I became a Chicago Cubs fan during and after college in Chicago, perhaps as atonement for early fan success.) We were driving from my grandparents' home in Brooklyn, listening to a game on the radio. A fly ball was hit on the infield and the Yankee announcer said, "Infield Fly Rule is in effect," the common phrase play-by-play announcers employ to describe a play on which the umpire has invoked the Rule—and which gives this book its title.

I asked my father what that meant and he explained, in understandable (and, looking back, largely accurate) terms, the Infield Fly Rule: When the batting team has runners on first-and-second or the bases loaded with less than two out and the batter hits an easily playable fly ball to an infielder, the batter is out and the runners can advance at their own risk. He went no further than that. He did not discuss infielder subterfuge. He did not discuss helpless baserunners who are "up a tree"[6] and unable to know whether to run or not. He did not discuss the possibility of a "cheap"[7] double play resulting from an infielder intentionally not catching the fly ball. He did not mention how calling the batter out eliminates the force play on the runners. In any event, I doubt my eight-year-old self could have understood the details or asked about the underlying policy preferences.

But it was enough. I was hooked. I knew and could explain the Infield Fly Rule in those simple general terms. I also sensed that this rule provided entrée into baseball knowledge—a code for those in the know about the game. To understand and explain the Infield Fly Rule is to truly understand, truly love, and truly "speak" baseball.[8] Of the game's interlocking complex of rules, the Infield Fly Rule is recognizable by name. Anyone who understands it, and appreciates it, must be a true and knowledgeable baseball fan. And those knowledgeable baseball fans know how to find one another.

Cartoonist Ron Morgan captured the sentiment:

"She's perfect! She even understands the
Infield Fly Rule."

© Ron Morgan. Reprinted with permission.

My fascination with the Infield Fly Rule remained inchoate until I reached law school in the mid–1990s. There I discovered that sport, particularly baseball, occupies a unique space in law and in the legal academy.

Which makes sense. Sport involves a system of organizing rules—laws—that must be understood, interpreted, and applied by those playing and supervising the game, within an adjudicative process allowing the games to proceed.[9] Sport contains such "essential institutional features as legislatures, adjudicators, and the union of primary and secondary rules."[10] In fact, soccer, cricket, and rugby—ever-different than games at the core of American life—are expressly governed by "laws" rather than "rules."[11] Understanding sports rules can help us understand ordinary law and ordinary legal systems. Legal scholar Mitchell Berman calls this the "jurisprudence of sport": "Sport warrants and repays exacting analysis. This is partly because sports present intellectual problems that are intrinsically interesting and challenging, and partly because those problems are often structurally analogous, sometimes structurally identical, to problems that arise in domains of life of greater intrinsic importance."[12] Berman has recently worked with another legal scholar, Richard Friedman, to write a book and design a law-school course studying sports as legal systems.[13]

Just as law can be grounded in a complex interaction of cost-benefit considerations and incentives and disincentives to conduct for society at large,[14] sports rules create a framework for the game, with the cost-benefit exchanges in a game situation incentivizing players to act or not act in certain ways. To take a simple example: A pitcher wanting to retaliate for his teammate having been hit by a pitch may be less likely to do so if the retaliation results in the tying run scoring or the retaliating pitcher's ejection from the game.[15] Or if the pitcher must appear at the plate in a game or league played without a designated hitter.

Baseball is, and long has been, unique among sports as a target of jurisprudence-of-sport analysis, for using "legal insights to inform the world of baseball and baseball insights to inform the world of law."[16] One scholar argues that law and baseball form a unique field of interdisciplinary study.[17] A federal judge, mourning the absence of baseball from his life during the 1994–95 player strike and the cancellation of the 1994 World Series, linked baseball to an ordinary water-law case by peppering his opinion with footnotes and baseball-related tangential musings.[18]

In the introduction to *Baseball and the American Legal Mind*, a compilation of essays and materials exploring the intersection of law and baseball, editors (and legal scholars) Spencer Weber Waller, Neil Cohen, and Paul Finkelman explain that "baseball is a highly legalistic game with a far more elaborate set of rules than any other sport."[19] These rules are inflexible, inconsistent, and complicated, making their interpretation an especially complex task.[20] In baseball, every pitch and every play requires a ruling.[21] We could imagine a long stretch in a basketball game in which teams exchange baskets, missed shots, and rebounds on both ends of the floor, with the clock moving, players running from one end to the other, and officials making no calls or signals. Such a stretch with no formal pronouncements from a game official, even if only to establish the obvious (the pitch is a strike, the batter is out on a caught fly ball), is impossible and unimaginable in baseball.

Legal scholars explain statutory interpretation through the changing strike zone[22] or the infamous George Brett Pine Tar Game in 1983.[23] A famous (if apocryphal) baseball story about a discussion among three umpires explains competing models of judging—one umpire says, "I call them as I see 'em"; one umpire says, "I call 'em as they are"; and one umpire says, "They ain't nothing until I call 'em."[24]

It is no accident that Chief Justice John H. Roberts—searching during his 2005 Senate confirmation hearing for a sports metaphor for his vision of judging—turned to baseball, umpires, and balls-and-strikes:

> Judges are like umpires. Umpires don't make the rules, they apply them. The role of an umpire and a judge is critical. They make sure everybody plays by the rules, but it is a limited role. Nobody ever went to a ball game to see the umpire.
> I will remember that it's my job to call balls and strikes, and not to pitch or bat.[25]

Roberts was criticized for an overly simplistic vision of both judging and umpiring.[26] The point for our purposes is that he chose an umpire calling balls and strikes rather than, for example, a football referee calling pass interference, a basketball referee calling a late-game foul,[27] or a soccer official calling Offside[28] (the last obviously would not have flown in an American political arena).

Within this baseball-centric world of law and legal academia, the Infield Fly Rule occupies its own pedestal. Its pride of place begins with 1975 publication of *Aside: The Common Law Origins of the Infield Fly Rule*, an unsigned student work in the UNIVERSITY OF PENNSYLVANIA LAW REVIEW,[29] later attributed to William Stevens, who went on to a successful career as an attorney.[30] In eight lighthearted pages, Stevens described the Rule's origins, history, and evolution, then analogized that evolution to development of the Common Law and Common Law rules. Many baseball fans *cum* legal academics, no doubt regretting not thinking of the idea first, rushed to respond, recast, and rebuild on the interpretive power of the Infield Fly Rule.[31] Waller and Cohen argued at a different point that "[l]egal scholars simply cannot keep their hands off the infield fly rule—either substantively or as a metaphor."[32] Commentators have used the Rule to illustrate all manner of judicial issues, concepts, developments, and rules.[33] Judges have done the same in deciding cases, comparing the Infield Fly Rule to the rules for initiating civil litigation or for proving sexual harassment,[34] even where the analogy did not work. And to return from legal metaphor to baseball rule, one federal judge and his law clerk took the time, on those same pages of University of Pennsylvania Law Review, to criticize the Rule as part of baseball and to urge its repeal.[35]

This legal and scholarly fascination (obsession?) confirms my childhood instinct about the Infield Fly Rule as the entrée to baseball and as the mark of one in the know about the game. Perhaps it is the Rule's complexity and perceived incomprehensibility in which attorneys revel. Perhaps it is because everyone believes they understand the Rule, but most do not—as rules analyst and consultant Rich Marazzi wrote, asking someone to explain the Infield Fly Rule produces answers that "vary from amusing to absurd."[36] Perhaps it is because the Rule is not intrinsic to baseball. It is not like using a bat to hit the ball or running around the bases. Recall the manager in the great *Bull Durham*, who insisted, "This is a simple game. You throw the ball, you catch the ball, you hit the ball."[37] He did not mention the Infield Fly Rule—which turns on not catching the ball, declining to do the simple thing around which the game is built. Baseball without the Infield Fly Rule still would be recognizable as baseball; it would not, Stevens wrote, devolve into "bladderball."[38] Perhaps it rests on the Rule's perceived uniqueness, the belief that it is a specialized rule covering a specialized situation, with no parallel elsewhere in baseball or in any other sport. The Infield Fly Rule stands alone, offering an inviting target for study.

While past study has used the Infield Fly Rule as a metaphor or lens to explore broader ideas about law and legal rules, my goal in these pages is the inverse—to use legal ideas to explore the Infield Fly Rule as it relates to itself, to baseball, and to other sports. I have several goals for this book. I show that the Rule is explicable, understandable, and necessary to a functional way of playing baseball; it is not unique or anomalous in its underlying logic, either within baseball or within other sports. Even if baseball without the Infield Fly Rule would be recognizable as baseball, it would be an inferior version of baseball. I defend the Rule as part of the internal rules, strategy, logic, ethos, and structure of baseball. I show the pervasiveness and effect of similar rules resting on similar ideas in baseball and in other sports. And I provide a framework for understanding and identifying game situations in which infield-fly-type rules are necessary and proper and those in which such rules are unnecessary or inappropriate.

This book is 40 years in the making, hearkening to that car ride in which I first learned the Rule. In the pages that follow, I combine my rudimentary understanding of the Infield Fly Rule of 1977 with the knowledge and analytical skills I have gained as a lawyer and legal scholar. I hope to use them to paint a full picture of the history and development of the Rule as law, of its place in baseball, and of the place of its underlying ideas throughout baseball and all sport.

For you, the reader, I hope it is worth the ride.

Introduction

An infield fly is "a fair fly ball (not including a line dive nor an attempted bunt) which can be caught by an infielder with ordinary effort, when first and second, or first, second and third bases are occupied, before two are out."[1] Ordinary effort means "the effort that a fielder of average skill at a position in that league or classification of leagues should exhibit on a play, with due consideration given to the condition of the field and weather conditions."[2] If a batter hits an infield fly, as defined, the batter is out, the runners are not forced to advance, although they may run at their own risk.[3]

The accepted, and logical, justification for the Rule is that it prevents the defense from turning a "cheap" double play by an act of defensive deception.[4] Without the Rule, an infielder could intentionally not catch that easily playable fly ball, then turn a double (or even triple) play on force-outs on the baserunners (not the batter), who would be unable to beat the throws to the next bases. Because the batter is out under the Infield Fly Rule, regardless of whether the ball is caught, the baserunners are not forced to advance, removing the possibility of a force-out double play involving them.

On paper, that all sounds simple and straightforward, both in definition and rationale. While baseball has had the Rule for one season in 1890 and continuously since the mid–1890s, it was not often remarked upon; it was simply part of the game. As discussed in the Preface, it was a source of fascination for judges and legal scholars, including myself. But baseball fans seemed to accept it without much discussion, notice, or, arguably, understanding.[5]

Public discussion and perception changed in the bottom of the eighth inning of the 2012 National League Wildcard Game, on one infield fly that thrust the Rule back into fan consciousness and the baseball conversation. That play also triggered my interest in writing about the Rule, leading to this book.

The St. Louis Cardinals faced the Atlanta Braves in Atlanta. Trailing 6–3, the Braves had runners on first-and-second/one-out. A high fly ball was hit into shallow left field, a fair distance from the infield dirt. Cardinal shortstop Pete Kozma chased the ball onto the outfield grass and appeared to be settled under it, facing the infield, waving his arms, and waiting for the ball to come down. Without warning, he ran forward and away from the ball, which fell in the area he had vacated, at the feet of leftfielder Matt Holliday charging in from behind and to Kozma's left. It appeared that Kozma ran off when he heard Holliday coming from behind. The baserunners, both of whom had moved halfway to the next bases, advanced easily.

Umpire Sam Holbrook, stationed along the leftfield line (post-season games use crews of six umpires, with an umpire in the outfield along each foul line), invoked the Infield Fly Rule, declaring the batter out, with the runners advancing on the live ball. Rather than having bases loaded with one out and the go-ahead run at the plate, the Braves ended the play with runners on second and third with two out. The call triggered confusion among the teams and a protest of the play (which Major League Baseball summarily rejected[6]). It also triggered outrage among Braves fans, who threw debris onto the field, delaying the game for almost 20 minutes. It all short-circuited a Braves rally; they did not score in the inning and lost the game by the same 6–3 score.[7]

Sports media spent the following days debating the play and the correctness of the call. Initial reaction was critical,[8] although many criticisms reflected common misunderstandings about the Rule. "He was not in the infield," some said—not recognizing that the umpire is not to apply the Rule "by some arbitrary limitation such as the grass."[9] The "umpire waited too long to make the call," others said—although the umpire may be unable to determine whether a fly ball is playable with ordinary effort until it is on its descent or almost in the fielder's glove, and some umpires believe the proper time to invoke the Rule is when the ball is on its downward flight.

Harold Reynolds, a former Major League infielder and at the time commentator at ESPN, defended the call in detail. He dissected the video, showing how and when Kozma was sufficiently settled under the ball to catch it with ordinary effort and how and when the umpire recognized that and made the call. Reynolds found and analyzed a comparable play from a 2012 regular-season game between the Philadelphia Phillies and Chicago Cubs, in which the Cubs shortstop went similarly far into shallow left field and the umpire waited similarly long to declare infield fly until the shortstop had stopped running back and was stationary and waiting for the ball to come down into his glove for the easy catch. Consensus soon developed that Holbrook got it right—or at least that his call was not unreasonable.[10]

Criticism in some corners shifted from the correctness of this call to the general wisdom and logic of the Infield Fly Rule, with some urging that the Rule was outdated, unwarranted, unnecessary, and ripe for repeal. Many questioned the Rule's wisdom in its early days, when players resisted the idea of not having to catch a batted ball for an out and everyone—fans, players, and umpires—was trying to figure it out.[11] But the Internet amplifies voices. A short-lived web site called "Abolish the IFR" offered a host of arguments for the Rule's repeal. I wrote several online pieces about that call, offering embryonic versions of the arguments that form the basis of this book, to which readers responded with criticisms of the Rule's existence.[12] Why, people wondered, have the Infield Fly Rule, but no special rule for many other baseball situations that (superficially) resemble the infield-fly situation? Why, people wondered, is there no equivalent of the Infield Fly Rule in other sports, and does that not suggest that it does not belong in baseball? These reactions surprised me, as they upended my long-standing presumption that everyone revered the Infield Fly Rule as much as I and other legal scholars did. Three years later, Judge Andrew Guilford, a baseball- and Los Angeles Dodgers–loving judge on the United States District Court for the Central District of California, and Joel Mallord, his law clerk at the time, co-authored the first sustained, reasoned, scholarly argument for repeal in the pages of University of Pennsylvania Law Review[13]—ironically, and intentionally, the journal that published William Stevens' original *Aside*, launched the Infield Fly Rule into the legal canon, and stirred legal and academic interest in the Rule.

There is and has been no serious discussion within Major League Baseball or among its officials to repeal or rethink the Infield Fly Rule; the Rule is not going anywhere. Nevertheless, the matter is joined, even if only in the pages of law journals and in certain corners of the Internet.

Baseball is in a unique period. The 2003 publication of the book *Moneyball*[14] and the rise of advanced metrics for understanding and evaluating baseball[15] have changed how the game is played on the field, how teams make personnel decisions and otherwise manage themselves, the in-game strategies that offenses and defenses employ, and how fans watch and understand the game. The stolen base and the sacrifice bunt have fallen from grace, in favor of working counts and getting on base by any means.[16] Infields increasingly employ dramatic shifts against pull hitters, stationing three infielders on one side of second base and leaving one player to cover the entire rest of the infield, or stationing the second baseman in shallow right field against left-handed power hitters.[17] The game is increasingly dominated by the three true outcomes of strikeouts, home runs, and walks, the three outcomes that reflect the one-on-one battle between pitcher and batter, with no influence from the other eight defensive players.[18]

Changes to the way the game is played prompt rule changes or discussion of rule changes—sometimes to halt a development, other times to codify it, other times to correct perceived defects in the game. MLB has considered limiting defensive shifts to reduce the effect of that strategy, in hopes of expanding offense and increasing scoring.[19] MLB now requires baserunners to slide into home rather than crash into the catcher, eliminating collisions out of a greater awareness of player health and safety.[20] MLB has created and altered rules to speed games and prevent players from delaying play, with the goal of making the game more attractive to fans living in a faster culture. Rules limit the number of mound visits and the time of inning breaks and pitching changes.[21] Baseball has considered, but not yet adopted, a pitch clock. Beginning in 2017, a batter is awarded first base on an intentional walk on a signal from the fielding team's dugout, without the pitcher having to intentionally throw four pitches outside the strike zone.[22] The "Batter's Box Rule" requires a batter to keep one foot in the batter's box throughout an at-bat and prohibits players from delaying the game by leaving the box, at the risk of an umpire warning and league discipline.[23] MLB lowered the pitcher's mound following the 1968 season to correct a perceived overwhelming imbalance in favor of pitching and against hitting.[24]

Some of these changes have triggered complaints from fans, old-time players, and others, who view the changes as confusing, as softening the game, and as pointless. The merits of these changes aside, the modern game, and the unique concerns and ideas involved, creates room for changes in strategy and thus in rules.

With so much of the game being rethought, there is no reason not to turn our attention to the venerated Infield Fly Rule. Perhaps, as Guilford and Mallord argue, the rules should leave infielders free to seek double plays by not catching fair fly balls and should leave baserunners free to dare them to do so, allowing us to see what strategy and excitement results.[25]

This book praises the Infield Fly Rule, rather than burying it. The Rule's rationales, justifications, and defenses hold, even in the modern game. The Rule remains as necessary and appropriate in 2018 as in 1894, when the powers-that-be decided they did, in fact, need a special rule for this game situation. Even if baseball remains recognizable as baseball without the Infield Fly Rule, it is better baseball with it. None of the arguments and criticisms offered against the Rule (distinct from criticisms of one call in the 2012 NLWC or concerns about application of the Rule on particular plays) withstands scrutiny. This book explains why that is.

Defending the Infield Fly Rule does not mean not rethinking it and its foundations. The Rule originated in 19th-century conceptions of sportsmanship and amateurism—the defense should not get a "cheap" double play through deception and subterfuge that strategically exploits holes in the rules in a situation in which the baserunners have no chance.[26] Those policy concerns fail as modern justifications. Our conceptions of sportsmanship have evolved, as baseball long ago became a professional sport in which the goal is to win the game, irrespective of gentlemanliness.[27] And we recognize, accept, and even celebrate subterfuge and deception throughout baseball.[28] As baseball executive (and scion of a baseball family) Andy MacPhail said in 2003, "There is a culture of deception in this game. It's been in this game for 100 years. I do not look at this in terms of ethics. It's the culture of the game."[29] If baseball accepts deception in other areas of the game, there is no reason to reject it with respect to double plays on uncaught infield fly balls.

But the loss of the anti-deception and anti-subterfuge justifications does not compel repeal of the Rule. It remains justified for other reasons resting on other foundations, reasons that do not turn on outdated notions of sportsmanship, amateurism, and the proper conduct of the gentleman-athlete.

My goal is to reverse-engineer the Infield Fly Rule—beginning from its existence, exploring the Rule and the circumstances in which it applies, and determining what makes those situations sufficiently unique to warrant a unique rule. What I propose and defend in the following pages is that the special features of the game situation in which the Infield Fly Rule arises together create particular and peculiar problems within the game that demand a particular and peculiar rule.

Recall the elements of what I label an "infield-fly situation"—runners on first and second or bases loaded, less than two out, and a fair fly ball that is easily playable by an infielder. Four characteristics together define this game situation. They create a framework that justifies the Infield Fly Rule and that can evaluate other baseball situations for the need for analogous special rules, and that can evaluate situations in other sports for the need for analogous special rules.

I sketch the four characteristics here, then explore them in detail throughout the book.

(1) One side of the play (in this case the fielding team) intentionally acts contrary to ordinary athletic expectations, failing to perform the expected athletic skills in the expected manner and in the way players ordinarily want to perform them. That side intentionally fails to seek "excellence in executing the particular athletic virtues that the sport is centrally designed to showcase and reward."[30] Without the Infield Fly Rule, the infielder intentionally fails to catch an easily playable fair fly ball, something he ordinarily wants to do and ordinarily does and something that he fails to do here only by intentionally acting contrary to athletic expectations.

(2) The play produces a one-sided, extraordinary, and inequitable cost-benefit disparity, with one side gaining overwhelming benefits while incurring few or no meaningful costs and the other side incurring overwhelming costs while gaining no meaningful benefits. Without the Infield Fly Rule, the defense gets a double play and perhaps a triple play rather than one out on the fly ball, while the offense incurs multiple outs, loses baserunners, and may see the end of its turn at bat.

(3) There is extraordinary and one-sided disparity in the power of each team to control or influence the play. One team (the defense) controls the play, the other (the offense) is powerless to counter or respond to its strategic move.

(4) The combination of (2) and (3) gives the advantaged team the perverse incentive to act on (1) most or even every time the game situation arises. Without the Infield Fly Rule, the potential for the benefits of a double (or triple) play on an intentional non-catch and the inability of the offense to stop or counter that move incentivizes infielders to intentionally not catch the easily playable fair fly ball whenever an infield-fly situation arises.

The confluence of these four characteristics in a game situation necessitates a special rule to prevent one team from gaining these extraordinary and one-sided benefits. I call these "limiting rules," because they limit a team's strategic options and its ability to seek or gain that inequitable cost-benefit advantage. Limiting rules operate in one of two ways. The rule might expressly prohibit a team from intentionally acting contrary to ordinary athletic expectations. Or it might impose a specific outcome on the play, eliminating the potential cost-benefit advantage to be gained, thereby eliminating the perverse incentive to intentionally act contrary to athletic expectations. The Infield Fly Rule adopts the latter approach. By calling the batter out and not forcing the baserunners to advance, it removes the possibility of a force-out double play on the baserunners. With no non-tag double play in the offing, the defense gains no advantage by not catching the easily playable fair fly ball; with no advantage to be gained, the perverse incentive to intentionally not catch the fair fly ball disappears.

This four-prong framework analyzes and explains many game situations to determine when a limiting rule is warranted and when it is not. The key is the presence of all defining characteristics. A limiting rule is required only when all four are present in a play, as with the infield-fly situation. If one or more characteristics is absent, no limiting rule is necessary or appropriate; the situation can be left to ordinary rules, practices, and strategies, as teams compete for advantages on plays.

Critics of the Infield Fly Rule begin from the premise that the infield-fly situation is not unique. Many game situations, in baseball and other sports, entail teams intentionally acting contrary to ordinary athletic expectations. And many game situations involve teams angling for cost-benefit advantages, even substantial ones. Yet most other game situations are not subject to limiting rules, with players left to battle for strategic advantage and benefits on the play, even via ordinarily unexpected acts. Either of two conclusions follows. One is that the Infield Fly Rule is unnecessary and should be repealed, leaving this game situation treated as the many comparable situations and left to the players' devices—this is the Guilford/Mallord position. The other is that these other situations should be subject to analogous limiting rules—baseball and other sports need more rules resting on the logic and structure of the Infield Fly Rule.

By offering a clearer assessment of the precise contours, details, and rationales for the infield-fly situation, this four-prong framework addresses and resolves those criticisms, revealing four things. The framework provides a precise understanding of what defines the infield-fly situation and what makes it unique. It shows that only one situation in baseball is comparable to the infield fly under these characteristics—an uncaught third strike, which is governed by its own limiting rule that rests on identical logic and function as the Infield Fly Rule. All other commonly proffered baseball situations are not analogous, each lacking one or more elements from this framework, and are properly left to the game's ordinary rules, practices, and strategies. Finally, the framework and analysis reveals a similar mix in other sports. Some game situations in other sports are structurally comparable to the infield-fly situation and are subject to analogous limiting rules that operate on the logic of the Infield Fly Rule, while most situations in other sports lack one or more defining characteristics and are properly left alone without a limiting rule, leaving players to pursue strategies in search of competitive advantage.

This book proceeds in multiple steps. Chapters 1 and 2 explore the history, text, application, and evolution of the Infield Fly Rule, then apply this four-part framework in greater depth and detail to form a comprehensive defense of the Rule as part of baseball.

Chapter 3 applies the framework to other baseball situations, offering two responses to critics of the Rule. It identifies several comparable situations and shows that each is governed by a limiting rule functioning in the same manner and logic as the Infield Fly Rule. And it considers a range of other baseball situations, showing why none is comparable for lack of one or more of the defining characteristics and why each is appropriately free from any limiting rule.

Chapter 4 applies the framework to other sports and the rules of other sports, identifying some situations that feature the four defining characteristics and that are subject to similar limiting rules and some situations that lack one or more of those characteristics and that remain appropriately free from any limiting rule. While not intended to be comprehensive, this chapter considers game situations and rules in football, basketball, soccer, and running and swimming racing.

The final chapter moves beyond policy arguments and into empirical analysis, measuring the Infield Fly Rule's effect on baseball as played on the field. It presents the results of a review of every actual or potential infield-fly call from eight Major League seasons (2010–2017). This chapter measures the frequency of the Rule's invocation, then considers how repeal might affect baseball by analyzing various measures of the Rule's effect on individual at-bats, innings, games, and seasons.

The Infield Fly Rule has enough layers to justify a dedicated book. My hope is that, by the end, readers will be as convinced as I am that baseball needs the Infield Fly Rule, that baseball is better for having the Rule, and that the arguments against the Rule do not withstand close scrutiny.

Chapter 1

A Brief History
of the Infield Fly Rule

Origin Story

The "trap ball," in which an infielder intentionally drops a playable fly ball to force-out baserunners while allowing the batter to reach first, is as old as the game, with newspaper accounts of the "peculiar strategy" dating to 1864.[1] The move was associated in early days with George Wright, the shortstop for the Cincinnati Red Stockings and a future Hall-of-Famer, an "alert and skillful infielder" with a "deft and delicate style" in playing balls off the ground.[2]

Wright's play featured in the June 1870 game between his Red Stockings and the Brooklyn Atlantics that at the time was labeled the "most exciting game on record" and "baseball's first truly great game."[3] The Atlantics defeated the Red Stockings 8–7 in Brooklyn in 11 innings, breaking the Red Stockings' 91-game winning streak. Wright brought his "strategic piece of play" out in the bottom of the tenth. Brooklyn had first-and-second/one-out when Wright began a double play "by dropping a fly ball" to "put the side out for a blank." Wright reportedly "cupped his hand as if to catch the ball but then it trickled through his hands to the ground" before fielding it and throwing to third base to force the runner from second, who relayed to second to force the runner from first.[4] Brooklyn fans were "furious with rage." "George was the victim of every name on the Rooter's calendar … but through the atmospheric blue streaks, his white teeth gleamed and glistened, provoking ability."[5]

The angry reaction by Brooklyn fans suggested less a problem with the play in itself and more the advantage this play gave the visiting team over their team. Fans, newspapers, and umpires generally praised the players who could execute the play and criticized early efforts to limit or eliminate "clever play."[6] Umpires imposed a slight limit by calling the batter out if the infielder held the ball for too long or where the misplay was plain; they grounded this not in a limit on what players could or could not do under the text of baseball's rules, but on inherent umpire discretion to enforce the spirit of the rules and ensure fair play.[7] But umpires in these early years ignored formal rules and league commands to declare batters out (and runners not forced to advance) where the infielder momentarily held the fly ball before deliberately dropping it.[8]

The Players' League barred the play for its lone season in 1890.[9] The National League adopted what became the Infield Fly Rule in 1894, although in reaction to a different play in a different game situation raising different issues. It was not a proto-version of the problematic play that had been around for three decades, but a distinct play that, once all the rule adjustments were complete, remained (and remains) legal. The rulemaking machinery activated, it took baseball's rulemakers nearly a decade to identify the real problem (reflected in Wright's non-catch 25 years earlier) and to calibrate the appropriate regulation.

In a May 1893 game between the New York Giants and Baltimore Orioles, the Orioles had a runner on first with less than two outs. The batter hit a pop-up on the infield towards Giants shortstop (and future Hall-of-Famer) John Montgomery Ward, with the runner on first retreating to the base, expecting Ward to catch the fly ball for the easy out. Instead, Ward intentionally allowed the ball to fall to the ground at his feet, untouched; he picked it up and threw to second base, forcing out the runner on first, as the batter reached first base safely. Ward wanted to get the fast runner off first base in favor of the batter, who had the "speed of an ice wagon."[10] (This was the common term of the era for a "player who runs slowly, resembling the labored movements of an ice wagon."[11]) Nothing in the rules prohibited or even deterred Ward's play. And unlike the outraged reaction to Wright's non-catch double play 23 years earlier, even the Baltimore paper credited Ward with "excellent judgment."[12] Excellent judgment from Ward is not surprising. He had graduated Columbia Law School, led early player efforts to unionize and gain basic employee rights, and enjoyed a successful post-playing career as an attorney; his biography marked him as a "clever baseball-ist."[13] This seemed another example of clever baseball-ing. It also was appropriate that the play occurred against the Orioles, a championship-caliber team throughout the 1890s known for rough play and for bending and shaping the rules to its advantage.[14]

During winter 1894, the National League adopted "Brush and Von der Ahe's rule" or the "trap ball rule." The "batter is out if he hits a fly ball that can be handled by an infielder while first base is occupied with only one out,"[15] although the umpire was not required to signal the out until after the play.[16] Rulemakers amended the rule the following year. The amended rule applied to first-and-second/one-out and bases-loaded/one-out; did not apply to first-base-only; and required that the umpire signal the batter out immediately rather than waiting for the end of the play. In 1901, the rule was extended to those base situations with none out.[17] The rule excluded (that is, batters would not be declared out) line drives in 1904 and bunts in 1920[18]; these changes limited the Rule to high, parabolic fly balls off a full swing. The name "Infield Fly Rule" took hold by 1909.[19] Taking Ward's excellent judgment in 1893 as a starting point, the basic structure of the Infield Fly Rule was in place in the National League within about a decade and has remained largely unchanged for more than a century.

This history and early evolution prompts several questions.

First is why the Rule evolved as it did in those early years and whether that evolution reflected rulemakers' initial failure to understand the real problem.[20] The 1894 rule applied to runner-on-first/one-out—the base-out situation Ward had faced the year before, where his goal in not catching the fly ball was to remove a faster runner from the basepaths in favor of a slower runner. But the only potential double play in that situation would involve the runner and the batter. And if the batter ran hard to first, as he was expected to do under the game's ethics and strategies, and the ball was hit high enough and with sufficient arc to trigger the rule, the batter should reach first base before a second throw could complete the double play. The real problem was a double (or triple) play involving force-outs on multiple baserunners—what had happened in the Red Stockings-Atlantics game a quarter-century prior. A special limiting rule was necessary only where force-outs were in effect at multiple bases, not including first base, and only when the defense needed to turn a double play. The 1895 and 1901 extensions of the Rule—to cover all multiple-force-out situations whenever there were less than two outs—resolved those concerns. Baseball historian Peter Morris argues that the 1894 rule was supposed to reach all multiple-force situations with less than two out; the subsequent amendments clarified rather than changed the rule's meaning, eliminating confusion over the League's original intent and establishing in the text what League umpires were doing anyway.[21]

The second question is why the League decided to ban the play in 1894. The play had been around for 30 years, had generally been praised, and was not common. The initial rule was met with "outrage" by players and fans alike—one infielder folded his arms and made no effort to make the catch during a game, since it no longer was necessary to "catch that kind of ball."[22]

Morris offers three reasons. First was competitive balance, as rulemakers believed it unfair to allow a high-advantage play that only a few players on a few teams could execute.[23] Second was the difficulty intentional drops produced and the arguments they triggered,[24] although rulemakers ameliorated that concern with the 1895 amendment requiring umpires to invoke the rule while the ball was in the air rather than waiting until after the drop. Third, the play "had lost its novelty and aesthetic appeal," with two developments rendering it "tricky" and "clumsy" rather than clever. The creation and improvement in fielders' gloves made it easier for players to "juggle" the ball as it traveled to the ground, and improvements to playing fields made it less likely a ball would strike a pebble or other obstacle and take a funny bounce. The challenge of controlling the uncaught ball, scooping it off the ground, and making the initial throw to begin the double play was gone, making the play look like "cold-blooded murder."[25]

This last point frames the Rule as an anti-subterfuge or anti-deception provision. As baseball historian Harold Seymour explains, the "whole idea is to prevent the defense from making a double play by subterfuge, at a time when the offense is helpless to prevent it, rather than by skill and speed."[26] The League sought to impose a gentleman's code, and a "gentleman, when playing a game, does not act in a manner so unexpected as to constitute trickery" and "does not attempt to profit by his own unethical conduct."[27] Baseball should reflect the original spirit "of the amateur, of the gentleman, and of the sportsman,"[28] where victory was not to be pursued by any means permissible under the language of the rules but violative of the spirit of those rules.

This does not mean that baseball was a gentleman's game. The game of the late 19th century was notorious for its lawlessness and for players pushing the limits of the game and its rules. Rulemakers nevertheless could, and did strive for a more genteel and less win-at-all-costs sport.

The proliferation of rules, written or otherwise, to stop or promote some conduct served not to preserve amateurism, but as a mark of the game's professionalization. Paul Dickson describes former Major Leaguer and broadcaster Joe Garagiola's argument that the game's many rules reflected the imperative for professional baseball players and teams to win. A professional game was a "far cry from the game of boyhood dreams," and the rules of how to play that real game were part of what players had to understand and adjust to.[29]

In his history of baseball's early years, Seymour describes the problem that the Infield Fly Rule remedied: "No matter what the runners did, a double play could be made. If they clung to the bases, the infielder could drop the ball intentionally, forcing them off their bases to make room for the batter, in which case they could be put out. If they took a chance and ran, the fielder could make a simple catch and double them off base."[30]

To understand why, consider what happens in that situation without the Infield Fly Rule. If the infielder does not catch the fair fly ball, the batter becomes a runner,[31] the baserunners are forced to advance to the next bases,[32] and they likely will be put out before reaching safely. If a baserunner takes a chance and runs to the next base and the infielder catches the fly ball, the runner will be doubled off at the prior base for having failed to retouch on a caught fly ball.[33] And there is an additional wrinkle. The ball is playable by an infielder, meaning it likely is in or near the infield, leaving the infielders with short and quick throws. Not only must each runner choose between running or waiting, but he cannot stray too far from his current base while he waits—if he leads too far towards the next base and the ball is caught, he can be doubled off on a short throw. Both runners must remain on or within a few steps of his current base to see how the play develops and what the infielder does with the ball—leaving them too far to run (perhaps 80–85 feet) and unable to beat the throws to the next bases. A 1911 newspaper story described the runners as "up a tree."[34]

George Wright and his Red Stockings teammates made that confusion part of the deception. According to one report of an 1872 game, Wright's teammates yelled for him to drop a fly ball, causing the baserunners to advance, only for Wright to catch the ball and start an easy triple play. A later account of the same game reported that Wright's teammates yelled for him to drop the fly ball, Wright yelled "no," causing the runners to hold, then he dropped the ball to start a triple play. Regardless of which version is correct, both "illustrate the hopeless dilemma that the play could present to base runners."[35] And improvements to gloves and playing fields exacerbated the problem by making the play easier for the defense, leaving baserunners with no chance.[36]

Defenses can turn this double play with one or two throws, depending on where the ball is hit, which is the closest base to the infielder playing the ball, and how far the baserunners retreat. Imagine runners on first-and-second and a ball hit to the left side of the infield, with the shortstop settling under the ball and the runners retreating to their current bases. Once the ball lands on the ground, the shortstop has two options. One is to throw to the third baseman covering third for the force-out on the runner on second, then for the third baseman to throw to the second baseman covering second for the double play on the runner on first (a 6–5–4 double play if you are scoring at home)—this is what George Wright did in that 1870 Brooklyn game. A faster option, if the runner on second has retreated all the way to the base, is a double play on one throw from the shortstop to the second baseman covering second. The second baseman first tags the runner; because the batted ball touched the ground and the batter became a runner, the runner on second is required to advance to third and can be tagged out, even if standing on second base, a base to which he no longer is entitled. The second baseman then steps on second base, forcing out the runner on first, who similarly was forced to advance when the ball landed on the ground. (The second baseman must proceed in that order—if he steps on the base before tagging the runner, it forces out the runner on first, but removes the force on the runner at second, who is safely standing on second base.[37])

The Rule was not without its confusion and controversy, given the number of amendments to the text during that first decade, whether for clarification or change. In a 1901 California League game, the umpire called the batter out on an infield fly with only a runner on first, although the rule had changed to require at least two baserunners.[38] In 1905, National League President Harry Pulliam reportedly instructed umpires to invoke the rule even with only a runner on first, where the batter was slower than the baserunner and the infielder might have had incentive to drop the ball intentionally; umpires largely ignored the command.[39] A June 1911 story complained of season-long problems the Pittsburgh Pirates encountered with umpires and the Rule, as "this particular section of base ball code has stirred up bother all along the line."[40]

The Text

By 1920, the Infield Fly Rule as we know it was in place. Despite initially positive fan and media reaction to the strategic efforts of Wright, Ward, and others, consensus developed that this play was inconsistent with the proper way to play baseball and should be discouraged, if not outlawed.

In its current form, the Infield Fly Rule provides as follows:

> An INFIELD FLY is a fair fly ball (not including a line drive nor an attempted bunt) which can be caught by an infielder with ordinary effort, when first and second, or first, second and third bases are occupied, before two are out. The pitcher, catcher and any outfielder who stations himself in the infield on the play shall be considered infielders for the purpose of this rule.
>
> When it seems apparent that a batted ball will be an Infield Fly, the umpire shall immediately declare "Infield Fly" for the benefit of the runners. If the ball is near the baselines, the umpire shall declare "Infield Fly, if Fair." The ball is alive and runners may advance at the risk of the ball being caught, or retouch and advance after the ball is touched, the same as on any fly ball. If the hit becomes a foul ball, it is treated the same as any foul.

> If a declared Infield Fly is allowed to fall untouched to the ground, and bounces foul before passing first or third base, it is a foul ball. If a declared Infield Fly falls untouched to the ground outside the baseline, and bounces fair before passing first or third base, it is an Infield Fly.[41]

A batter is out if an Infield Fly is declared.[42]

The definition is followed by an official Comment:

> On the infield fly rule the umpire is to rule whether the ball could ordinarily have been handled by an infielder-not by some arbitrary limitation such as the grass, or the base lines. The umpire must rule also that a ball is an infield fly, even if handled by an outfielder, if, in the umpire's judgment, the ball could have been as easily handled by an infielder. The infield fly is in no sense to be considered an appeal play. The umpire's judgment must govern, and the decision should be made immediately.
>
> When an infield fly rule is called, runners may advance at their own risk. If on an infield fly rule, the infielder intentionally drops a fair ball, the ball remains in play despite the provisions of Rule 5.09(a)(12) (Rule 6.05(1)). The infield fly rule takes precedence.
>
> If interference is called during an Infield Fly, the ball remains alive until it is determined whether the ball is fair or foul. If fair, both the runner who interfered with the fielder and the batter are out. If foul, even if caught, the runner is out and the batter returns to bat.[43]

The definition of infield fly cross-references "ordinary effort," defined as "the effort that a fielder of average skill at a position in that league or classification of leagues should exhibit on a play, with due consideration given to the condition of the field and weather conditions."[44] A Comment to that definition clarifies that this "is an objective standard in regard to any particular fielder. In other words, even if a fielder makes his best effort, if that effort falls short of what an average fielder at that position in that league would have made in a situation, the official scorer should charge that fielder with an error."[45] The question is not whether this fair fly ball was easily catchable by this infielder at this moment, but whether a fair fly ball hit in this space would have been easily catchable by the average infielder in the league.

The Rule's language and commentary show that the colloquial shorthand explanation of the rule, if followed, is largely accurate. If runners are on first and second or the bases are loaded with less than two out, we have an "infield-fly situation," a game situation in which the Infield Fly Rule might be invoked. If the batter hits a fair fly ball that is not a line drive or a bunt and that the umpire determines can be easily caught by an infielder, the Infield Fly Rule is in effect—the batter is out whether the infielder catches the fly ball or not, the runners are not forced to advance (as they ordinarily would be if the batter becomes a runner on an uncaught fly ball), although they may run at their own risk if the ball is not caught.

Yet the Infield Fly Rule has faced more than a century's worth of criticisms of its complexity and incomprehensibility—journalist John Dickerson complained that the Rule is more complex and more misunderstood than any Papal decree.[46] Read carefully, however, the text reveals a rule that, while requiring umpireal judgment based on multiple considerations, is straight-forward and readily understandable in its terms and application. A close focus on the text also resolves common misconceptions.

The batted ball must be a fair fly ball. It need not be on the infield and need not be handled by an infielder, so long as an infielder could play it with ordinary effort somewhere on the field. Seymour explains this element as a reaction to an early defensive strategy to foil the original rule—teams would have an outfielder race in to play balls near the infield.[47] Because the Rule applies if an infielder could have caught the ball, even if someone else plays it, this strategy does not avoid an infield-fly call. An outfielder stationed on the infield at the time of the pitch is treated as an infielder, making the rule applicable to any batted ball he could catch with ordinary effort.

Bunts and line drives are excluded, so the Rule applies only to balls hit off full swings with sufficient parabolic arc. Identifying something as a non-line-drive fly ball becomes tricky with a "humpback liner," a cross between a line drive and pop fly that travels like a line drive, although sometimes higher, then sinks precipitously to become a ground ball.[48] But this is a judgment that umpires are trained to make. So is whether a batted ball is a bunt, depending on how full the batter's swing.

Although umpires are instructed to disregard "some arbitrary limitation such as the grass, or the base line" and to apply the Rule to balls hit beyond the infield, a logical link remains between the infield's geographic boundaries and ordinary effort. The closer the ball is to the infield, the more likely an average infielder can catch it with ordinary effort; he does not have to run as far to get the ball, has more time to position himself and settle under the ball, and has more time to make the throws for the double play if the ball is not caught. The closer the ball is to the infield, the more likely the unwanted double play. The throws, especially the initial throw, are shorter and quicker. The baserunners must remain at or near their current bases. If they stray too far to the next base, the shorter throw makes it more likely they will be doubled off if the ball is caught. But by staying close, they have further to run to the next base, giving the infielders more time to make the necessary throw or throws. The converse holds for balls hit further from the infield—baserunners can lead further to the next base, leaving them less distance to run to the next base if the ball is not caught but enough time to retreat to the current base if the ball is caught.

Umpires must declare infield fly "immediately" for the benefit of the baserunners. Some erroneously interpret this to require that the umpire invoke the rule early, which explains criticism that the infield-fly call in the 2012 NLWC was made too late.[49] Immediacy must be understood in light of the Rule's other elements. The umpire must declare infield fly immediately upon determining that the Rule should be in effect—upon determining that this is a fair fly ball playable by an infielder with ordinary effort in an appropriate base-out situation. The Rule does not dictate when the umpire can or should make that determination, which is a subject of debate among umpires.

When the Rule is invoked, the batter is called out. If the infielder catches the ball, the batter is out on the caught fly ball.[50] The runners may retouch and advance, as on any caught fly ball. If the infielder does not catch it, the batter is treated as if the ball is caught, with the infielder who would have caught it credited with a put out.[51] The uncaught ball remains alive and the runners can advance at their own risk, as on any other ball that lands on the ground in fair territory.

In either case, the batter never becomes a runner. The baserunners are not forced to advance and must be tagged out if they try to do so, a point one commentator argues should be made explicit in the text or commentary to the Rule.[52] But saying a runner can advance at his own risk means he is not forced to run and takes his chances in doing so. The tag requirement is present by implication. If a batter becomes a runner, the runner (or runners) immediately ahead of him on base are forced to advance.[53] It follows that if a batter does not become a runner because he is out on a caught fly ball, the runners immediately ahead of him are not forced to advance and must be tagged out if they attempt to do so. If the rules need not tell infielders they must tag a runner trying to advance on an ordinary caught fly ball, they need not tell infielders they must tag a runner trying to advance on an infield-fly call that creates the equivalent of a caught fly ball—when the batter again does not become a runner.

The Umpireal View

Criticisms of the Infield Fly Rule are often framed as criticisms of the umpires charged with applying it. Initial objections to the Rule reflected concerns that it gave umpires too much to do.[54] A 1911 story from the *Evening Star* (Washington, D.C.) complained that some umpires had only "'vague ideas' concerning the rule, with many failing to announce whether the batter is out and different umpires interpreting the rule differently." The writer placed blame for confusion over the then-relatively new rule "wholly with the arbitrators," who "collect between $2000 and $4000 per six months' work for laboring two hours a day [and] ought to have enough leisure time to acquire a working knowledge of the base ball code."[55]

A complete exploration of the Infield Fly Rule looks beyond the text and legal analysis of the text to consider how those arbitrators manage its many details and nuances. I looked for the views of three people who teach the Infield Fly Rule to those who work with and around it. On the umpires' side, I spoke with Jim Evans and Brent Rice. Evans was a Major League umpire for 27 years, was the founder and chief instructor of the Jim Evans Academy of Professional Umpiring until 2012, and since 2014 has worked as a special advisor on umpiring for the President of Minor League Baseball. He long has been recognized as the foremost expert on baseball's rules. Rice was a Minor League umpire for 13 years, and since 2008 has been chief instructor at the Harry Wendelstedt Umpire School, one of two umpiring academies whose graduates are placed in Minor League umpiring jobs and on the track to umpiring in Major League Baseball. On the teams' side, I spoke with Rich Marazzi, a long-time commentator on baseball rules, including as author of the 1980 book *The Rules and Lore of Baseball*. Since 2004, Marazzi has worked as a rules consultant for numerous Major League teams, teaching players, coaches, and staff about rule changes and developments. Marazzi provides in-season reports about rule-related incidents; his job is to make players and managers more aware of the rules and rule-related issues, thus better able to gain strategic benefits and to avoid strategic losses.

Several themes and ideas emerged from my conversations with the three.

Extra-Textual Considerations

Umpires introduce several extra-textual considerations in operationalizing the Infield Fly Rule. They reduce the Rule to two considerations not mentioned in the text—whether the ball has sufficient arc and whether the fielder gets "comfortably underneath"[56] the ball. These are heuristics, shorthand for the textual elements of whether a batted ball is a fly ball (not a line drive) and whether it is playable with ordinary effort; they provide umpires more concrete clues to look for in judging the play while the ball is in flight. If an infielder can settle comfortably underneath the ball, standing in position waiting for it to come down to him, it is playable with ordinary effort. If the ball has enough parabolic arc, it is a fly ball and not a line drive, although Evans and Rice acknowledge that umpires sometimes struggle with humpback liners.

These heuristics reflect the player movements that umpires look for. Arc and settled comfortably suggest a stationary infielder, standing in position to catch a ball that travelled in a parabolic arc and is falling straight down into his glove. They therefore suggest a fly ball on which a stationary and positioned infielder could easily pull his glove away or move a step in either direction so as not to stand directly underneath the ball; the ball would fall untouched at his feet, placing him in position to easily pick it off the ground and make the necessary throw to begin the double play on the baserunners. In other words, an infielder who is settled comfortably under a batted ball with sufficient arc is in position to catch the ball—or to intentionally not catch it and begin the double play that the Infield Fly Rule is designed to eliminate. By contrast, an infielder not settled comfortably underneath a ball—if he was still running or his body was not positioned properly when the ball landed on the ground—would have a more difficult time controlling an uncaught ball off the ground or making the necessary throw to begin the double play.

In deciding whether to invoke the Rule on an individual play, umpires account for the Rule's purpose of protecting baserunners from an unfair double play and keeping the defense from obtaining an unfair advantage. Rice reminds students that under the text, an umpire could declare infield fly on a ball hit to the left field wall—an infielder could settle comfortably under that ball if the infielder were fast enough to cover the distance and the ball hit high enough to give him time to cover the distance. But an umpire would never invoke the Rule on such a ball, because there would be no chance of a double play and no chance of unfair defensive advantage if the infielder intentionally did not catch a ball at the wall. Purpose overrides isolated text.

These purposive considerations allow umpires to adapt the Rule to the modern game. Modern infielders possess greater range, enabling them to easily get underneath and catch many balls that travel quite far onto the outfield grass. They wear larger and better gloves than when the Rule was born, meaning most non-catches are, in fact, intentional. Umpires adjust for that greater range and fielding ability in deciding whether an infielder got underneath the ball in time and whether he put himself in position to intentionally not catch it and turn the double play if infield fly were not declared.

Infield Shifts and the Infield Fly Rule

Teams increasingly incorporate defensive shifts, positioning players in different places, often at extremes, to respond to a batter's tendencies.

The defense may place three and even four infielders on one side of second base against a pull hitter or position the second baseman in shallow right field against a left-handed power hitter.

Defensive shifts affect the Infield Fly Rule in three ways.

The shift makes some balls hit on the infield less playable with ordinary effort than they would have been with ordinary defensive positioning. Evans illustrates the point with a test for his students. He announces the situation as first-and-second/one-out, fungoes a pop-up next to third base, and asks whether Infield Fly should be called; students invariably respond that it should, seeing a softly hit fair fly ball on the infield in the appropriate base-out situation. But the correct answer is that they cannot know. Because Evans never told them where the third baseman or shortstop were positioned, they cannot determine whether the batted ball was playable by an infielder with ordinary effort. If on a left-handed batter the third baseman shifts to where the shortstop usually plays and the shortstop shifts to the right side of the infield, a ball hit near the third base bag arguably is not playable with ordinary effort; no infielder was positioned there at the start of the play and the third baseman must run further to settle comfortably under the ball.

Rice offers a textual reason not to invoke the Rule when the ball is hit to a shifted second baseman stationed in right field. Just as an outfielder stationed on the infield at the beginning of a play is deemed an infielder to whom the Rule may apply, an infielder stationed in the outfield at the start of the play should not be treated as an infielder, so the Rule should not apply on a fly ball that he can catch.

On the other hand, if the second baseman is stationed in shallow right field for the pitch, he has less distance to run to get himself comfortably underneath a ball hit 30 or 40 beyond the infield that infielders routinely run back to catch. Evans and Rice agree that the question shifts to the possibility or likelihood of a double play from that distance—what would an infielder be able to do if he intentionally let the ball fall to the ground. Evans argues that the Rule is properly invoked on balls hit that far into the outfield. Rice says that umpires are more likely to invoke on such balls on the left side of the field than the right, because a shorter throw puts out the lead runner advancing from second to third if the umpire does not declare and the force-out remains in effect.

Shifts may not significantly affect application of the Infield Fly Rule because they are employed less often, or are less extreme, in infield-fly situations. With multiple baserunners, the defense needs fielders in position to cover the bases, particularly third. If a team employs a big shift to the right side against a left-handed batter with runners on first and second, the runner on second might steal third base standing up, since the third baseman, playing in the shortstop position, cannot reach third to receive the throw from the catcher. With infielders in more traditional positions, most fly balls on the infield in this game situation become playable with ordinary effort.

Timing of the Call

One controversy is over the umpire's timing in invoking the Rule. The text requires that the umpire "immediately" declare infield fly, expressly for the benefit of the baserunners. That means immediately upon determining that the Rule should be invoked—that a fair fly ball is playable by an infielder with ordinary effort in the appropriate base-out situation, based on the infielder settling comfortably beneath a ball hit with sufficient arc. An umpire cannot declare it sooner than that moment.

Evans and Rice agree that the cardinal sin for umpires, and the common mistake for new umpires, is declaring infield fly too early. The batter is out as soon as the umpire declares, an irrevocable determination, even if the play develops differently than the umpire anticipates or expects. A premature infield-fly declaration prevents the umpire from seeing how the play evolves and reacting accordingly, freezing the play and taking it out of the players' hands.

But there are competing schools about the appropriate moment to invoke. Evans teaches that the call should come when the ball is at the apex of its flight, based on what the umpire observes as the ball begins its descent. Rice teaches umpires to wait longer. He argues that whether a ball is playable with ordinary effort is indicated not by the flight of the ball, but by the action or inaction of the infielders. As soon as the umpire realizes the ball is hit in the air, he shifts his focus to the fielders and what they do on the play, rather than watching the flight of the ball. But this means it may not be clear to the umpire that the ball could have been caught with ordinary effort until it is in the fielder's glove or has landed on the ground. Neither approach necessarily produces more or fewer infield-fly calls. In waiting to see what happens on the ball's descent, the need for the call may become more obvious (as the infielder takes the additional time to settle under the ball) or less obvious (as the wind catches the ball and carries it away from the waiting infielder).

Umpires must train themselves not to be too anxious to make the call, although umpire practice may increase the chances of a premature call. When a batter comes to the plate in an infield-fly situation, umpires signal one another (usually each touching the bill of his cap) as a group reminder to be alert for the call. Evans suggests that this cues the umpires into the possibility of the Rule arising before play begins by having them think specifically about infield fly. While this is important in managing the game, it may lead to a premature call because the Rule is on their minds.

A late call creates different concerns, depending on whether the umpire invokes the Rule or declines to invoke the rule.

A late invocation does not hurt the offense. Calling infield fly puts the batter out, removing the force on the advancing baserunners. But the baserunners' obligations remain the same on the batted ball regardless of when the umpire declares infield fly. They cannot do anything until they see whether the infielder catches the ball—they must tag up if the fly ball is caught (and infielders catch almost every ball on which the Rule is invoked), while they can, but need not, run immediately if the ball falls to the ground. Those choices are not affected by the timing of the umpire's declaration of infield fly—the players respond as they would on any catch or any non-catch under the Rule.

A late invocation could create problems for the defense on an unintentional non-catch on which baserunners attempt to advance. The infielders may not know whether the force-out remains in effect (if the Rule was not invoked and the batter is not out) or whether they must tag the advancing runners (if the Rule was invoked and the batter is out), thus they may not know what to do on the advancing runners. But infielders almost always catch the fly ball regardless of whether the umpire declares, so the timing of the invocation does not affect what they do. And baserunners rarely attempt to advance on the few balls that are not caught.

A late invocation creates the greatest problems for the umpires. They must declare the batter out and remove him from first base when he believed he had reached safely, although any advancement by the baserunners, including runs scored, stands. This precipitates arguments, ejections, and official protests. And in the 2012 NLWC, it precipitated fans showering the field with debris and delaying the game for nearly 20 minutes.

A late non-invocation on an uncaught ball creates problems for everyone. It confuses infielders in the same way as a late invocation—on an unintentional drop, they may be uncertain whether they must tag the baserunners. It also confuses baserunners. Knowing that infield fly could be called at any time up to when the ball hits the ground or the infielder's glove, they retreat to their current bases to wait for the call or the catch. But if the umpire does not invoke and the infielder does not catch the ball (whether intentionally or unintentionally), the baserunners are suddenly and unexpectedly forced to advance and likely will be unable to reach the next bases safely, certainly on any ball hit on or near the infield. That late non-call disadvantages the baserunners in the precise way the Rule is designed to avoid.

Evans teaches umpires to avoid that problem by declaring infield fly on any close play in which there is a "reasonable doubt" as to whether the Rule might be satisfied. Marazzi describes this as erring on the side of caution. In law, this can be describes as a presumption or default rule. On a close or uncertain play that could go either way, the default is that it is an infield fly and the umpire should err in favor of invoking. This protects the baserunners, who can retreat and remain safely on their current bases if the ball is not caught when the Rule is in effect.

Location Concerns

One difficult application comes on balls hit in what Evans calls "no-man's land," the area on the infield grass behind the pitcher's mound. Although the ball is hit on the infield, any infielder playing at normal depth must run a fair distance to settle comfortably underneath the ball, unless it is hit sufficiently high.

Rice says the Rule typically should be invoked on such balls, despite the distance the infielder must run on the play. The Rule requires that the fair fly ball be playable with ordinary effort by "an infielder," not by any specific infielder and not by the infielder who attempts to catch the ball. A ball hit behind the mound can be caught with ordinary effort by the pitcher. Established baseball strategy on pop-ups near the mound is for the pitcher to get out of the way and let another infielder catch the ball, even if he has further to run to the ball. For infield-fly purposes, however, an infielder, the pitcher, was positioned near that spot when the ball was hit and could have caught the ball with ordinary effort; that is all the Rule requires. That someone else ran a longer distance to play the ball does not change that.

Rice defends invoking on these balls in light of the Rule's purpose. This would be a prime area for the defense to turn an easy double play off an intentionally uncaught ball against trapped baserunners. If the ball falls to the grass in this area, the throw(s) for the double play will be short and quick, allowing the baserunners no time to advance. And runners must remain close to their current bases on a ball hit in the middle of the infield, because the throws to double them off their current bases will be short and quick if they stray too far.

Understanding the Rule

The most consistent concern among the interview subjects is that no one understands the Infield Fly Rule. Players, other than a few strategic thinkers, either never grasp it or their athletic instincts override their knowledge. This explains mistakes on both sides of the ball. Baserunners forget that, if infield fly is in effect, they need not run, causing them to run into the double play from which the Infield Fly Rule is designed to protect them. Infielders forget that, because the batter is out (whether on the call or the catch), if the baserunners do advance, it is a tag play rather than a force play. I explore both problems further in the next section of Chapter 1. Rice and Evans say umpiring students are always surprised to learn the Rule's minutiae. For example, they are confused that the infield bears no express correlation to whether the Rule is in effect. It can be invoked on balls hit quite far into the outfield, but may not be invoked on a ball landing on the infield dirt, as Evans' fungo play demonstrates.

The general lack of deep understanding leads to an additional oddity for umpires—arguments from both managers on the same play. Rice and Evans both recall plays in which the batting team's manager complained that his batter was called out even though the ball was not caught (ignoring that the call protected his baserunners against a likely double play), followed by the fielding team's manager complaining that his team would have been able to turn a double play if the umpire had not invoked the Rule.

Evans, Marazzi, and Rice believe that, without the Infield Fly Rule, infielders would immediately begin intentionally failing to catch easily playable fair fly balls in search of double plays; Evans remarked that infielders would begin trying it "last inning." He guesstimated that the defense would succeed in turning the double play on roughly 75 percent of the balls on which the Rule is now invoked. Teams would coach players to do it regularly, seeing it as a way to get out of a jam. In their view, in other words, the Infield Fly Rule succeeds in its stated purpose of preventing that unwanted double play. Removing the Rule from the game would recreate the problem baseball's rulemakers have been trying to eliminate for more than a century.

Marazzi is troubled by any suggestion that the Rule be repealed, believing that reintroducing such trickery, in a way that reduces offense and scoring, would make a "travesty" or "farce" out of the game. Rice is agnostic about the Rule's wisdom, primarily wanting to keep it for the sake of nostalgia and the fact that it has been around so long as to become a deep part of baseball's history. He believes that most umpires are similarly agnostic about its merits; they do not care what the rules are, so long as they are clear, understandable, and easily applied. Whether that clarity is present as to the Infield Fly Rule, as written and applied, remains the subject of debate and of this book.

Modern Story

As part of this project, I watched every infield-fly call (plays on which the Rule was invoked and balls on which it might have been called) for eight Major League Baseball seasons (2010–2017). Chapter 5 presents the quantitative results of this study and their normative implications. Watching every call provided a wealth of specific plays to illustrate the Rule and its effects. Whatever happened on the infield-fly plays in this eight-year period was not new. In his 1980 exploration of baseball's rules, Marazzi's section on the Infield Fly Rule describes strikingly similar plays from decades earlier, in both the Major and Minor Leagues.[57]

While the myth of the Infield Fly Rule increases attention on this game situation, the Rule has rendered the mine run of plays uneventful. In all but a small handful of plays, the infielder catches the easily playable fair fly ball hit near the infield, as he would on any ordinary fly ball, and the baserunners stay put, as they would on an ordinary fly ball hit near the infield. The only difference is the umpire's declaration and the broadcast announcement that "infield fly rule is in effect." Because the batter is out when infield fly is declared, the catch has no legal effect and is merely "for posterity," as one announcer put it. But because the infielder catches the ball, the Rule's effects are not obvious to anyone observing the play—it appears that the batter is out because the infielder catches the fly ball and is credited with a put-out. It is not obvious that baserunners are being protected against a strategic bind.

Some plays do not proceed as ordinary fly balls, however. And these plays reveal much about the Rule, its purposes, its success in achieving that purpose, and its function within baseball.

2012 NLWC

Recent fan and announcer interest (as opposed to interest of legal scholars) in the Infield Fly Rule begins with the call from the 2012 NLWC, discussed in the Introduction. The play thrust the Rule into public consciousness and public discussion, while setting me down the road of this writing project. As described, initial reaction was outrage—Braves fans delaying the game for almost 20 minutes by throwing debris on the field rivaled Brooklyn fans directing a blue streak at George Wright in 1870. While media commentary also was initially critical, consensus developed that the call was correct, or at least not unreasonable.

Regardless of the call's metaphysical correctness, the play illustrates important points about the Rule.

The play was not out of the ordinary. Although the ball traveled quite far into left field, it did not travel much further than balls on which the Rule is regularly invoked. The ball also remained well within the range of Cardinal shortstop Pete Kozma—and since Kozma was about an average National League shortstop in 2012[58] within the range of the shortstop of average skill. Kozma had stopped running, was stationary and settled under the ball, was facing the infield, and was waving his arms above his head, a signal to his teammates that he was ready to catch the ball. Umpire Sam Holbrook declared infield fly immediately after Kozma did that, indicating that he was watching the fielder and not the ball for signals of ordinary effort, as Rice urges. (Holbrook is an instructor at the Wendelstedt School, where Rice is the supervising instructor.) It appears that Kozma would have caught the ball had he not run off at the last instant when he heard left-fielder Matt Holliday coming, the ball landing roughly where Kozma had been standing seconds earlier.

The Infield Fly Rule applies even if the ball is handled by an outfielder in the first instance, so long as it could have been handled by an infielder. It thus did not matter that Holliday, not Kozma, picked the uncaught ball off the ground. And umpires are consistent about this. Infield fly was declared in an April 2015 game between the Washington Nationals and Philadelphia Phillies, where the Phillies leftfielder called off the shortstop and caught the fly ball while running towards the infield. The outfielder was closer to the infield when he caught that ball than Kozma was in the NLWC.

The presence of additional post-season umpires stationed along the foul lines may have affected this play. Holbrook was the left-field umpire; when he declared infield fly, he was positioned along the left-field foul line, on a horizontal line to where Kozma had stopped to wait for the ball, with a clear, unbroken view of the shortstop "comfortably underneath" the ball. But perspective, an umpire's view and angle on the play, affects what he sees and calls. In a regular-season game staffed by four umpires, the call would have been with the third-base umpire, who would have run along the foul line from behind third base to follow the play, leaving him below the line of the shortstop and the ball, observing from a different angle that might have produced a different call. This does not mean that Holbrook was right or wrong in invoking the Rule, since the play requires an exercise of judgment from the umpire's angle. It means that the answer depends on the additional variable of the umpire's positioning and perspective on the play. Rice suggests that Holbrook's flatter view made it more difficult to judge how far into the outfield the ball and the infielder had traveled; an umpire trailing the play might have seen that differently.

Finally, this play offers a baseball-based illustration of two competing methods of statutory interpretation—textualism and purposivism. Textualism focuses on the text of the rule,[59] while purposivism accounts for the rule's underlying purpose and the ends the rulemaking body sought to accomplish in enacting that rule.[60] A textualist applies the rule when the text requires, while a purposivist invokes a rule in circumstances that implicate the evil the rule is designed to eliminate, even if the text pushes towards a different result. Accepting that Holbrook accurately observed Kozma settled comfortably underneath the ball and that the ball unquestionably had sufficient arc—such that it was a fair fly ball playable by an infielder with ordinary effort in an appropriate base-out situation—these competing interpretive methods perhaps compel different results on this play.

The call was correct as a textual matter. There were runners on first and second with one out. It was a fair fly ball hit with sufficient arc. Kozma, an infielder, could have caught the ball with ordinary effort, based on the settled-comfortably heuristic. The text of the Infield Fly Rule, as MLB umpires interpret it, requires nothing more. Indeed, given Rice's argument that a ball hit to the left-field wall could be an infield fly under the plain text, this play certainly qualified.

A purposivist approach introduces additional considerations. The purpose of the Infield Fly Rule—the evil the Rule is designed to eliminate—is the force-out double play on multiple baserunners forced to advance by the infielder intentionally not catching the easily playable fair fly ball. But video indicates that a double play was impossible on this play. The ball and Kozma traveled far enough into the outfield that both baserunners moved halfway to the next bases while waiting on the play and both easily advanced once the ball fell to the ground, just as they easily could have retreated safely to their original bases had the ball been caught. They were not the trapped, "up-a-tree" baserunners the Rule seeks to protect. Because the lead runner moved far from second base, the single-throw/tag-the-runner/tag-the-bag double play was not an option and any double play would have required two throws. The first throw to get the lead runner at third would have been so far that, even if it put out the lead runner, the trailing runner easily would have reached second base safely ahead of the relay (assuming he ran hard). Video seems to show that Kozma always planned to catch this ball and only failed to do so because of an unintentional miscommunication with his teammate. A purposivist umpire might not invoke the Rule here, knowing that a double play on the non-catch was impossible and the infielder was not attempting to manipulate the play. The play did not implicate the evil the Infield Fly Rule was designed to eliminate.

Purposivism also considers who a rule seeks to protect and who will be protected on any play. (Courts sometimes describe this as whether a party falls within a law's "zone of interest," within the class of people and activities Congress wanted to protect by enacting a law.[61]) But that reveals a second unique feature of this play—it benefited the defense at the expense of the offense. Given the impossibility of a double play and the unintentionality of Kozma's non-catch, the Braves would have had the bases loaded, including the tying run on first, with one out had infield fly not been declared. Instead, they were left with runners on second and third with two outs. While a good scoring opportunity, it placed them in a worse base-out situation than they would have been had infield fly not been called, while leaving the Cardinals in a slightly better position.

Rice teaches a purposivist approach to the Rule. He wants umpires to account for the possibility of the double play and the Rule's purpose of protecting baserunners as background considerations before invoking. Holbrook must have determined that the ball remained close enough to the infield to make a double play possible.

This play remains the touchstone for current discussions of the Infield Fly Rule. Announcers routinely invoke its memory in reporting plays on which the Rule has been called, particularly on balls that travel further into the outfield—the comparison to whether the ball was as far out as the ball in the NLWC is inevitable. Some announcers have become more inclined to discuss the Rule's details or purposes. In a September 2016 game on which infield fly had been declared, Houston Astros announcers offered a complete and correct tutorial on the Rule, its purpose of eliminating the cheap double play, and why that purpose is implicated only with runners on first and second or bases loaded, so long as the batter runs hard to first.

Non-Invocation and Non-Catches

Although the batter is out on the infield-fly call and the baserunners are not forced to advance, the Infield Fly Rule does not eliminate all gamesmanship on fair fly balls in infield-fly situations. An infielder still might intentionally fail to catch the ball, hoping to create an opportunity for additional benefits under the rules. He might hope the umpire will not invoke or even try to fool him into not invoking, enabling the defense to turn a double play. He might try to fool the baserunners into doing something stupid or instinctual when the ball lands on the ground. Or he might try to do both.

An umpire's failure to invoke the Rule places the offense in the same disadvantageous position as if the Rule did not exist, leaving a situation that infielders might exploit, either intentionally or unintentionally.

Intentional Non-Catches

A July 2013 game between the Minnesota Twins and Los Angeles Angels of Anaheim shows intentional exploitation, where the umpire's failure to invoke produced a double-play on an intentional non-catch. This is the critical play in my eight-year study of the Infield Fly Rule. It provides a concrete, non-speculative, non-counter-factual example of why the Rule exists, why it remains necessary, and why it would be possible, likely, and enticing for infielders to intentionally fail to catch fly balls in search of double plays if baseball were to repeal the Rule.

Trailing 1–0 in the top of the ninth, the Twins had first-and-second/none-out, an infield-fly situation. The batter hit a ball off his fists, lofting a low, looping, soft pop to the right of the pitcher's mound. Angels pitcher Ernesto Frieri drifted toward the ball, as both baserunners, expecting him to catch the ball, retreated to their bases and the batter trotted up the first-base line in the ritual of running-out the batted ball. It looked like a typical infield fly, in which the Rule would be invoked, the ball would be caught anyway, and the runners would stay put.

But Frieri stopped moving one step before he was directly underneath the ball, allowing it to fall to the ground, untouched, at his feet. No umpire signaled infield fly. Frieri picked the ball and threw to first base to put out the batter (who was about halfway up the line when the ball landed on the ground). The first baseman and shortstop then executed a run-down to tag out the runner on first (who no longer was forced to advance, since the batter was out at first) between first and second, with the runner on second advancing safely to third. At the end of the play, the Twins had the tying run on third, but two out. They failed to score in the inning and lost the game, 1–0.[62]

This play appears to have warranted an infield-fly call—NBC Sports headlined a web article "Isn't This Why We Have an Infield Fly Rule?"[63] The pitcher could have caught the ball by taking one more step to his right and putting his glove up. But he made an obvious and intentional decision to not stand directly underneath the ball and to not put up his glove, allowing the ball to fall untouched at his feet. Both baserunners were trapped and up a tree—they had retreated to their current bases and could not have hoped to outrun throws to the next bases.

The resulting double play, involving the batter and one baserunner, was different than the one the rulemakers feared and that the Rule seeks to prevent. But that does not make a meaningful difference. Frieri made a reasonable move here—the ball was not hit very high in the air, it landed roughly halfway between the mound and first base, and the runner was not sprinting up the line, leaving a short throw and easy first out. Nor does it make life easier for the baserunner on first. Although he was not forced to advance once the batter was put out at first (thus the reason he had to be tagged out in the rundown), he could not have remained near first as the play developed—the first baseman would have caught the throw from Frieri, tagged the runner, then stepped on first base to complete the double play (that single-throw double play often occurs at second base). In any event, that the pitcher pursued one double play does not mean that other, better double plays were not likely. With the runner on second retreating, Frieri also could have thrown to the shortstop covering for the single-throw/tag-the-runner/tag-the-base double play there. Or he could have wheeled and thrown to third base to start a third-to-second double play on the forced baserunners. He even could have wheeled and thrown to third to start a third-to-first double play on one forced baserunner and the jogging batter. The combination of the ball on the infield grass and the non-call offered the defense a wealth of options.

Following the game, the umpires explained that, while the ball had sufficient arc to warrant invoking the Rule, the pitcher was not comfortably underneath the ball to catch it.[64] That explanation makes the call shakier, not stronger. The pitcher was comfortable and settled in his position—he was standing still, no longer moving or running to get into position. He could have caught the ball simply by raising his glove. He was not directly underneath the ball, but only because he intentionally stopped moving. He wanted the ball to land in front of him so he was positioned to pick the ball and throw it; standing directly beneath the ball would have left him less able to play the ball off the ground. This perhaps reveals a problem with the umpires' "comfortably underneath" heuristic to define when a ball is playable with ordinary effort—the infielder's best position is not directly underneath the descending ball, but one step behind it.

A better argument against declaring infield fly on this play might have been that the ball did not have sufficient arc, that it was more of a humpback liner, hit lower and dropping quickly. Indeed, the ball was hit low enough that the batter could be thrown out at first, which typically does not happen on infield flies with sufficient arc. While the batter was not sprinting up the line (he only began running hard once the ball landed on the ground and he realized the umpire had not invoked), a true fly ball is typically high enough that the batter easily reaches first base before the ball lands. The problematic double play involves multiple baserunners, who cannot run immediately, not one baserunner and the batter who can and should run immediately. That batter could be included on the double play suggests the ball was not hit high enough to warrant a call. On the other hand, the ball fell straight down to the ground, rather than carrying forward through the infield, as would a typical line drive; this suggests sufficient arc to justify invoking the Rule.

Although an outlier, this play illustrates why the Infield Fly Rule exists and how it affects the game. A double play is a plausible, perhaps probable, outcome on intentionally uncaught fly balls such as this one, hit on or close to the infield where the infielder has time to position himself. Even with the Rule, a smart infielder can create a double play by positioning himself to fool the umpire into not invoking. It follows that, without the Rule, intentionally not catching fair fly balls in search of double plays would become common and widespread practice.

Unintentional Non-Catches and Non-Invocation

A 2017 game between the Orioles and Boston Red Sox demonstrates unintentional exploitation, where the umpire's failure to declare infield fly on an unintentional non-catch produced a triple play.

The Red Sox were batting with first-and-second/none-out, when the batter popped the ball into shallow left field, approximately 20 feet onto the outfield grass behind the shortstop. Orioles shortstop J.J. Hardy backpedaled, stopped, and waved his right arm above his head, signaling his readiness to catch the ball and warning the leftfielder to stay back. But the ball drifted behind and to his right, falling to the ground. The baserunners, seeing Hardy going back and expecting the Rule would be in effect, retreated to their bases. But the umpire never declared infield fly, meaning the batter was not out and the runners were forced to advance. Hardy grabbed the ball off the ground and threw to the second baseman at the bag, who tagged the runner on second for the out, stepped on the bag to put out the runner on first, then threw to first base to complete an inning-ending triple play on the batter. The baserunners, confused as to why infield fly was not called, stood helplessly in place as they were tagged out, unsure whether to run or retreat. The batter, expecting infield fly to be declared, turned toward the dugout before touching first base.[65]

The Rule could have been invoked on this play. Hardy (an excellent defensive shortstop) was settled comfortably under the ball and telling everyone around him he was ready to catch it, at least until the last instant, by putting up his arm and yelling "I got it." The ball was close to the infield on the left side, about 20 feet onto the outfield grass and easily playable by the shortstop; the first throw following the unintentional non-catch was short and easy, with the retreating runners unable to make up the ground. This looks like a play on which, without the Rule, an infielder might seek the double play through an intentional non-catch, knowing the baserunners must retreat.

The Orioles turned a nearly identical triple play in 2000 on a ball hit to the same spot on the field in the same situation. On that play, the shortstop settled directly underneath the ball, then intentionally and obviously stepped back at the last instant so the ball fell at his feet, before picking the ball and throwing to second for the same tag-the-runner/step-on-the-bag/throw-to-first triple play.[66]

This play demonstrates how an umpire's approach to the timing of the infield-fly call affects the outcome of an individual play. Under Jim Evans' model of invoking with the ball at its apex, the umpire should have invoked here—when the ball was at its apex, Hardy appeared settled, able, and ready to handle the fly ball with ordinary effort. But under the Brent Rice model of waiting for the ball to descend, the non-call was appropriate, as it accounts for an infielder misjudging the ball or for the ball carrying away from him at the last instant, as happened on this play.

The Special Problem of Non-Invocation

These two plays highlight one ironic point—umpires' failure to invoke the Rule may disadvantage the offense more than would the complete absence (or repeal) of the Rule. Non-invocation of an existing rule subverts player expectations, as their efforts to conform to expected rules work against them. The existence of a rule designed to protect baserunners lulls them into a false security that disadvantages them if the rule is not put into effect on the play. On both non-catches, the baserunners retreated, expecting that infield fly would be called and not hinting or even faking at advancing. They believed they were safe where they were on the play, without concern for being forced to advance. Similarly, neither batter ran hard up the line or ran all the way to first base, expecting the ball to be caught or to be called out under the Rule.

The difference between non-existence and non-invocation most affects batters, as an unanticipated non-call of an existing rule scrambles expectations. With no Infield Fly Rule, a batter always would hustle to first base; while it is likely he will be out when the infielder catches the easily playable fly ball, there is a chance the infielder will drop it and the batter needs to reach first base should that happen. A batter would move on an infield fly as he does on a fly ball to the outfield. With the Rule, the batter assumes he is out even if the ball is not caught, so running hard or continuing to the base should be unnecessary. And when the umpire does not invoke the rule when the offensive players expect him to, it places the batter at a unique disadvantage.

In his role as rules consultant, Rich Marazzi offered several recommendations on how baserunners and batters should handle "no call" infield-fly situations such as the one from the Orioles-Red Sox game. Batters must run hard and all the way to first base on all plays, to allow for the non-call/non-catch that allows him to reach safely, however unlikely it might be. Baserunners should not retreat to their current bases on balls that carry into the outfield, but should lead at least a few steps toward the next base. How far he leads depends on the location of the ball. In the Orioles-Red Sox game, the runner on second could not lead very far, because the ball was close to him on the left side of the field, although the runner on first could (and did) move nearly halfway to the next base. On a ball hit to the right side of the field (where, Rice argues, umpires are less likely to invoke), the runner on second can take a larger lead towards third base.

In Marazzi's view, the worst this play should have gone for the Red Sox was one force-out on the lead baserunner heading to third, with the runner on first safely reaching second and the batter safely reaching first. The batter should have continued running to first, and the runner on first, having taken a 40-foot lead towards second, should have continued in that direction once the ball hit the ground. Even if the runner on second remained there, the runner on first was entitled to that base once the ball landed, the batter became a runner, and the runners were forced to advance. The runner on second could have been tagged out, even if standing on second base, but the runner on first would have been safe at second if he reached before the infielder tagged the base.

However the Red Sox baserunners should have reacted, that option was not available to the Twins runners in their game against the Angels. They remained unavoidably helpless, where the ball landed in the middle of the infield grass and neither runner had an opportunity to lead far enough to the next base to avoid being thrown out.

Intentional Non-Catches and Fooling Everyone

The more likely goal of an infielder in intentionally not catching the fair fly ball, even when the Rule exists and infield fly is declared, is to fool the runners into a baserunning mistake that might produce a double play. With the batter out on the infield-fly call, the defense must put out one napping baserunner to complete the double play (and to end the inning if one man were out), and may be able to turn a triple play if the ball is hit to the right place on the field or if both baserunners are napping. One critic of the original 1894 Rule, sportswriter John H. Gruber, expressed concern for these "dull-headed men" who run themselves into multiple outs.[67] While the strategy typically does not work against alert baserunners, the attempt is costless for the defense, so long as the infielder can control the ball when it lands on the ground.

Consider a May 2015 game between the Washington Nationals and Atlanta Braves. With the Nationals batting with first-and-second/none-out, the batter hit a soft fly ball just onto the outfield grass behind shortstop, clearly high enough to justify an infield-fly call; the Braves shortstop backed up, then allowed the ball to fall at his feet, scooped it, and made a snap throw to second. Recognizing what the shortstop was doing and that infield fly had been declared, the runner stayed safely on the base.

For the Braves shortstop, however, it was worth a shot. He knew he was going to get one out on the batter from the infield-fly call, so there was no reason to catch the ball. And assuming he handled the ball and made a good snap throw, nothing was lost by trying to catch the runner unawares. Alternatively, the shortstop may have allowed the ball to fall to the ground hoping to fool the umpire into not invoking the Rule, meaning the snap throw could have begun a tag-the-runner/step-on-the-base double play.

The announcers acknowledged the clever baseball-ing by all involved. One emphasized that "that's why the Infield Fly Rule exists, because it prevents the infielder from turning a double play on a play like that." They credited the umpire for making the correct call and the baserunner for knowing the rules, being aware of the call, and having the presence of mind to not stray too far from the base. Implicitly, they also credited the shortstop for giving it a shot. In an August 2017 game against Texas, the Angels shortstop wore a grin on his face as he allowed a similar batted ball to fall to the ground in the same situation, knowing that his gambit would not succeed but having fun in the attempt.

Not every player has the presence of mind not to be fooled. Many baserunners never shake the athletic instinct to run whenever a batted ball touches the ground in a force-out situation, forgetting the details of the game situation and the Infield Fly Rule in favor of muscle memory sharpened by years of playing baseball. I identified numerous plays on which the umpire declared infield fly and called the batter out, the infielder unintentionally dropped or failed to catch the fly ball, and one or more baserunners started for the next base, with varying results. This sample is not unique—similar plays have occurred in baseball over the years.[68]

Running on the unintentionally uncaught ball most frequently works to the offense's detriment. On fly balls on the infield or shallow outfield grass, infielders can pick the ball off the ground and tag or throw out a confused runner who ran when he did not have to. This outcome is consistent with the Infield Fly Rule. While designed to protect baserunners, it permits them to run at their own risk and to bear the cost of the risk not paying off. Put differently, the Infield Fly Rule protects the batting team against an unfair force-out double play it cannot control; it does not protect the batting team against a double play resulting from its own stupid mistakes.

Consider several examples.

In April 2016, the Philadelphia Phillies had first-and-second/one-out against the New York Mets. The Mets third baseman could not catch a fly ball on the infield grass between third base and the mound, as the wind carried the ball behind him. The umpire called the batter out on the infield fly, but both runners ran when the ball hit the ground. The runner on second advanced to third, but the runner on first got caught between the bases and was tagged out in a rundown for an inning-ending double play. The Mets announcer criticized that runner in sharpest terms, as "a player who didn't know the Infield Fly Rule."

In an August 2015 Cincinnati Reds-Kansas City Royals game, the Reds had bases-loaded/one-out. The batter hit a soft fly ball about halfway up the first baseline that fell to the ground untouched because of miscommunication between the pitcher and first baseman. The umpire declared infield fly, putting the batter out. Yet the runner on third broke when the ball landed and was easily tagged out at home. The Reds announcers expressed shock, wondering "when's the last time you saw that in a Major-League game."

The answer would have been a game between the Toronto Blue Jays and Cleveland Indians three months earlier. On a pop-up caught by the pitcher to the left of the mound, the runner on second ran halfway to third without tagging up for no obvious reason and was doubled off when he could not get back to second in time.

Confusion is not one-sided. It sometimes works to the offense's advantage, as when infielders neglect to tag the baserunners advancing on an uncaught fly ball on which the Rule was invoked. A rule designed to protect the offense from an inherent disadvantage affirmatively benefits it.

This occurred in an August 2017 Texas-Anaheim game. With the Angels batting with first-and-second/one-out, the Rangers catcher dropped a pop fly in front of the pitcher's mound. The first-base umpire declared infield fly by raising his arm, but no one noticed. The Rangers first baseman fielded the dropped ball and threw to third ahead of the advancing baserunner, who the third-base umpire initially called out on a force play. When the plate umpire and the first-base umpire conferred and realized the latter had declared infield fly, the batter was called out and the runner on third called safe, since he had not been tagged. The Rangers manager objected to the change of call, although his team gained an out on the play either way. Despite there being two outs in the inning, he preferred having first-and-second (the situation if the Rule had not been invoked, the lead runner was out at third, and the batter reached first base safely) to having second-and-third (the situation with the invocation, in which the batter was out and the runners advanced safely).

Confusion over what runners and fielders must do again left the Phillies on the short end of an infield-fly play, this time in a 2014 game that produced a run for the Mets. The Mets had bases-loaded/one-out. The Phillies second baseman was unable to catch a soft fly ball on the edge of the outfield grass, as the ball drifted to his right. The umpire declared infield fly, putting the batter out. The runner on third broke for home when the ball hit the ground; the second baseman was unable to quickly play the ball and threw high, allowing the runner to slide home safely. It was not clear from video whether the catcher was aware that the force was off and he had to tag the runner (which would have been difficult on the high throw).

Some plays are marked by one or both teams forgetting the rules, producing confusion and a comedy of errors. The ultimate beneficiary on the play depends on who makes the biggest and the last mistake.

In an April 2010 game between the Mets and Braves, the Mets had first-and-second/one-out. The batter popped a ball between the third baseman and shortstop on the cut-out portion of the infield grass near third. The umpire declared infield fly. The third baseman cut in front of the shortstop to catch the ball, but it hit off the heel of his glove and bounced towards home. When the ball hit the ground, both base runners ran and the batter continued to first. The catcher picked the ball off the ground near home, walked towards first base, and flipped the ball to the first baseman standing on the bag, who then tagged the batter standing on the base. Unfortunately for the Braves, neither move had any legal effect. The batter was out on the infield-fly call, so tagging him or tagging first base did nothing. Because the ball had landed on the ground, the runner on first could advance to second at his own risk, which he did. He was not required to retouch before advancing to second, so tagging first base did not put him out. At this point, the play looked like the 2012 NLWC infield-fly call: the batter out on the call, the runners advancing on the non-catch.

But by walking the ball up the line, the catcher vacated home. In the confusion of the defense taking unnecessary steps while failing to create an out, the runner who had advanced from second to third broke for the uncovered plate. He beat the throw home with a head-first slide past the pitcher covering. The Mets, who had been leading 3–2 at the time, won 5–2, so the additional run did not provide the margin of victory.

To find a game in which the defense's lack of awareness or knowledge of the Rule was outcome-determinative, we go to Japan for a 2015 game between the Hiroshima Toyo Carp and Tokyo's Yomiuri Giants featuring a walk-off[69] infield fly.

Batting in the bottom of the ninth of a tie game, the Carp had bases-loaded/one-out. The batter hit a high pop fly on the grass in front of the home-plate circle. The third-base umpire signaled infield fly. The catcher, first baseman, and third baseman converged on the ball, then allowed it to fall untouched among them, all apparently having lost sight of it. The baserunner on third broke for home when the ball landed on the ground. The catcher grabbed the ball and stepped on home ahead of the runner, but did not tag him. The batter having been called out on the infield fly removed the force play; the runner on third no longer was forced to run, making it a tag play at home. Following an argument and an umpire conference, in which the third-base umpire informed his colleagues that he had declared infield fly, the runner was called safe because of the lack of a tag and the game ended in a Carp victory.

Finally, consider a May 2014 game between the Mets and Dodgers, with the Dodgers batting with first-and-second/none-out. The batter hit a fly ball into short right-center; the ball drifted to the right and behind the Mets second baseman, falling to the ground untouched. It is unclear from the video what the second baseman was doing; it appears he both misplayed the ball as it drifted away from him and pulled up and allowed it to fall to the ground. In any event, the umpire declared infield fly, with both runners breaking for the next bases when the ball hit the ground. The runner on second easily advanced to third. The second baseman threw the ball to the shortstop standing on second base, who caught it while the runner on first was still more than five feet away from second. But the shortstop, believing the runner was out on the force when he caught the ball, stepped away from the play without tagging the runner, who continued to the base. Because no force was in effect and the runner could only be put out on the tag, the umpire gave no signal, since the play was not over; had the runner continued to the base and stayed there, he would have been safe. Fortunately for the Mets, the runner also was unaware of the situation. Believing he was forced out at second when the shortstop caught the ball, he overran second and stopped, looking to the umpire for some signal that was not forthcoming because, again, the play was not over. Seeing that, the shortstop finally tagged the runner for the out, completing the double play. The defense came out ahead on the play, having the advantage of the last move but not the last mistake.

This play is notable for another reason—the only ones aware of the situation seemed to be the Mets broadcasters. Recognizing that infield fly had been declared, one shouted instructions to the Mets shortstop, in loud and frustrated tones: "You can tag [the runner] out! Oh, but he didn't tag him! You need to tag him!" His partner can be heard groaning "Oh, my god." Both expressed clear relief when the runner, standing confusedly three steps off the base, was finally tagged out.

It would be easy to attribute these recent examples to "players these days not knowing the rules or respecting the game as they did back in my day," as a loss for the code and guidelines of the game.[70] But players misunderstanding what to do under the Infield Fly Rule seems as old as the game itself. In *Rules and Lore*, Marazzi describes two infield-fly plays—one from 1961 and one from 1972—identical to the one described above. The defense believed it only had to touch the base, the runner believed he had been forced out and began trotting off the field without the umpire having declared him out, and the infielder tagged the runner out to complete the double play when he figured out what was going on.[71]

Other Uncaught Fair Fly Balls

By the early 1900s, the Infield Fly Rule controlled this game situation, leaving the original trap ball (or Brush and Von der Ahe's) rule as a historical relic superseded by a specific rule that better addressed the problem.

As the Infield Fly Rule assumed its current form by 1920, however, holes remained. There was no rule to handle balls hit well beyond the infield that only could be caught with ordinary effort by an outfielder. There was no rule for situations in which a force was in effect at only one base—runner on first or runners on first-and-third. There was no rule for uncaught or intentionally dropped line drives or bunts. As with the rule that evolved into the Infield Fly Rule, baseball proceeded in fits and starts in addressing the problem.

A 1939 rule prohibited outfielders from intentionally dropping the ball in an infield-fly situation. Although a double play was less likely on a ball hit into the outfield because of the greater distance for the throws, the original concerns for subterfuge, deception, and confusion of the baserunners justified the broader limitation. In 1942, the rule was expanded to cover all intentional drops by all players whenever there was at least one force in effect on the bases—first only, first-and-third, and infield-fly situations.

In 1975, baseball enacted the modern version of the trap ball rule, as a separate, although complementary, regulation to the Infield Fly Rule. A batter is out if an "infielder intentionally drops a fair fly ball or line drive with first, first and second, first and third, or first, second and third base occupied before two are out. The ball is dead and the runner or runners shall return to their original base or bases."[72]

By its terms, the rule is limited in four important respects. A batter is not out when an infielder tries to catch the ball but unintentionally drops it, a judgment call for the umpire. The rule applies to all balls hit in the air, including bunts and line drives. An approved ruling clarifies that the batter is not out if the infielder allows the ball to fall to the ground untouched, intentionally or not.

Most importantly, this rule yields to the Infield Fly when they overlap.[73] This means two things. First, while the ball ordinarily is dead on an intentional drop, it remains alive and the runners can advance at their own risk if the intentional drop occurs in an infield-fly situation. Second, while intentional drop cannot be invoked on a ball that falls to the ground untouched, Infield Fly can be. In the handful of infield-fly situations in recent seasons in which infielders intentionally did not catch the fly ball in an effort to fool the baserunners or the umpire, they always let the ball fall untouched, rather than allowing it to hit their gloves and drop to the ground.

The historical irony is that the play by John Montgomery Ward in that 1893 Giants-Orioles game—the catalyst for the new rule and 120 years of experimentation and amendment—remains legal. The Infield Fly Rule would not apply because there was only a runner on first base. The modern intentional-drop rule would not bar the play because Ward allowed the ball to fall to the ground untouched, rather than intentionally dropping it or intentionally having it hit his glove and fall to the ground.

The intentional non-catch with a runner on first remains part of the modern game. Maury Wills, a star shortstop for the Dodgers, practiced it regularly.[74] Detroit Tigers second-baseman Ian Kinsler pulled it in a 2016 game against the Rangers, allowing the ball to fall softly between his feet by leaving his hands down to avoid touching the ball on its descent.[75]

The play is sufficiently rare that Kinsler's move confused everyone. The umpires had to confer to ensure they made the correct call, then had to explain it to the Rangers manager. The announcers similarly could not figure out what to make of the play. They began by talking about the Infield Fly Rule, even while acknowledging it should not apply with a runner on first base only. They then discussed whether Kinsler had failed to sufficiently "sell" his fake to the umpire and whether his non-catch was too obvious in its intentionality. This concern for deception and intentionality hearkened back to the 1890s, when umpires policed deception that was inconsistent with the spirit of the game,[76] or to 1905, when NL President Pulliam encouraged umpires to police obvious intentional non-catches where the batter was slower than the baserunner.[77] But the current rule does not care about the fielder's intent—Kinsler's intent was obvious, as he did not bother raising his glove—if the ball lands on the ground untouched.

The modern intentional-drop rule played a small, unspoken role in one of the most controversial plays in World Series history. In the bottom of the sixth inning of Game 4 of the 1978 World Series against the Dodgers, the New York Yankees had first-and-second/one-out. The Yankee batter hit a low, knee-high, sinking line drive to the left of Dodger shortstop Bill Russell. Russell shuffled to his left, caught the ball around shin-level, dropped it, and chased it down as it rolled off his glove and towards second base. He barehanded the ball, stepped on second for the force out, and threw to first for what would have been an inning-ending (and rally-killing) double play.

That double play was thwarted when Russell's relay hit Reggie Jackson, the runner on first standing between first and second, and caromed into right field. This allowed the batter to reach first safely and the runner on second, who had advanced to third when the batted ball hit the ground, to score. Although Jackson already was out on the force at second, he had not left the base path, seemingly confused by the play. The umpires ruled that Jackson had not interfered with the throw, although replay shows Jackson thrusting his right hip to the side as the ball approached him. Had the throw not hit Jackson, the batter certainly would have been out at first to complete the double play.

The play remains infamous for the failure to call interference.[78] But the Infield Fly Rule and the intentional-drop rule played initial silent roles, requiring umpires to make several decisions before reaching whether Jackson interfered.

All four umpires were aware that this was an infield-fly situation, likely having signaled to one another prior to the pitch. And all four had to decide that the Infield Fly Rule should not be put into effect on a ball hit in the air with first-and-second/one-out. This was an easy determination, as the ball was obviously a line drive, lacking the height and parabolic arc umpires look for.

Next, the second-base umpire had to determine that Russell had not intentionally dropped the line drive, because the intentional-drop prohibition applies to line drives. Had the drop been deemed intentional, Piniella would have been out and the play dead, with the baserunners remaining at first and second. This was a closer decision. Russell appeared to close his glove before the ball got there, allowing the ball to strike the tip of his glove, although it is difficult to tell whether that was intentional or whether he mistimed the ball. In judging the drop unintentional, the umpire likely observed Russell's body language, how far the ball rolled away from him after he dropped it, and the way he scrambled after it, all of which suggested lack of intent and a player trying to catch up to a miscue. Alternatively, Russell successfully "sold" the play, making the drop look sufficiently unintentional precisely to avoid the call and give himself the chance at a double play. Unfortunately for the Dodgers, Russell's sales job was thwarted by a historic non-call on runner interference.

* * *

This chapter explored what the Infield Fly Rule and related rules look like, how they began and evolved, and how they have been applied over 120 years of baseball. With that background, Chapter 2 turns to a deeper exploration of the underlying reasons and policy justifications for the Infield Fly Rule within baseball's logic, structure, ethics, strategies, and rules. It offers a comprehensive legal defense of the Rule's current existence, scope, and reach as part of the game.

Defending the Infield Fly Rule

With the history and evolution of the Infield Fly Rule behind us, we turn to the crux of this book—a defense and justification for the Infield Fly Rule as a necessary and appropriate part of baseball, in light of the game's rules, logic, structure, strategies, and ethics. Baseball needs the Infield Fly Rule and would be a lesser game without it.

Rethinking the Historical Argument

Attempting to square a modern defense of the Infield Fly Rule with its history presents one challenge—the explanations and justifications offered in 1894 are no longer salient in the modern game. The Rule grew from the developing perception that the intentional drop had become more tricky and deceptive than clever, thereby inconsistent with a degree of gentility and sportsmanship that rulemakers wished to instill.[1] But these have become outdated and irrelevant relics of a "kinder, gentler America."[2] We accept that athletes are professionals and should, within the basic rules of the game, seek any advantage in pursuit of victory and be rewarded for it. The imperative to win—and the imperative to understand the rules, to know how to play according to them, and to use them to one's benefit— differentiates professional baseball from the games played by children.[3]

That historical assumption also is inaccurate. Deception, trickery, and subterfuge are and always have been an essential part of baseball. As long-time executive Andy MacPhail put it, "There is a culture of deception in this game. It's been in this game for 100 years. I do not look at this in terms of ethics. It's the culture of the game."[4] Jason Turbow and Michael Duca describe this as "a soft-focus that turns lines that are sharply delineated in the view of an outsider into so much gray area at the level of the playing field." They capture it this way: "Deceiving an umpire is cheating, but deceiving an opponent … is simply hard-nosed competition."[5]

History aside, any discussion of rules and practices must account for a modern game in a modern society, in which the "rude coarseness of the twenty-first century" creates "an era that embraces both risk and subterfuge." In the modern game played in the modern world, "subterfuge can be applauded as clever rather than condemned as devious."[6] That ideal is reflected in the sentiment among players that "if you're not cheating, you're not trying."[7] Cheating is admired, almost a sacrament, such that there is no line between "smart" play and "cheating."[8] There is a reason that, 120 years later, John Montgomery Ward is remembered not as a cheater but as a "clever baseball-ist" and that both Ward and Wright sit in the National Baseball Hall of Fame in Cooperstown.

Baseball is replete with accepted and lauded examples of trickery and deception, within the rules of the game, in the never-ending search for competitive advantage.[9] Consider the following:

- The hidden-ball trick, defined in *The Dickson Baseball Dictionary* as a "time-honored legal ruse." A player, usually an infielder, hides the ball hoping the baserunner believes the ball had been returned to the pitcher and steps off the base, then tags the runner out. The play was popular in the late 19th century, and despite criticisms and attempts to eliminate it as "unprofessional," it survives to this day.[10]
- Infielders pantomime catching or throwing the ball, even though it has traveled well into the outfield; the goal of these feints is to fool and slow a baserunner who does not know where the ball is and tries to rely on the fielders' movements for a clue. Commentators credit this move with helping the Minnesota Twins defeat the Atlanta Braves in the 1991 World Series. With Game 7 tied 0–0, a Braves batter hit a long drive to the outfield wall that should have allowed the Braves' Lonnie Smith to score from first base. But Twins infielder Chuck Knoblauch pretended he already had received the relay throw from the outfielder, causing Smith, watching Knoblauch rather than the ball, to hesitate near second base; that hesitation forced Smith to stop at third on the play, where he was stranded. The Twins won Game 7, and the Series, in the tenth inning.
- Pitching is the art of deception. The point is to fool batters as to the type of pitch and where it is going, making it more difficult for them to hit. The changeup is deceptive by definition—a pitch thrown with the same windup, motion, hand position, arm angle, and arm speed as a fastball, but as much as 15 or 20 miles per

hour slower and with particular movement; the point is to fool the batter on that pitch and to make the pitcher's fastball seem faster.[11] Effective pitchers "hide the ball" in their pitching motion, making it more difficult for the batter to see, follow, and hit.[12]

- The rules attempt to delineate acceptable and unacceptable deceptions. Pitchers cannot deceive baserunners by faking pick-off throws to first or third base, although they can fake a throw to second. In 2013, baseball amended the balk rule to outlaw one notorious pick-off deception—the right-handed pitcher faking a throw to third, then wheeling to throw to first, hoping to catch that runner too far off the base.[13]
- Players steal signs, teams accept that opponents will try to steal signs, and it is up to each team to protect their own.[14] The 1951 New York Giants famously employed an elaborate system of stolen signs—aided by having a clubhouse behind centerfield in their home Polo Grounds—in staging their historic comeback from 14 games behind the Brooklyn Dodgers to win the National League pennant.[15]

Limits on deception derive not from formal prohibitions, but from an elaborate code of unwritten rules, established within "the rough-and-tumble game on the field in which players fight for an edge." These practices or mores reflect "rules that serious fans already know and new fans need to learn in order to speak baseball."[16]

Rule changes outlawing deceptive practices often are motivated by something other than a need or desire to eliminate subterfuge or to promote gentility and sportsmanship. Baseball eliminated the fake-to-third-spin-to-first pickoff not because it was deceptive, but because it annoyed and upset fans who believed it was a balk (which it was not prior to 2013) or a waste of time that rarely worked (which it was).[17]

What does this have to do with the Infield Fly Rule? Intentionally not catching a fair fly ball is nowhere near the deception *cum* cheating that triggers controversy. To the extent an intentional non-catch is deceptive, it deceives the opponent, making it hard-nosed competition rather than cheating.[18]

Deception constitutes a small part of what enables the double play on an uncaught fly ball in the infield-fly situation. Left to his own devices without the limitations imposed by the Infield Fly Rule, an infielder must disguise his intentions, keeping the baserunners guessing as to whether he will catch the ball and whether they should attempt to advance or not—recall George Wright and his teammates arguing about whether he would or should catch a fly ball. But infielders can do this without being deceptive. The infield fly does not require the active deception of catching-then-dropping the ball, since the umpire declares infield fly while the ball is in the air and before it reaches the fielder's glove. The infielder disguises future intentions more than he presently deceives anyone; to return to the pitcher comparison, it is more akin to the accepted practice of hiding the ball on delivery than to the prohibited practice of faking a pick-off throw.

Baseball's modern (and, in reality, longstanding and historical) ethos places the onus on the opposing team to avoid being deceived. Subject to the unwritten rules, cheating and deception constitute routine practices in the business of baseball.

A Modern Defense of the Infield Fly Rule

But if the modern game views deception differently, then the Infield Fly Rule's original anti-deception justification no longer holds—whether because the game always has accepted deception and rulemakers were deluding themselves by insisting on a limiting rule in 1894 or because the modern game accepts a greater degree of deception, rendering the limiting rule a relic of a different age. It becomes time to reject the Infield Fly Rule.[19] Or at least to question its survival.

The Rule might survive because of what legal scholars call "path dependence," in which "an outcome or decision is shaped in specific and systematic ways by the historical path leading to it." Path dependence occurs because once an initial decision has been made and followed, it is "less costly to continue down that same path than it is to change to a different path," as a "step in one direction decreases the cost (or increases the benefit) of an additional step in the same direction."[20]

Baseball established the modern Infield Fly Rule more than a century ago. Whether the original purpose holds, everyone in the game has devoted the time, cost, and energy to learning that Rule and conforming their behavior to it—infielders almost always attempt to catch fair fly balls and almost always do so; baserunners learn (or should learn) that they are not forced to run on an uncaught ball and must be tagged out if they do; infielders learn (or should learn) that they must tag the runners if they run; and umpires have developed a shorthand and procedures for identifying when the Rule should be in effect and how to apply it. Path dependence says it is less costly and less burdensome for everyone to continue along that same path than it would be to force everyone to adjust their conduct to an amended Rule and to a new legal reality in the game.

The solution to path dependence is to become aware of it and to recognize the appropriate time to jump off that path. But that is often easier said than done. Baseball—a backward-looking, tradition-bound sport in which "purists" abound[21]—is especially susceptible to path dependence and to becoming locked into the way things have been done because that is the way they have been done for more than a century. Former umpire and current umpire instructor Brent Rice identifies nostalgia and the Rule's deep-seated part of baseball history as the primary reason he would retain it.

A second, more principled way to justify the continued existence of the Infield Fly Rule is to identify different explanations and justifications for it. The Rule can be reverse-engineered—begin from its long-standing existence, identify what defines the situation and what makes it unique, and look for a basis that might explain and justify (or not justify) the limiting rule. This exercise reveals that the Infield Fly Rule is not a product of path dependence on no-longer-valid rationales. It is a warranted and necessary part of modern baseball—not for outdated sportsmanship-and-deception reasons offered in 1895, but for reasons sounding in concerns that remain relevant in the modern game.

The Infield Fly Rule is grounded in highly and uniquely inequitable cost-benefit disparities, one-sided and extraordinary strategic imbalances, and perverse incentives. It is grounded in baseball's rules maintaining essentially equitable (even if not equal) cost-benefit exchanges between opposing teams in game situations, avoiding situations of forced inequity. It also is grounded in the game's aesthetics—about what makes a visually and competitively pleasing game, the on-field plays and strategies the rules should incentivize, and the on-field plays and strategies the rules should disincentivize, if not prohibit outright. The Infield Fly Rule does not form the core of baseball—baseball without the Infield Fly Rule would still be recognizable as baseball.[22] But it would be baseball played in a different way at times, with players attempting plays and producing outcomes that are both extraordinarily and one-sidedly inequitable and aesthetically displeasing. Rather than a relic of the 19th century, the Infield Fly Rule reflects concerns that resonate in the modern game and in the realities of the special game situation to which the Rule applies.

Recall what constitutes an infield-fly situation and a play in which the Infield Fly Rule might be put into effect. There are fewer than two outs in the inning. There are runners on first and second or the bases are loaded—in other words, there are force-outs in effect at two or more bases (other than first base), two or more baserunners must try to advance on any ball that lands on the ground in fair territory when the batter becomes a runner, and two or more baserunners can be put out at the next base by the infielder stepping on the base without having to tag that runner. The batter has hit a fair fly ball that is not a line drive or bunt and that is easily catchable by the average infielder. The ball likely is on or near the infield (so not hit far or hard), hit reasonably high in the air and in a parabolic arc, and the infielder is settled comfortably beneath the ball waiting for it to come down. This leaves the infielder with options—he can catch the ball on the fly for the out on the batter; he can drop the ball in a controlled fashion; or he can allow it land untouched on the ground at his feet, standing in a fielding position from which he quickly can handle the ball off the ground and throw to an appropriate base.

Without an Infield Fly Rule, those baserunners are in a bind—"up a tree," as that 1911 newspaper story put it.[23] But they are trapped not by infielder deception, but by the limitations that baseball's ordinary rules and practices impose on them, depending on whether a batted ball is in the air or on the ground. Harold Seymour explains the problem: "No matter what the runners did, a double play could be made. If they clung to the bases, the infielder could drop the ball intentionally, forcing them off their bases to make room for the batter, in which case they could be put out. If they took a chance and ran, the fielder could make a simple catch and double them off base."[24] We can elaborate on Seymour's point by imagining what might happen absent an Infield Fly Rule.

Baserunners in this situation cannot run if a fly ball is caught unless they retouch, while they must run immediately if the ball lands on the ground and the batter becomes a runner. What options does a baserunner have? If he remains at his current base (as he ordinarily would on a fly ball near enough to the infield to be playable by an infielder with ordinary effort) and the ball is not caught, he will be forced out at the next base. If he takes a chance and runs on the hit and the infielder catches the easily playable fly ball for the out on the batter, the baserunner will be doubled off at his previous base (as might his fellow baserunner, producing a triple play). The baserunner also lacks the option of leading between the bases while he waits, given the likely proximity of the ball to the infield. If the baserunner strays too far from his current base into No-Man's Land and the ball is caught, he will be unable to retreat in time to avoid the double play. He thus must remain on or near the base (within about three to five steps or five to ten feet), giving him time to safely retreat on the catch. But if the infielder does not catch the fly ball, the baserunner now has too far to run to beat the throw to the next base, since those throws will be short and quick. And because the baserunner is forced to advance when the ball lands on the ground and the batter becomes a runner, the infielders need only step on the base and throw, without having to tag the runners.

With a force-out in effect at multiple bases and no Infield Fly Rule, the defense can turn that uncaught fly ball into a double play with two short throws to force the lead runners. With bases-loaded/none out, a ball hit in the right spot on the field might produce a triple play on three short throws. The defense might turn a double play on a single throw—picking the ball up and throwing to second base, where the covering infielder can tag the runner on second (who stayed near the base fearing the fly ball would be caught) before he can advance to third, then step on second base to force the runner from first (who never had a chance to run to second). Alternatively, the defense can turn a double play on the threat of an uncaught fly ball. Fearing the non-catch double play, a baserunner might run immediately, or at least lead farther towards the next base to give him time to beat the throw. Seeing that, the infielder can catch the fair fly ball and double the baserunner off his previous base. This is the gamesmanship and uncertainty that George Wright mastered.[25]

The question is what, if anything, is special or unique about this game situation and these possibilities that demands a limiting rule. I propose a framework for identifying and defining a special class of game situations in baseball (and, in Chapter 4, other sports). Plays falling within this framework feature all of four defining characteristics, working in combination. I will briefly describe the four characteristics here, then elaborate on each and explain how the Infield Fly fits this framework and those characteristics.

(1) In the game situation, one team or player intentionally acts contrary to ordinary athletic expectations. He intentionally fails to perform the expected athletic skills in the expected manner. Or he does the opposite of what he ordinarily wants to do or is expected to do on the field, according to the game's ordinary structures, rules, practices, ethics, and strategies. The player intentionally and willfully fails to seek what legal scholar Mitchell Berman calls "excellence in executing the particular athletic virtues that the sport is centrally designed to showcase and reward."[26] This could involve either a player intentionally doing what he ordinarily does not want to do or a player intentionally failing to do what he ordinarily wants to do.

(2) Because a team or player engages in number (1), that team or player gains a one-sided, extraordinary, unique, and inequitable cost-benefit advantage, an advantage well beyond what it would gain on the same play acting within ordinary expectations in executing the game's athletic skills and virtues. One side obtains extraordinary benefits and incurs no meaningful costs, while the other side incurs extraordinary costs and gains no meaningful benefits. This is different than the bilateral cost-benefit exchanges that characterize ordinary competition; it is a unilateral, one-

sided, and highly imbalanced exchange, with all costs going one way and all benefits the other.

(3) One team possesses extraordinary and one-sided control or influence over the play. The team acting contrary to athletic expectations in search of the inequitable and one-sided cost-benefit advantage exercises exclusive control over the play and can manipulate and bend the situation to its will, at least with proper execution of the play. The team burdened by extraordinary costs is unable to meaningfully respond or counter the opponent's actions within the game's ordinary structures, rules, practices, ethics, and strategies. That is, there is nothing Team A can do to stop Team X from intentionally acting contrary to athletic expectations and nothing Team A can do to avoid or minimize the extraordinary costs it incurs. There is no strategic interchange, no cat-and-mouse game in which each side jockeys for competitive advantage. Given the rules and strictures of the sport, the game situation is overwhelmingly weighted in favor of one team and against the other. And the cost-incurring team can do nothing to change that.

(4) The combination of numbers (2) and (3) creates for the advantaged team a perverse incentive to attempt number (1), most, many, or even every time the game situation arises. The cost-benefit advantage for the advantaged team is so great, inequitable, and one-sided, and the opposing team so powerless to respond or counter. The game situation thus incentivizes the team to act contrary to ordinary athletic expectations whenever it arises, whether by intentionally failing to perform the expected skills in the expected manner or by intentionally performing the opposite of those skills.

If, but only if, each defining characteristic is present on a play or game situation, this framework dictates that a special, situation-specific rule becomes necessary and appropriate. I refer to such rules as "limiting rules" because they limit (or eliminate) the strategic options available to one team, thereby limiting the power of that team to manipulate the situation in search of that inequitable and one-sided cost-benefit advantage. A limiting rule functions in either of two ways. It may prohibit players from intentionally acting contrary to ordinary expectations—from intentionally failing to seek excellence in executing the athletic virtues and from intentionally failing to perform the expected skills in the expected manner—by imposing a penalty or sanction for intentionally doing so. Or, more commonly, it eliminates the inequitable cost-benefit advantage to be gained on the play, thereby removing the perverse incentive to intentionally act contrary to ordinary athletic expectations. Either way, the limiting rule maintains cost-benefit equity within the game situation and ensures that the play cannot produce extraordinary, unilateral, and one-sided benefits for one team or impose extraordinary, unilateral, and one-sided costs on the other.

This framework does not require limiting rules in every game situation or even every game situation that might produce cost-benefit disadvantages and disparities. If one or more defining characteristics is absent from a play that situation falls outside this framework and a limiting rule is not necessary or appropriate, at least not for the same policy reasons. A limiting rule may be appropriate for other reasons, notably the game's aesthetics and a sense of the "right way" to play the game. But the rule is not, and should not be, imposed for reasons of cost-benefit equity.

The framework is concededly subjective. Reasonable minds may differ over when a cost-benefit disparity is sufficiently inequitable or extraordinary, although one-sidedness should be easy to identify. Reasonable minds may differ over when one side is sufficiently unable to influence a play as to be helpless. Reasonable minds may differ over what the game's ordinary structures, rules, practices, ethics, aesthetics, and strategies entail and when players act consistent with or contrary to them. Reasonable minds may differ over what the game's athletic virtues entail and when someone intentionally fails to achieve excellence in executing them. And reasonable minds may differ over a game's aesthetics and the "right way" to play.

These four characteristics are not selected at random or arbitrarily. Rather, they are baked into the structure of plays. They form the play's foundation—the basic structure of the game situation, players' behavior within that game situation, and how the rules should respond.

The Framework Applied

Even if subjective, this framework provides a way to view the infield-fly situation and to explain and justify the Infield Fly Rule, which remains the quintessential example of a limiting rule in baseball and in all sports. The risk in this game situation is that infielders will intentionally not catch an easily playable fair fly ball, choosing instead to turn the double (or even triple) play by forcing-out multiple otherwise-helpless baserunners. The Infield Fly Rule stops infielders from turning that double play through the intentional non-catch by limiting it to one out on the batter and removing the force-out on the baserunners, thereby eliminating the perverse incentive for infielders to intentionally fail to catch that fair fly ball. With no double play in the offing, the infielders have nothing to gain from intentionally failing to catch the fair fly ball.

1. Intentional failure to perform expected athletic skills in the expected manner.

The double play arises in the infield-fly situation because an infielder intentionally fails to perform the expected athletic skills and to demonstrate athletic virtue in the manner that an infielder ordinarily wants to perform them, consistent with the game's ordinary structures, rules, practices, ethics, aesthetics, and strategies. Infielders ordinarily want, and are expected, to catch fair fly balls that are playable with ordinary effort; they ordinarily do not want to intentionally drop or not catch such balls. Infielders ordinarily want to make the simple play of catching the batted ball on the fly to put the batter out, rather than the complicated and riskier play of not catching the fly ball and trying to throw runners out on the bases. The natural and expected consequence of an easily playable fair fly ball to an infielder is one out on the batter from the infielder catching the ball—that is the DNA of the play. Any other outcome departs the game's ordinary expectations.

The intentionality of the non-catch is essential to understanding the Infield Fly Rule. Although infielders sometimes drop balls on which the Rule is in effect, almost all those drops (all but five or six in the eight seasons I examined) are unintentional, the occasional miscue that is part of baseball. But an infielder can do less to take advantage of an unintentional non-catch, with a ball he wanted to catch but misplayed. The infield fly in the 2012 NLWC illustrates the point. Because Cardinals shortstop Pete Kozma wanted to catch the ball, neither he nor the outfielder who fielded the ball off the ground was prepared for the non-catch or in position to do something with the ball off the ground. An infielder can do more with an intentional non-catch. Knowing he does not want to catch the fly ball, he can set himself in good fielding position, control how and where the ball falls to the ground, and be ready to quickly and cleanly play the ball off the ground and throw it to the appropriate base. Ideally, the infielder will field the ball the way Tigers infielder Ian Kinsler did on his non-catch in 2016[27] or the way Angels pitcher Ernesto Frieri did on the 2013 non-call[28]: Not settled directly beneath the ball, allowing it to land softly between his feet, and making the short, easy throw to force-out the first baserunner.

This characteristic is subject to several counter-arguments as applied to an infield fly.

The pitcher has performed his expected athletic skills in the expected manner on this play and should be rewarded for that performance—he threw a pitch that induced the batter to hit a weak, shallow fly ball that an infielder can catch easily. But the expected outcome of that great pitch is one out on a fly-out—the infielder catches the batted ball out of the air, putting the batter out for one out. Anything more on the play results from a distinct move by the infielder to intentionally not catch the batted ball—intentionally not doing what he ordinarily wants to do. The pitcher has not "earned" anything more than that. Moreover, not every easy pop-fly is the result of a good pitch simpliciter—sometimes a pitcher gets away with a bad pitch (in the sense of it being too close to the strike zone and without movement) that a batter fails to hit well.

A second counter-argument is that the infielder demonstrates great athletic skills and virtues on an intentional non-catch—one infielder must cleanly field the ball once it lands on the ground and make a quick and accurate throw, while he and his teammates make the catches, throws, and tags necessary to complete the double play. There is skill involved in not catching a fly ball in a way that allows the fielder to play the ball off the ground and put out the baserunners. And if, through their strategic choices to run, feint, or hold, baserunners pressure the defense, the infielder displays and highlights his athletic skills by handling that more-challenging play.[29] In other words, infielders seek excellence in executing the athletic virtues when they create a double play off the intentionally uncaught fly ball. Only the initial non-catch of the fly ball is out of the ordinary; the rest is a display of baseball skill. And because players demonstrate athletic skill and virtue on the play, the situation should be left to bear the strategic risks of the infielder catching or not catching the ball and making the appropriate play.

This brings aesthetics and appearances to the fore as distinct considerations in the design of any sport. The rules should create a game that is not only competitively and equitably balanced, but aesthetically pleasing to play and watch. Baseball's rulemakers can reasonably prefer that infielders catch (or at least not intentionally fail to catch) easily playable fair fly balls, believing that the game is more pleasing for fans to watch when players catch the ball. Even if there is nothing deceptive about the resulting double play and even if the risks to both sides create chaos that creates excitement,[30] those considerations can be outweighed by the aesthetic preference of not having infielders routinely dropping or not catching easily playable balls.

Aesthetic considerations alone may justify rules banning or controlling some practices and strategies, although the analysis leading to that result looks different than what leads to a true limiting rule. Baseball outlawed the fake-to-third-fake-to-first-pick-off play (making it a balk[31]) for purely aesthetic reasons—the desire to stop a silly play that confused fans and never worked.

The game's aesthetics inform what constitutes ordinary athletic expectations and what constitutes a player acting consistent with or contrary to athletic virtues. Even if there are athletic skills and virtues in an infielder playing an intentional non-catch off the ground and making the necessary moves and throws to complete the double play ahead of the baserunners, the distaste for the appearances around intentionally dropped or uncaught balls reasonably might carry the day. Aesthetics also gain power in combination with the other three characteristics. An instinct towards playing the game the "right way" justifies certain limitations on what players remain free to do on the field.

2. One-sided inequitable cost-benefit disparity.

Imagine baseball without the Infield Fly Rule. And imagine the outcome on an uncaught easily playable fair fly ball if the infielders are able to make the necessary throws and catches without error once the ball lands on the ground. The intentional non-catch in this game situation creates a substantial and overwhelmingly inequitable cost-benefit disparity that runs entirely in one direction. One team receives substantial benefits while incurring no meaningful costs, while the other incurs substantial costs while receiving no meaningful benefits. And the benefits received and costs incurred are significantly greater than otherwise expected or incurred on the play compared with the result had everyone acted according to the game's ordinary structures, rules, practices, ethics, and strategies.

The defense likely gets two outs on the non-catch by turning a force-out double play on two baserunners trying advance (which bases those outs are recorded depends on the base-out situation and where the fly ball is hit). A triple play is possible in a bases-loaded/none-out situation on a fly ball hit to the right spot on the field (likely close to a base, allowing a short initial throw). The best outcome for the defense is that it gets out of the inning on a double play (where there had been one out in the inning) or a triple play (where there had been none out and the bases loaded). The multiple-killing ends the batting team's turn at bat and its opportunity to score runs, gives the defense its next opportunity to score runs, and moves the game a half-inning closer to its conclusion. The worst outcome is a double play that leaves two outs and a runner on first (if there had been first-and-second) or runners on first-and-second (if the bases had been loaded). And the defense gains these multiple outs at no cost or disadvantage, leaving it substantially better off than if the infielder had caught the fly ball.

The offense experiences everything described above as substantial costs. It incurs multiple outs and loses multiple baserunners and runners in scoring position. A triple play (with none out) or double play (with one out) ends one of its nine precious opportunities to score runs and brings it closer to the end of the game. And the offense gains no benefits on the play, always leaving it worse off than if the infielder had caught the fly ball. The offense "loses" on the play, beyond what it expected or anticipated.

Contrast this with the relatively equitable, two-way cost-benefit distribution if the infielder performs the expected athletic skills in the expected manner and catches the easily playable fair fly ball. The defense gets one out on the batter, bringing it closer to the end of the inning (a benefit); the catch does not end the inning or bring that team to bat and it still faces the next batter with multiple baserunners, at least one in scoring position (all costs). The offense loses an out (a cost); it retains its turn at bat and its opportunity to score and still has multiple runners on base, at least one in scoring position (all benefits). In other words, each side incurs some costs and gains some benefits, on a relatively even, two-way exchange, far from the extraordinary one-sided disparity resulting from the non-catch.

Again, reasonable minds may differ over when costs and benefits become extraordinary or one-sided (a point I discuss later as to other plays in baseball and as to other sports). Reasonable minds may differ about whether any imbalance should be regarded as overly inequitable—one may argue that creating cost-benefit imbalance is the goal of baseball and all efforts to gain all advantages and impose all disadvantages, no matter how wide, should be praised, protected, and celebrated.

This reflects a normative choice for rulemakers in selecting among competing possible rules. If the question is whether the Infield Fly Rule is rationally justified, the demonstrable disparity in costs and benefits for each team suggests it is. Nor can there be any doubt that the source of the cost-benefit disparity is number (1), the defense intentionally not performing the athletic skill it ordinarily wants to perform of catching an easily playable fair fly ball.

3. One-sided disparity in control or influence on the play.

The defense is in complete control of the infield-fly situation and how the play proceeds. The offense is helpless to respond or counter the defensive strategy and has no way to avoid the costs imposed on the play.

Consider how the defense controls this play. The fair fly ball is playable by an infielder with ordinary effort, which means the ball could be caught easily by a Major League infielder of average ability. The ball is hit straight up in the air (it cannot be a line drive), likely high in the air (umpires look for sufficient parabolic arc), but not very hard or far. The play unfolds slowly; the height of the ball leaves the infielder time to get into position, settle comfortably underneath the ball, and wait for it to come down. Although artificial boundaries such as the outfield grass do not dictate the rule's applicability, the ball likely is near, if not on, the infield (as to be playable by the infielder with ordinary effort). Location has several effects. The infielder does not have very far to run to get into his position comfortably underneath the ball. He can stand and wait, think the play through, know where the runners are and what they are doing (retreating, advancing, or leading part way between the bases), and allow the ball to fall straight to the ground at his feet in a way that he can surround and control. The proximity to the infield, especially to the left side of the infield, means the first (or only) throw to a base to get the lead runner will be short and quick. The softness of the hit and the infielder's ability to settle comfortably underneath it means he can wait until the last instant to decide whether to catch the fly ball (even from his knees) or allow it to fall at his feet. He can disguise his intentions to get the runners to commit to running or staying put, then catch or not catch the ball accordingly once he knows their move. The ordinary effort required on these fair fly balls cuts both ways. All the things that make it easy for an average infielder to catch the ball make it easy for an average infielder to intentionally not catch it in pursuit of the force-out double play.

Other infielders have time to become part of, and to influence, this slow-developing play. While the ball is in the air and their teammate settles comfortably beneath it, they move to their proper positions to receive and make the throws for the multiple force-outs on the baserunners. Especially important in the common first-and-second situation is for the shortstop or second baseman to cover second, ready to receive the throw for the single-throw/tag-the-runner/step-on-the-base double play. Like George Wright's Cincinnati teammates, the other infielders can communicate with their teammate about what the baserunners are doing, whether he should catch the fly ball, and which base to throw to for the double play.

The defense incurs one risk—botching the play. The ball might take a bad or unexpected bounce when it lands on the ground that the infielder cannot control. Or one or more throws might not be accurate. But the likelihood of an error by a Major-League infielder is relatively low—less than 2.5 percent.[32] (I consider this point in later chapters.) And the quality of modern fields reduces (although does not eliminate) the risk of bad bounces.[33]

More importantly, the infielders control how cleanly they play the ball or how accurately they make the throws—the batting team does not cause or even influence those miscues. Any defensive skill must balance against the absence and impossibility of any competing skill from the offense—the batting team cannot do anything to change the course of the play or to avoid the costs. As Seymour argues, no matter what the baserunners do, they risk a double play; they are trapped, helpless, and entirely reactive.

They must run if the ball is not caught, but cannot run (without retouching) if the ball is caught. They must wait on the infielder to catch or not catch, then react accordingly. But given the nature and location of the hit—high, not hard, likely on or close to the infield—they cannot stray too far from their current bases as they wait, lest they be doubled off (as happened in a 2015 game—the runner on second inexplicably ran halfway to third on a low pop-up that was caught in front of the pitcher's mound and was easily doubled-off at second). The baserunners retreat and remain a few steps from their current bases, allowing them to return safely when the ball is caught. They now must run 80-plus feet from a standing start when the ball is not caught, attempting to outrun one or two relatively short throws to the bases—something they are unlikely to be able to do.

In his critique of the Rule, Judge Guilford argues that the infielder's choice of whether to catch the ball and the baserunners' choice of whether to run could precipitate an interesting cat-and-mouse game, in which each tries to guess what the other will do and each tries to draw a move from the other.[34] An infielder might catch or not catch at random and the baserunners might risk running at random, hoping to pick the "right" play. But the control disparity remains because the defense retains first-mover advantage, with the baserunners always reactive. The infielder's decision to catch or not catch dictates what the baserunners are permitted to do under the rules—they must return to the current base or retouch before running if he catches, they must run immediately if he does not catch. If an infielder settled comfortably beneath the ball knows the runners are moving (because his teammates talk him through the play), he catches the ball and doubles (or triples) them at their prior bases. If he knows the runners are holding and retreating, he lets the ball fall to the ground and doubles them at the next bases.

Nothing limits the defense's control over the play. At best, a runner might pressure the fielder into misplaying the ball or making a bad throw, whether by charging to the next base or convincingly feinting in that direction. But if both sides properly perform the necessary athletic skills and virtues, the defense never relinquishes the control advantage.

The defensive advantage in this situation increases without the Infield Fly Rule, because the rule change gives infielders incentive to practice and hone the unique skills involved in intentionally not catching fly balls and gives teams an incentive to develop plays and strategies around it. Because current rules largely eliminate the intentionally uncaught fly ball double play from the game, it is pointless for players to practice or teams to strategize for the situation. Other than the occasional attempt to fool a runner into committing or an umpire into not declaring infield fly, there is no reason for infielders to not catch the fly ball. That lack of practice shows in the defensive confusion on the occasional unintentional drop, with fielders uncertain about whether they must tag baserunners.

Repeal the Infield Fly Rule, however, and teams and players gain incentive to practice and strategize. Professional infielders would become quite skillful at the new athletic virtues involved in the play—waiting until the last instant to catch or not catch the fly ball, catching and throwing from their knees to disguise their intent until the last instant, keeping the runners guessing, and letting the ball land on the ground in a way that is easy to pick, control, and throw. Improving these necessary infielder skills enhances the inherent defensive advantage and offensive disadvantage, increasing the likelihood of the double play and the cost-benefit advantage for the defense. Baserunners' fakes become less effective the more infielders and teams practice, improve, and perfect this play.

Finally, one might argue that the batting team does not lack control on the play. Rather, the batter failed to exercise the control he had—he failed to achieve excellence in executing athletic virtues—when he "barely tick[ed] the bottom of the ball and produce[d] a pop-up" that an infielder could easily catch.[35] In other words, the batting team lacks control because the batter did a poor job of hitting; had he better performed his job, his teammates on the base paths would not be up a tree. It follows that we should reward the athletic virtue of the pitcher whose good pitch induced this weak hit by allowing his team to get as many outs as possible on the play.

Control and influence over a play are measured once the play has begun, not before. "The play" includes the fly ball occurring after the pitch and what each side can do once the pitch is hit—the equities of control over that situation. Otherwise, we might play this out in an infinite regression. If the two baserunners had done something different in their respective at-bats (such as hitting home runs or not getting on base at all), the batting team would not have runners on first and second with fewer than two out and would not be at risk of a double play on the uncaught pop-up. Or if the batter had done an even worse job than an easy popup and instead swung and missed, failing to put the ball in play at all. It might even follow that the offense would have been better off had the runners not reached base at all, because it would protect the offense from the risk of the inequitable double play.

4. Perverse incentives.

The fourth characteristic is the key to this framework. The extraordinary, inequitable, and one-sided cost-benefit advantage to be gained by one team combined with the one-sided control that team wields over the play gives it a perverse incentive to intentionally fail to perform the expected athletic skills in the expected manner virtually every time (or most times) the appropriate game situation arises.

Return to baseball without the Infield Fly Rule. The cost-benefit imbalance of the potential double play—high benefits and no costs to the defense and high costs and no benefits to the offense—combined with the defense's total control over the play incentivizes the unexpected athletic move of intentionally not catching the easily playable fair fly ball. The benefits to the defense are sufficiently great and the costs sufficiently low (or non-existent) that infielders will ignore the ordinary athletic virtues and the simple play—catching the easily catchable ball to put out the batter—in favor of the riskier move of pursuing a double play by not catching the ball. The extraordinary benefits—two (and perhaps three) outs instead of one, fewer runners on base and in scoring position, perhaps the end of the opponent's turn at bat—incentivize that intentional non-catch.

Without the Infield Fly Rule, this would represent the only baseball situation in which the defense consistently achieves a substantially more optimal outcome, and makes itself substantially better off, by intentionally not catching a batted ball in fair territory. The perverse incentive is present most times the situation arises, regardless of circumstance and regardless of who is involved in the play for the batting team. That the batter, who will reach base, might be faster than the baserunners put out on the base paths (the inverse of the John Montgomery Ward play and the batter with the speed of an ice wagon) does not change those incentives. The defense would prefer two outs and one fast runner on first to one out that leaves two slower runners on base and in scoring position. And when, as is often the case, the double play would end the inning on a one-out fly ball, the incentive for the intentional non-catch grows further.

Infield Fly Rule Reconsidered

The Infield Fly Rule responds to this combination of four defining characteristics baked into the infield-fly situation. By declaring the batter out, removing the force-outs on the baserunners, and not forcing them to advance when the ball lands on the ground, the Rule eliminates the possibility of a force-out double play on an uncaught fly ball. This deprives the fielding team of the extraordinary, inequitable, and one-sided cost-benefit advantage through a play the offense cannot counter. That, in turn, eliminates the perverse incentive for an infielder to intentionally not catch the easily playable fair fly ball—the defense gains no additional advantage from the non-catch, so it has no reason to take the risk of intentionally not catching the fly ball. This is a paradigmatic limiting rule—it limits the defense's strategic options, thereby eliminating the cost-benefit disparity and the perverse incentives to act contrary to expectations in pursuit of that disparity.

The precise operation of the Infield Fly Rule is telling under this framework. The Rule does not prohibit the targeted conduct, as infielders remain free to intentionally not catch easily playable fair fly balls. Rather, the Rule strips the defense of any reason to intentionally not catch the easily play fair fly ball. It imposes the expected outcome on the play with the expected cost-benefit allocation, the same result as if the infielder performs his athletic skills and virtues as ordinarily expected and catches the easily playable fair fly ball. By imposing that outcome, the Rule removes any incentive for infielders to intentionally not catch the ball, because there is nothing more to gain.

The outcome of the play is the same whether the infielder catches the batted ball, drops it, or lets it fall to the ground untouched and whether he acts intentionally or unintentionally. The batter is out, the runners are not forced to advance (although they may run at their own risk, without a force play), the offense continues its at-bat with one more out and likely the same baserunner situation. Not catching the fly ball will not produce a double or triple play or otherwise provide the defense with a greater benefit than catching it. An infielder therefore has no incentive to do anything other than catch a fair fly ball.

Measuring the Scope of the Infield Fly Rule

Any limiting rule must eliminate extraordinary cost-benefit disparities and perverse incentives in situations containing all four characteristics. But it should not reach game situations lacking one or more of those characteristics, which do not produce the same cost-benefit disparities or provide the same perverse incentives.

The Infield Fly Rule breaks into nine component elements: (1) force-outs in effect on two or more baserunners other than the batter (meaning runners on first and second or bases loaded); (2) fewer than two out; (3) the batted ball is a fly ball; (4) the batted ball is in fair territory; (5) the batted ball is not a bunt; (6) the batted ball is not a line drive; (7) the batted ball can be caught by an infielder; (8) the batted ball can be caught with ordinary effort, meaning it is a routine play for the average infielder in the league; and (9) runners can advance at their own risk, but are not forced to advance.

The following section explores each component of the infield-fly situation and the current Rule, considers how altering or removing an element satisfies one or more of the defining characteristics from the game situation, and shows why eliminating one characteristic eliminates the need for a limiting rule in that revised situation. This framework reveals that the Infield Fly Rule not only is necessary, but is properly drafted to apply only to situations appropriately subject to a limiting rule, but not to many similar-but-distinguishable situations that should not.

1. Force-outs in effect on two or more baserunners.

Not having a force-out in effect on two or more baserunners could mean a force-out in effect at one base—first-base-only or first-and-third, with a force only in effect at second base. It also could mean that no force-out is in effect at any base, such as second only, third only, or second-and-third.

The common theme is that the defense cannot turn a double (much less triple) play on an intentionally uncaught fly ball through force-outs on multiple baserunners, because there are not multiple baserunners and forced to run when the ball lands on the ground.

With only one possible force-out, the defense has little incentive to intentionally not catch the fly ball. The result on the play will be one out, whether on the batter because the infielder catches the ball or on the baserunner forced at second base while the batter reaches first base safely, and leaves a runner on first (or first and third). This produces an equitable and two-way cost-benefit exchange—the offense gives up one out but continues batting with the same number of base runners at the same bases, while the defense gets one out but still must deal with the same number of baserunners at the same bases. The defense's easiest and safest move in this situation is the ordinarily expected one—catch the fly ball, get the one out on the batter, and keep the baserunners in place. And when no force-outs are in effect, the defense loses all incentive to intentionally not catch the fly ball, because catching the fly ball is the only way to guarantee an out on the play.

The intentional non-catch with one force-out in effect produces a small cost-benefit advantage for the defense, and small incentive for infielders to intentionally not catch the fly ball, if the defense can exchange a fast runner on first for a slow batter. This is what Ward did in 1893 and what infielders occasionally do today, as with the Tigers' Kinsler in 2016. But the advantage gained rarely will be sufficiently overwhelming or one-sided to warrant a limiting rule. During the 2016 season, for example, a batting team's run expectancy (the average number of runs a team scores in an inning from a given base-out situation to the end of that inning)[36] with runner-on-first/one-out was approximately 0.5 runs and with runner-on-first/two-out was approximately 0.2 runs.[37] Those numbers perhaps move slightly when the difference between the baserunner on first and the batter is dramatic—the Ice Wagon of 1893 or trading all-time steals leader Rickey Henderson[38] as the baserunner for Prince Fielder, a large, lumbering slugger of the '00s.[39] But differences in speed rarely are so pronounced. And the relative decline of the stolen base in recent years decreases the value to the defense of getting the faster runner off the bases.[40] Any additional benefit to the defense and cost to the offense is far smaller than the benefits gained and costs incurred from a double play. The praise heaped on Kinsler for this play in 2016—and the initial confusion the play caused players, coaches, umpires, and announcers—demonstrates how infrequently infielders attempt the move.[41] Although it remains a limited option, the small cost-benefit advantage is rarely worth the effort.

With only one (or no) force-outs in effect, a double play is possible only if one of two things occurs. The batter might fail to run hard to first base and be unable to beat the relay throw to complete the double play. But this should not happen on a ball hit high enough to constitute a non-line-drive fly ball, if the batter hustles up the line. There also might be a double play on a tag play on a baserunner who runs at his own risk when not forced to advance. Either situation lacks the second and third characteristics—extreme one-sided cost-benefit disparity and disparity in control over the play. Any double play results from the offense's poor decisionmaking and execution, voluntarily undertaken rather than forced on them by the game's structures. The batter should have hustled to first base; the baserunner should have been smarter in choosing when and whether to advance.

This situation also shows that the Infield Fly Rule is more about one-sided cost-benefit inequities than about the aesthetics or deception of intentionally uncaught fair fly balls. Rulemakers only limited or eliminated the incentive for an intentional non-catch when two force-outs are in effect on the basepaths, not when only one force-out is in effect. They were not concerned about infielders intentionally not catching all fair fly balls, despite the aesthetic considerations, only intentionally not catching fair fly balls when the non-catch produces the one-sided and inequitable cost-benefit disparity of a force-out double play involving multiple baserunners. Without that disparity or with a more-even cost-benefit exchange, aesthetics and subterfuge were not sufficient concerns to command a limiting rule.

Having the applicability of the Infield Fly Rule depend on the number of forced baserunners and the number of outs gained on the play arguably maps onto visceral fan reactions to each situation. As discussed in Chapter 1, John Montgomery Ward was lauded for his "excellent judgment," even by opposing fans and media, on his 1893 non-catch,[42] while George Wright's 1870 non-catch outraged opposing Brooklyn fans, who showered him with an array of insults and profanities.[43] One difference between the two plays is the outcome—Ward's non-catch produced the same single out, only trading one baserunner for another at first, while Wright's non-catch produced an inning-ending double play. The disparate fan reactions suggests an instinctual understanding that the difference matters.

2. Less than two outs.

The easiest and most obvious limitation on the reach of the Infield Fly Rule is its non-application when two are out in the inning. The only reasonable move for the defense is the simple one—catch the fair fly ball for the easy one out to end the inning. No other strategy produces better results and other strategies threaten worse results.

With two outs, the defense needs only one out to end the inning, so the outcome of the play will always be one out. The defense gains no cost-benefit advantage, much less an overwhelming one, by intentionally not catching the fly ball. It gains the same benefits and the offense incurs the same costs whether the infielder catches the fly ball to put out the batter or plays it off the ground and forces-out a baserunner. The inability to gain an extra out eliminates the fourth characteristic—the defense lacks any perverse incentive to intentionally not catch the ball; the simplest and least risky way to get the needed one out is to catch the easily playable fair fly ball.

In fact, incentives run in the opposite direction with two out, because not catching the fly ball places the defense at a substantial disadvantage. Baserunners run immediately on any batted ball with two outs and need not wait for the ball to land on the ground; they no longer worry about being doubled-off, as the inning ends when the fly ball is caught. Like a hustling batter (who should run as soon as he hits the ball), a hustling baserunner runs on contact with two out and should reach the next base safely before the high fly ball can fall to the ground and the infielder can grab it and make the necessary throw. The force-out on the uncaught ball becomes a difficult (if not impossible) play for the defense; this gives infielders even less incentive to intentionally not catch the ball, because the catch is the only way to guarantee an out.

3. Fly ball.

The defining characteristics in the infield-fly situation derive from the batted ball being a fly ball—hence the name of the Rule. The defense gains the extraordinary cost-benefit advantage of the double play on two baserunners only by trapping them, making them wait near their current bases to see if the ball is caught, and leaving them too far to reach the next bases safely to avoid the double play on a-non-catch. The defense's one-sided control over the play depends on the infielder manipulating whether to catch the ball in the air and disguising his intention, forcing the baserunners to wait helplessly to see what happens. All of which creates the perverse incentive for the defense to intentionally not perform the expected athletic skill by intentionally not catching the ball.

But baserunners only must wait in this way, creating the defensive advantages, on fly balls. Each of these elements disappears on ground balls.

The baserunners can (indeed must) run immediately when the ball is hit on the ground, making it easier to reach the next base in time. This gives baserunners greater influence over the play. It also strips infielders of the choice of whether to catch the ball, because the defense gets any outs on a ground ball only by performing the expected athletic virtue of catching the batted ball. If the infielder does not catch it, it may roll through the infield and into the outfield. If he bobbles or otherwise does not handle it cleanly, he may be unable to throw out any of the runners, all of whom ran immediately. And a non-catch on the groundball leaves him less able to make the multiple throws necessary to turn a double play and gain the extraordinary one-sided cost-benefit advantage.

Given these outcomes, there is no perverse incentive for the defense to intentionally not catch a groundball, where doing so leaves it with no chance for multiple outs on a double play and may leave it with no outs at all.

4. Not a line drive.

Exclusive defensive control and manipulation also is absent on a line drive. That, in turn, removes the perverse incentive to intentionally not catch the batted ball in search of an inequitable, one-sided cost-benefit advantage.

Line drives are less likely to be playable by an infielder with ordinary effort, and infielders are less able to control and manipulate them. Line drives hit harder and lower, affording the infielder no (or less) time to position himself, settle under the ball, allow it to fall, and play it off the ground. He may have to move quickly in one direction; he may have to jump, run, dive, slide, or reach to play the ball. He may be less able to control how the ball bounces or rolls once it hits the ground and he may have to scramble after it when it lands.

An untouched, uncaught line drive does not travel in a parabola and fall straight to the ground at the feet of a waiting, settled infielder. It continues flying in a straight line through the infield and into the outfield for a hit, leaving the infielder no chance to make any play once the ball lands on the ground. He can keep the ball near him and on the infield only if he catches-then-drops the ball or knocks it down. But knocking the ball down may not leave him in position to easily control the ball, pick it up, and begin the double play; he may be too busy scrambling after it to play it quickly and cleanly. And intentionally dropping a line drive runs afoul of the intentional-drop rule, resulting in the batter being called out and the ball being dead,[44] leaving the defense with the same one out, but depriving it of the opportunity for a double play. The incentive therefore runs to catching the batted ball.

In enforcing the Infield Fly Rule, umpires must judge whether a batted ball is a fly ball, a line drive, or, as often happens, something in between, the humpback liner that travels like a line drive, generally lower than a fly ball, then sinks downward to the ground, playing like a ground ball.[45] A humpback liner travels in something of a parabola and is not hit very hard or far (often struck off the handle or the end of the bat), although with less height and arc than a fly ball. Like a line drive, its lower trajectory leaves the infielder less time to position himself and settle underneath the ball. In characterizing the hit, the umpire must predict what might happen to that batted ball if untouched—would it continue through the infield and onto the grass for a hit or would it drop at the infielder's feet, waiting to be picked up for the double play.

The Infield Fly Rule categorically excludes line drives. But this creates a potential fit problem. Because most true line drives travel hard and straight, they carry into the outfield if untouched; there is no exclusive defensive control and no perverse incentive for the infielder to intentionally not catch them. But some humpback liners produce the extraordinary cost-benefit disparity because they drop straight to the ground and are hit softly enough to be fielded easily and turned into double plays. The question—for rulemakers and umpires—is whether humpback liners are sufficiently rare or irregular that the better course is to exclude them from the Rule and accept the occasional inequitable double play as an unintended, but unavoidable, consequence.

Two plays illustrate the balance the rules and the umpires strike.

One is the infamous dropped line drive in Game 4 of the 1978 World Series (discussed in Chapter 1). Because Dodger shortstop Bill Russell knocked the ball down and because the umpire determined that Russell had not dropped the ball intentionally, he almost certainly would have completed an inning-ending 6–3 double play, an extraordinary and one-sided cost-benefit advantage, had the relay throw not struck the baserunner (who already had been called off) standing between first and second.

Even with the drop, however, this was a unique line drive that produced (or would have produced, but for the arguable interference) a unique double play. The momentum of both the dropped ball and Russell carried toward second base, placing both in better position for the double play. Had the ball bounced in a different direction or had Russell been moving away from second base, the double play would have been more difficult. Alternatively, had the umpire declared the drop intentional—not an unreasonable view of the play—the attempt at the double play would have failed, because the batter would have been declared out and the play declared dead under the intentional drop. This entire play proceeded more like a ground ball; the ball was hit low, barely above the ground, and Russell attempted the typical groundball double play involving a force-out on one baserunner and the batter, rather than the fly-ball double play on two forced baserunners that the Infield Fly Rule seeks to eliminate.

A more recent example occurred in Game Four of the 2016 NLCS between the Dodgers and Cubs. The Dodgers had first-and-second/one-out. The batter hit a broken-bat humpback liner towards Cubs second baseman Javier Baez, positioned on the edge of the outfield grass. Rather than charging to catch the ball on the fly, Baez took two steps backwards as the ball fell gently at his feet. Baez picked the ball up and threw to the shortstop covering second for the force-out on the runner at first; the shortstop started to throw to first to complete a 4–6–3 double play, then stopped, apparently because the first baseman was slow moving to cover the base. Instead, he wheeled and threw to third, eventually tagging out the runner from second to third in a rundown.

As with the '78 Series, this play was unique in several respects. The humpback liner was hit especially low, softly, and directly to Baez, who did not have to do anything other than step backwards, allow the ball to hit the ground, and play it off the ground. It again played like a grounder in the way it landed, and should have allowed for the typical 4–6–3 groundball double play involving the runner on first and the batter, but for the first baseman's slow reaction. The play required a bit of fielding skill, in that Baez could not catch-and-drop the ball, which would have violated the intentional-drop rule, but he had time to position himself to let the ball land on the ground and to play it cleanly as a groundball.

Both plays—and the double plays they should have produced—demonstrate the effect of rules operating at a categorical, rather than case-specific, level. The Infield Fly Rule excludes line drives because the typical line drive is hit hard, travels into the outfield if untouched, and is not easily controlled;

it therefore does not produce an easy double play involving multiple forced baserunners if not caught. That the occasional line drive might be hit softly or follow a trajectory that produces the cost-benefit inequity of a different double play does not mean the Infield Fly Rule should extend to line drives. The rules focus on the typical line drive—harder, lower, and faster, carrying into the outfield if untouched—that does not produce the extreme cost-benefit inequity. Because most uncaught line drives will not bounce so favorably as to regularly produce double plays, infielders generally lack the perverse incentive to intentionally not catch them in search of the same double play.

At the same time, the rare line-drive double play demonstrates why we need the limiting rule for true fly balls. It shows how easily infielders can turn a double play when they have time to set themselves and wait for a softly hit ball to land at their feet. And it shows how trapped baserunners are when having to wait at their current bases, unable to decide whether to run until the defense decides how to play the ball.

5. *Not a bunt.*

The exclusion of bunts from the Infield Fly Rule is the most recent change, adopted in 1920. A 1911 newspaper story complained about an umpire's failure to declare infield fly on a popped-up bunt.[46] This also may be the one element of the Rule that is difficult to justify under my framework.

On one hand, there might be something about a bunt in the infield-fly situation that warrants its exclusion from the Rule.

The nature of a bunted ball removes the exclusive and disparate defensive control over the play. A bunt typically does not travel as high in the air or with the same arc as a ball hit off a full swing; a popped bunt looks more like a humpback liner or even a groundball than a true fly ball. Infielders have less time or opportunity to settle comfortably under this lower-flying ball, often catching it on the run or dive, without setting themselves or preparing to play the ball off the ground. They are less able to control how and where the ball lands and how they play it off the ground, therefore less able to start the double play.

The exclusion of bunts also reflects the overall game situation. Teams generally bunt only in one infield-fly situation—first-and-second/none-out (a team occasionally bunts with first-and-second/one-out, where a National-League pitcher is batting). That bunt is almost always a sacrifice,[47] which flips the ordinary incentives. The batter intends to give himself up by not taking a full swing and not trying to hit the ball hard or far, while the runners, knowing the play is on, are ready and expecting to run as soon as the ball lands on the ground. Allowing the ball to fall to the ground plays into the offense's hands, giving them what they want. The defense thus thwarts the offensive strategy by catching the ball out of the air, putting out the batter without allowing the baserunners to advance into better scoring position. And because the runners are expecting to run, the defense is more likely to get a double play by catching the ball and doubling-off a runner at the previous base than allowing the ball to fall to the ground and getting force-outs on multiple baserunners.

In addition, defensive strategy against a sacrifice bunt may leave infielders out of position for a double play on multiple baserunners. Defenses often employ the "wheel" play—in a first-and-second bunt situation, the first and third basemen charge towards home to field the bunt, the shortstop covers third base for a possible play on the lead runner, and the second baseman covers first for the throw to get the batter on the sure out,[48] leaving no one covering second. This eliminates the third-to-second double play on the trapped baserunners, the evil the Infield Fly Rule seeks to avoid. Even if both baserunners wait to see if the ball is caught, the defense can get a force-out only on the lead runner going to third, but no one is covering second to get the trapped runner moving from first. Any double play in this situation must involve the batter. But if the bunt travels high enough to allow an infielder to settle comfortably under the ball and wait for it to land at his feet, a hustling batter should be able to reach first base in time to beat the relay throw. And with no one covering second base, a double play involving the trailing runner and the batter is impossible. If there is no way to complete the double play on multiple baserunners, the perverse incentive for the defense to intentionally not catch the popped bunt disappears; if it can get only one out on the play, it should make the easy play and catch the ball for the out, leaving the runners where they are.

The third-to-first double play remains possible only if the ball is not bunted high enough to allow the batter to reach first base ahead of the relay throw. But that suggests a popped bunt that did not go high in the air, playing more like a groundball, to which the Rule never applies. Even if bunts were not categorically excluded, a bunt that lacks sufficient arc is not subject to the Infield Fly Rule, just as a ball hit off a full swing that lacks sufficient arc is not subject to the Rule. Lower bunts play more like ground balls, on which we accept, and even expect, a double play involving one baserunner and the batter.

Alternatively, everything above is incorrect—excluding bunts is a mistake and popped bunts should be subject to the Infield Fly Rule (as they are subject to the intentional-drop rule), with the batter declared out and the baserunners not being forced to advance, but able to do so at their own risk if the ball is not caught. Marazzi takes this position, pointing to a triple play that the Seattle Mariners turned against the Blue Jays in 1995, when the Mariners pitcher allowed a popped bunt to fall to the ground untouched and began a triple play by throwing to second for the tag-the-runner/step-on-the-base double play (when the runner on second froze, expecting the bunt to be caught on the fly), followed by a relay throw to first to put out the batter.[49] Again, however, that the triple play involved the batter suggests the ball may not have been popped high enough to justify an infield-fly call, even if bunts were potentially subject to the Rule.

In any event, that the exclusion of bunts is arguably erroneous does not undermine the necessity of the Rule or render it invalid in its entirety. It perhaps means the Rule as written is not broad enough to serve its purpose and that one limitation, added two decades later as an afterthought, does not fit. If so, the solution is to expand the Infield Fly Rule to include popped bunts that otherwise implicate our framework and command a limiting rule. The remainder of the Rule should remain as is.

Excluding bunts introduces an additional judgment call for umpires—whether the batter took too much of a swing, so the batted ball ceased to be a bunt and became subject to the Rule. In a June 2017 game between the Dodgers and Milwaukee Brewers, the Dodger batter took a half-bunt/half-swing and sent a pop-up to the lip of the outfield grass between the first and second basemen; the umpire declared infield fly, although the batter (a pitcher in a National League game) was seeking to bunt in that situation. The infielder caught the ball and the runners did not advance, so the call did not affect the outcome of the play.

6. *Fair ball.*

This should be obvious, but is nevertheless worth discussing.

A batted ball that falls to the ground in foul territory, whether dropped or untouched, is dead.[50] The batter need not run, so he does not force the runners ahead of him to advance, eliminating any possibility for the defense to obtain the cost-benefit advantage of a double play by not catching the foul fly ball. It follows that an infielder never has perverse incentive to intentionally not catch an easily playable foul fly ball in search of a double play. Indeed, the incentive runs towards catching the ball, because the defense cannot otherwise ensure any outs on a foul ball. (A double play on a foul ball occurs only if the ball is caught and a baserunner retouches and is tagged out trying to advance.) The defense puts itself in a better position only by catching the foul ball. Failing to catch it leaves the defense in roughly the same position it was prior to the hit—same batter, same base-out situation, perhaps one more strike on the batter.

The literal and figurative line between fair and foul defines whether an infielder has perverse incentive to intentionally not catch the ball, thereby defining whether the Infield Fly Rule is needed as a limiting rule. If the batted ball remains in foul territory, the opportunity for an inequitable and one-sided cost-benefit advantage never materializes, thus neither does the perverse incentive. If the batted ball remains in fair territory, the opportunity for the inequitable double play creates the perverse incentive, necessitating the limiting rule.

The Rule accounts for that difference by requiring that the umpire declare "Infield Fly, if Fair" on balls hit near the foul line.[51] The declaration provides the baserunners and the infielders with notice of their options. If the ball stays foul, the infielders must catch the ball to attain even one out. If the ball stays fair, the batter is out (regardless of whether the infielder catches the ball), the baserunners are not forced to advance regardless of where the ball ends up, and no double play is in the offing unless the baserunners risk advancing on a non-force play.

7. *Playable by an infielder.*

The requirement that the ball be playable by an infielder functions as a proxy for the likelihood of that inequitable double play and the perverse incentives it creates.

A Comment to the Rule commands umpires to ignore "arbitrary" limitations such as the infield or the baseline.[52] In practice, however, a ball on or near the infield is more likely to be catchable by an infielder and more likely to produce an inequitable double play if the infielder intentionally fails to catch it. An outfielder positioned on the infield is treated as an infielder for purposes of the Rule, further recognizing that proximity to the infield triggers the concern for the uncaught-fly-ball double play and the reason for having the Rule. The call is more likely on a ball hit on the infield grass or dirt than elsewhere. The announcers in a September 2016 Mets-Braves game noted that infield fly had been declared on a ball "actually on the infield, which is always a treat."

Several things follow when a fly ball is on or near the infield and playable by an infielder. Proximity traps the baserunners. They must remain close to their current bases while waiting to see if the fly ball is caught, because a short throw will double them off if they stray too far. Because they must remain close to their current bases, they have further to run to reach the next bases on the non-catch. This increases the chances of any double play. If both baserunners must run 80 to 85 feet, the infielders will have time to make two throws. If the lead runner must remain close to his current base behind the short throw, it is easier for the defense to complete the single-throw/tag-the-runner/step-on-the-base double play.

A ball that cannot or will not be caught by an infielder (or by an outfielder stationed on the infield) with ordinary effort is likely not on or near the infield. On such a ball, the throws for the double play will be longer. The baserunners can lead further towards the next base as they wait, leaving them sufficient time to advance if the ball is not caught or retreat if it is; they can avoid the double play in either case. All of which makes the double play—the inequitable, one-sided extraordinary cost-benefit disparity the Infield Fly Rule seeks to eliminate—less likely on a ball further from the infield.

8. *Ordinary effort.*

The batted ball must be playable with ordinary effort, meaning the "effort that a fielder of average skill at a position in that league or classification of leagues should exhibit on a play, with due consideration given to the condition of the field and weather conditions." The Rule does not apply to difficult plays—where the ball is hit in a swirling wind or where the infielder must run, jump, or dive to catch the ball. Difficult catches eliminate all four defining characteristics.

The one-sided defensive control over the play, and the resulting possibility of an extraordinary cost-benefit advantage, derives from the ease of the catch. The defense turns the double play because the infielder can settle comfortably underneath the ball, wait for it to come down at his feet, and plan and prepare his next move. He controls how the ball lands, how he positions his body, and what he does when he picks the ball off the ground. He can disguise his intention, waiting until the last instant to decide whether to catch the ball or not, perhaps tempting the runners into committing to run or not. The ease of the play allows his teammates to communicate with him and to move into position to cover the bases for the double play.

That control disappears on a more difficult catch. The infielder may not be in as good position to play the ball if not settled comfortably and waiting for the ball, making it more difficult to pick and throw the ball off the ground. He also is less able to disguise his intentions or to fool the baserunners. This gives the runners a better chance to advance safely when the ball lands on the ground. The baserunners are less up a tree on a difficult play—they have greater control and influence when the play is not as easy for the defense. They may be more willing to run on a hard-to-handle ball, gambling that the infielder cannot make the difficult catch or throws. Aggressive baserunning may contribute to the difficulty of the play, as the pressure of the moving runners affects the catch and throw.

A difficult catch also lacks the aesthetic problems of infielders intentionally not performing the expected athletic skills and virtues in the expected manner. The more difficult the play—the less routine the play for an infielder of average ability—the less likely that the infielder's failure to catch the fair fly ball was intentional and unexpected. And the less likely the play reflects an infielder acting on a perverse incentive to intentionally not make a catch in search of a cost-benefit disparity.

As with playability by an infielder, there is a correlation among ordinary effort, location of the ball on the field, and likelihood of the double play. The closer to the infield, the less distance the infielder must run to catch the ball, the more likely the fly ball is playable with ordinary effort. The less distance he must run, the easier to settle comfortably underneath the ball and be in position to play the ball off the ground and make the necessary throws. All of which makes it easier to obtain the extraordinary cost-benefit advantage of the double play.

9. *Forced runners, running at own risk, and other double plays.*

Although the batter is out when the umpire declares infield fly, the ball remains alive if the infielder does not catch it. Because the batter is out and has not become a batter-runner to be put out at first, the baserunners are not forced to advance; they can remain at their current bases, as on any caught fly ball. Because the live ball landed on the ground, the baserunners may, but need not, try to advance at their own risk. If they do so, no force-out is in effect and they must be tagged out.

As a result, the Infield Fly Rule does not eliminate all double plays in this game situation. The defense could complete a double play by catching the fly ball for the out on the batter and doubling off a baserunner who strays too far from his base and fails to retouch. The defense also could turn a double play by not catching the fly ball but having the batter called out on the infield fly, then throwing out a baserunner trying to advance. Although not the force-out double play on multiple trapped baserunners the Rule seeks to eliminate, these double plays do provide the defense with an inequitable cost-benefit advantage. And the possibility of any double play preserves some perverse incentive for an infielder to intentionally not catch the fly ball, hoping to entice the runner into attempting to advance on the uncaught ball and running into an out. Infielders attempted this, although never successfully, in the eight MLB seasons studied.

What is missing here is the third characteristic of disparity in control, because the batting team now can influence and counter this play. The baserunners are not forced to advance and are free to remain at their current bases. And because most infield flies are hit on or near the infield, not running typically is the wiser choice. The decision to try to advance at the risk of being thrown out for a double play rests entirely and exclusively with the baserunners. Unlike the trapped baserunners who, absent the Infield Fly Rule, are forced to advance on the uncaught ball but have no hope of getting to the next bases safely, these baserunners avoid the double play by making smart choices about when and if to run. By eliminating the force and requiring that any runner who tries to advance be tagged out, the Rule also gives the offense additional control by making it easier for baserunners to advance safely and more difficult for the defense to complete the double play.

A baserunner's decision to run may be less a choice than a result of honed athletic instincts kicking in and causing him to run when he sees a batted ball land on the ground. The line between aggressive baserunning by a player trying to make something happen and recklessly risky baserunning is a fine one. But neither point matters. The rules need not save players from their own recklessness or misguided instincts, even where that recklessness provides one team with an inequitable cost-benefit advantage.

The Infield Fly Rule produces a situation in which, once infield fly is invoked and the batter is declared out, both teams exercise relatively equal levels of choice and influence on a sufficiently level playing field, each with the incentive to work the situation to its benefit. A baserunner might run on an unintentional non-catch to pressure the infielder into a bad drop or throw. Or a baserunner might run in the hope that the infielder will forget that, the batter having been called out, the runner must be tagged, allowing him to reach the next base safely. (Recall the instances of confusion by both infielders and runners, discussed in Chapter 1.)

Guilford and Mallord argue that repealing the Rule, and allowing the cat-and-mouse game between infielders and baserunners, would energize the game. As they explain in full:

> The strategic scenarios are fascinating. Imagine the second baseman trying to keep one eye on the runners and one on the ball while making a snap decision to catch or not to catch. He considers letting the ball drop so he can attempt a double or even triple play: he could throw to the catcher, who would then throw to third, who might even get a third out by throwing to second. But there are risks. If the runner at third base charges home while the ball is in the air, a dropped ball would allow him to score the tying run. On the other hand, if that runner is sufficiently convincing in faking to the plate, the fielder might be induced into the misplay of catching the ball with no prospects for more than one out on the play.
>
> Likewise, fielders might engage in feints and other deceptions with the ball in the air to induce the runners to make mistakes that might produce the elusive triple play. For instance, by slamming his fist into his glove at just the right time, a fielder might trick a runner facing the other way into believing a catch was made, causing the runner to scramble back to his base. The fielder could then let the ball drop and easily throw the runner out. Or in another example of trickery, the

fielder closest to the pop-up could back away from it as though to let the ball drop, while another fielder swoops in at the last second to make the catch.[53]

Although correct about excitement and strategy, they understate the imbalance in control over the play and overstate the baserunners' ability to influence the typical play in a non–Rule world in which the runners would be forced to advance on the uncaught ball. That imbalance convinced the National League to adopt the Rule in 1894.[54]

The Infield Fly Rule restores the excitement and strategic Guilford and Mallord seek. It creates the gamesmanship of infielders dropping the ball (or not) to trick the baserunners and of runners taking off (or not) to pressure the defense. By declaring the batter out and removing the force outs on the runners, however, the Rule restores a necessary balance on the play by making the strategic exchange more equitable, giving the runners the option of advancing or not advancing (rather than being forced), and giving both teams an opportunity to influence and gain advantage on the play.

An Overbroad Rule?

Accepting that the infield-fly situation warrants a limiting rule, the question remains whether the Infield Fly Rule, as written and applied, is the appropriate one. Perhaps the current version leaves gaps or fails to fully address the problems. Perhaps a different rule could limit strategic options to prevent one-sided cost-benefit disparities, while being better-tailored to the problems and benefits of the infield-fly situation.

One objection is that the Rule is over-inclusive; it reaches too many situations, including some that do not produce extraordinary one-sided cost-benefit disparities or perverse incentives. Although designed to eliminate the force-out double play on an intentionally uncaught fly ball, the Rule applies to all fair fly balls playable by an infielder with ordinary effort in the applicable base-out situation; it does not matter as a textual matter whether a double play is likely or even possible if the infielder does not catch the fly ball on a given play. That is, even if the infielder has no practical incentive to intentionally not catch that ball because the double play is so unlikely, the text requires the umpire to declare infield fly.

Umpires regularly invoke the Rule on balls hit well beyond the infield onto the outfield grass.[55] This created some of the controversy over the infield-fly call in the 2012 NLWC. That fly ball was playable by the shortstop with ordinary effort—he appeared stationary and settled under the ball. But the ball was hit so far into shallow left field that both baserunners had moved halfway to the next bases before the ball descended and both easily advanced when it landed on the ground. Even had the shortstop (absent the Infield Fly Rule) intentionally not caught the ball and positioned himself to try for the double play, the runner on second was far enough along that the one-throw/tag-the-runner-step-on-the-base double play at second was not in the offing and the initial throw to third for a third-to-second double play would have been too far to allow for a relay for the second out.

Even if a double play is possible on a play, infielders might not act on that perverse incentive in search of the inequitable one-sided cost-benefit advantage. They may choose to catch the easily playable fly ball for the sure out, eschewing the riskier double-play opportunity and the danger of bad bounces, throws, or misplays.

The perverse incentive ebbs and flows with the precise game situation and the location of the ball. Imagine a bases-loaded/none-out fly ball into the shallow outfield on the left side. A home-to-third double play (putting out the two lead runners) might be difficult, because the distance of the throw home might not allow time for the relay to complete the double play. There is a better chance at a third-to-second double play or a single-throw-to-second double play (because of the shorter initial throw). But that double play will not end the inning, meaning the runner on third scores. In such a situation, the benefits on the play no longer run in one direction; the defense gets multiple outs on the play, but the offense gains the benefit of a run scored. The defense must choose: get two outs but allow the run to score, or get one sure out and keep the run from scoring but face a continuing bases-loaded situation. The strategic choice may depend on the score and situation. A team leading by five runs in the ninth inning might go for the double play, while a team in a tie game will accept the easy single out and take its chances with the next batter. (This choice between multiple outs or preventing a run is not unusual in baseball. Many game situations put teams to that choice—for example, the routine strategic decision of whether to play the infield in with the bases loaded to cut the run at home or to leave the middle infielders at double-play depth, allowing for a ground-ball double play, even at the cost of a run.)

This problem is more pronounced on balls hit behind first base and along the foul line in shallow right field. Any throw to start the double play (to any base) will be long and difficult, perhaps prompting infielders always to take the sure out on the catch in that area of the field and never to act on the perverse incentive to intentionally not catch the fly ball.

The over-inclusiveness criticism prompts several responses.

First, it is impossible to know what would happen in a counter-factual baseball game played without the Infield Fly Rule. While baseball without the Rule would still be recognizable as baseball and would "not degenerate into bladderball,"[56] a change to any rule affects player conduct and team strategy in immeasurable and unknowable ways.

Second, legal rules are naturally overinclusive.[57] In trying to eliminate undesirable conduct while also creating an administrable rule, rulemakers paint with a broad brush, prohibiting the targeted conduct in all circumstances, even those that do not necessarily produce the evil the rule seeks to alleviate. Take a simple example. A municipality imposes a low speed limit on residential streets out of concern for the safety of people, especially children, walking and playing in the street and in adjacent yards, sidewalks, and driveways. But the reduced speed limit applies at 3 a.m., when no child (and likely no person) is playing or walking in or near the street. Nevertheless, the municipality retains and enforces the broad, over-inclusive rule—always drive at a reduced speed limit in a residential neighborhood, even when the evil the rule seeks to remedy is unlikely—because it is easier to administer. The enforcing official (police or courts) need not speculate about whether children or pedestrians were endangered in the circumstance; that children could be endangered in some cases is sufficient to support the categorical reduced speed limit in all cases.

So, too, with the Infield Fly Rule. Intentionally not catching the ball in some infield-fly situations could, absent the Rule, produce inequitable double plays. It thus is rational to enact and enforce a categorical limiting rule and to disincentivize infielders from intentionally not catching the ball in all infield-fly situations, even those that do not present the same (or any) double-play risk.

Third, the likelihood of the underlying evil does not disappear from the umpire's calculus. Rice explains that umpires do and should apply the Rule with its runner-protective purposes in mind, at least considering the likelihood of a double play when deciding whether to declare infield fly on an uncertain play.

Fourth, the relative rarity of the force-out double play does not undermine the point of having a rule to eliminate that double play. Within any system of rules, a prohibition on undesirable conduct is justified, even if the conduct and feared harm do not occur often, so long as the burdens of maintaining the prohibition do not exceed the benefits the prohibition provides.[58] To the extent baseball's rulemakers consider a force-out double play on the baserunners off an intentionally uncaught fly ball unjust or harmful within the game's structures and ethos—whether because of the cost-benefit disparity, the aesthetic concerns for intentionally uncaught fly balls, or both—it must eliminate such double plays, so long as the broader prohibition does not also eliminate beneficial activity.

Legal rules can be analyzed in terms of the risk of error—of erroneous application or non-application of the rule. Legal scholars distinguish Type I errors, or "false positives," from Type II errors, or "false negatives." A false positive occurs when a rule is applied in situations when it should not be applied, because the targeted evil is not implicated; the result is that desirable behavior is erroneously halted. A false negative occurs when a rule is not applied in situations when it should be applied, because the targeted evil is implicated; the result is that undesirable behavior, including the targeted evil, erroneously occurs.[59]

With respect to infield flies, a false positive means the Rule is invoked on a play in which a double play from an intentional non-catch is unlikely, so the infielder never had perverse incentive to intentionally not catch the fly ball. This, arguably, is the 2012 NLWC call. A false negative occurs when the Rule is not invoked on a play in which the inequitable double play is likely, leaving in place the perverse incentive and allowing the defense to gain the inequitable one-sided cost-benefit advantage of a double play. This is the double play following the non-call in the July 2013 Twins-Angels game or the triple play following the non-call in the 2017 Orioles-Red Sox game (both discussed in Chapter 1).

A false negative is more problematic than a false positive in applying the Infield Fly Rule—not invoking when the Rule should be invoked is more problematic than invoking when it should not be invoked. Calling infield fly when it should not have been called (perhaps the ball was not playable with ordinary effort) gives the defense an out it might not otherwise deserve if the infielder unintentionally fails to catch the ball. But most such plays impose no serious costs on the offense—the runners usually remain at their current bases. The 2012 NLWC play is the rare example (one of two in my eight-year study) in which multiple runners advanced and the batter reached first base safely on a non-catch, causing the umpires to remove the batter from first base because infield fly was declared. Even then, however, the baserunners advanced, so the offense gained some benefit.

But not declaring infield fly when it should be declared disadvantages the offense as much as, if not more than, not having the Rule at all. With the batter not out, the baserunners are forced to advance and will run into a probable double play, given the location of the batted ball, the short throws, and the fact that the runners have too far to run to beat those throws. That double play becomes easier when, expecting infield fly to be called, the baserunners do not attempt to advance, relying on the anticipated security of the Infield Fly Rule.

Given the disparity between the harmlessness of false positives and the problems created by false negatives, umpires adopt a presumption of the Infield Fly Rule, making invocation the default. On a close play that could go either way, the umpire should presume that it is a fair fly ball playable by an infielder with ordinary effort and invoke the Rule, unless facts show that the fair fly ball is not playable by an infielder with ordinary effort. If what the umpire sees does not point definitively to a conclusion or if the umpire is uncertain, he should conclude that the ball is playable with ordinary effort, declare "infield fly," and put the Rule in effect. This captures former umpire Jim Evans' argument that if the umpire entertains "reasonable doubt" about whether to invoke the Rule, he should invoke. In the majority of cases, presuming that infield fly should be called protects the offense from the force-out double play, consistent with the Rule's purposes, while imposing no additional burden on the defense. That should outweigh the occasional play in which an erroneous invocation deprives the offense of the benefit of the batter reaching first base.

Rulemakers also must consider administrative costs associated with a rule's enforcement. When increased enforcement of an over-inclusive rule increases costs, it may be better to adopt a narrower rule that produces less enforcement, but also fewer false positives.[60] The Infield Fly Rule's costs include the difficulty for umpires in identifying plays warranting invocation, given the subjectivity of the necessary judgments. Costs also include player, manager, media, and fan confusion, controversy, and anger from an erroneous or disputed call, especially if it is perceived as an unwarranted invocation of the Rule (a false positive). Perhaps the Rule as drafted is not costless if fans respond to a call by hurling debris on the field and delaying the game for 20 minutes. A final possible cost is the loss of additional excitement from the cat-and-mouse game between infielders and baserunners that might result if infielders were free to seek any competitive advantage through any means.

An Alternative Approach?

If some limiting rule is necessary and appropriate, the second question is whether the current iteration of the Infield Fly Rule is right for the task. Perhaps a different rule, as written or as applied, could achieve the desired end of eliminating extraordinary one-sided cost-benefit disparities without the same overinclusiveness and the same costs.

Rulemakers might reorient the Rule around its purpose. A modified rule might require the umpire to find a reasonable possibility (or likelihood or probability or reasonable probability or some other standard) of a double play should the infielder intentionally not catch the fly ball. That is, the text would expressly incorporate the purposivist considerations that Rice suggests umpires silently and unthinkingly apply. This eliminates the over-inclusiveness problem, as the Rule would not apply where, in the umpire's judgment, there is no realistic possibility of the targeted evil of an inequitable double play, even if the ball is otherwise playable by an infielder with ordinary effort.

But this would be difficult to administer, imposing heightened enforcement costs that the current Rule avoids. To determine the likelihood of a double play while the ball is in the air, an umpire must speculate—guess—about what might hypothetically happen if the fly ball is not caught, if the baserunners run, if the infielder picks up the ball, and if the infielders make the necessary throws. The umpire must do this based on no information, before the play has begun and before anyone knows where the ball will land, how it will bounce, and what the baserunners and infielders will do. And all while the umpire should be focused on the infielders' movements, not on the ball or the baserunners.

Faced with that difficulty, umpires likely would compensate by adopting proxies for likelihood of the double play. One proxy might be playability with ordinary effort, looking to whether the infielder has settled comfortably under the ball. Or umpires might effectively limit infield flies to the infield grass and dirt, where the short first throw and the need for runners to remain closer to their current bases increases the probability of the double play. Either proxy returns us to the current rule, but without the clear textual basis.

Umpireal speculation about what might happen on a play also is unprecedented under baseball's rules. Consider how umpires award bases when a ball, once in play, winds up in the stands. If a batted ball lands in fair territory beyond first or third base and then bounces or rolls out of play, the batter and runners are awarded two bases from where they began the play.[61] This result holds regardless of what might have happened had the ball remained in play—if a slow batter would have stayed at first base, a fast batter might have reached third, or a fast runner on first would have advanced three bases and scored. Rulemakers chose not to rely on additional, hypothetical judgments, opting for an overinclusive rule providing a set outcome based on one piece of known information—where everyone was at the beginning of the play—without requiring umpires to predict the future or engage the counter-factual.

Rulemakers took the same approach to the infield-fly situation. All fair fly balls easily catchable by an infielder are subject to the limiting rule, without requiring umpires to speculate about what might happen on the play should the infielder not catch the ball.

A second possibility is to rely exclusively on the intentional-drop rule, the descendant of the original trap ball, or Brush and Von der Ahe's, rule, which similarly seeks to protect baserunners against confusion and cost-benefit disparity resulting from infielders intentionally not catching fly balls.[62] This rule applies whenever there is a force-out in effect at one or more bases, including infield-fly situations (in which force-outs are in effect at two or three bases). If this general prohibition sufficiently deters infielders from intentionally failing to catch fly balls in search of the inequitable cost-benefit advantage, perhaps the specific Infield Fly Rule is unnecessary.

This alternative approach fails for several reasons.

The intentional-drop rule prohibits an infielder from intentionally dropping the ball, but permits him to intentionally not catch the ball by allowing it to fall to the ground untouched.[63] That leaves the baserunners in the same bind in an infield-fly situation. The batter would not be out on the untouched ball, therefore the baserunners are forced to run while being powerless to counter the play (for all the reasons discussed in this chapter). The inequitable cost-benefit disparity in the infield-fly situation comes not from infielders intentionally dropping the fair fly ball, but from infielders intentionally not catching the fair fly ball. Because the intentional-drop rule only reaches a drop, not an untouched non-catch, it is insufficient to prevent the unique harm of the force-out double play in the infield-fly situation. The broader, specialized Infield Fly Rule remains necessary.

It also is not clear that the intentional-drop rule functions better as a limiting rule. The Infield Fly Rule is criticized for turning on vague, subjective, and difficult judgments, such as whether the ball could be caught with "ordinary effort" or whether it "could ordinarily have been handled by an infielder." But the intentional drop rule is no better in this regard. It requires umpires to decide a similarly subjective and difficult issue of the infielder's intent in dropping the ball, usually based on reading subtle movements as the infielder tries to catch the ball and based on what happens to the ball and the infielder after the drop. It makes no sense to trade one difficult, ambiguous legal standard for another. The Infield Fly Rule arguably incorporates infielder intent by proxy—if a fly ball can be easily caught by an average Major League infielder, there is a roughly 98 percent chance that the failure to catch the ball was intentional (based on the median fielding percentage for infielders.[64])

Finally, if the goal is to protect the batting team, the Infield Fly Rule provides an additional benefit. Under the intentional-drop rule, the ball is dead when it hits the ground and the baserunners remain where they are; under the Infield Fly Rule, the uncaught ball remains alive and the runners can advance at their own risk. This offers baserunners the opportunity to advance if the infielders do not handle the ball off the ground or if they forget to tag the runners on the non-force play. That extra benefit offers additional deterrence against infielders intentionally not catching the ball, lest the offense take advantage of any miscue.

*   *   *

These four defining characteristics create a framework for understanding and justifying, even in reverse, the Infield Fly Rule. The framework explains the scope and reach of the Rule and why it applies as it does, as well as why it properly does not reach and apply to certain game situations that are excluded from its text and its ambit. In the next chapter, I use this framework to explore other baseball plays and game situations, considering whether they are or should be subject to limiting rules akin to the Infield Fly Rule, based on the presence or absence of the four defining characteristics.

Chapter 3

Infield Fly Rule
Throughout Baseball

Chapter 2 established a framework to explain and justify the Infield Fly Rule as a response to the confluence of four characteristics in the infield-fly situation—one team intentionally not performing the expected athletic skills in the expected manner; a highly inequitable, one-sided cost-benefit disparity in favor of one team; exclusive disparate influence over the play in favor of one team with no possible response from the other; and perverse incentives for one team to intentionally not perform those expected athletic skills in the expected manner whenever the game situation arises. The unique presence of all four characteristics in a game situation warrants a limiting rule to prohibit the unexpected athletic play or to eliminate the perverse incentive, thereby preventing one team from obtaining the extraordinary cost-benefit advantage.

The common criticism of the Infield Fly Rule is that it is underinclusive. Why, the argument goes, have a limiting rule for this game situation, but not for a host of baseball situations that appear comparable, if not identical, yet remain subject to ordinary rules and strategies, with players free to seek extreme cost-benefit advantage without strategic limitation. No rule prevents or disenticvizes an infielder from intentionally not catching a fair fly ball with a runner on first base to get a speedy runner off the base paths— the rules allow John Montgomery Ward's 1893 play that sent baseball down the road to the Infield Fly Rule, and the occasional modern infielder repeats the move. No rule prevents or disincentivizes an outfielder from intentionally dropping a deep foul fly ball with a runner on third to keep that runner from retouching and scoring. No rule prevents or disincentivizes a pitcher from intentionally walking the opposing team's best hitter to face a weaker hitter in a more-optimal base-out situation. Yet all appear to involve the defense acting contrary to its expected interests in search of a cost-benefit advantage.

That underinclusiveness leads to either of two conclusions. If a limiting rule is necessary and appropriate in the infield-fly situation, it is necessary and appropriate in these and other game situations. If a limiting rule is not necessary or appropriate in these and other game situations, it is not necessary or appropriate in the infield-fly situation and the Infield Fly Rule should be repealed. This choice holds unless there are meaningful differences between the infield-fly situation and other baseball plays, as reflected in this framework and the four defining characteristics.

Applying this framework to different baseball situations shows that the underinclusiveness criticism fails along three lines.

First, the infield-fly situation is unique. Only one baseball play is genuinely comparable—a catcher intentionally not catching a third strike with a force in effect at one or more bases. And that play is subject to a limiting rule that has been around as long as the Infield Fly Rule and functions in a similar fashion. This suggests that baseball approaches similar situations in a similar manner with similar limiting rules.

Second, MLB recently encountered a new rule interpretation that had the unintended effect of creating a risk of cost-benefit disparities and perverse incentives similar to those in the infield-fly situation. Its response was to withdraw the problematic interpretation, functionally creating a limiting rule that eliminated the perverse incentive. In other words, MLB recognized a situation in which the four characteristics were present and responded with a limiting rule.

Third, every other baseball play and situation offered as an analogy to the infield-fly situation is not analogous or comparable. All lack one or more of the defining characteristics established in this framework. And absent all four characteristics, a limiting rule is not necessary or proper. The Infield Fly Rule is not under-inclusive. Rather, other baseball situations are distinguishable under this framework. They should be left to the game's ordinary rules and strategies because, unlike the infield fly, they can be left to those rules and strategies without creating overwhelming cost-benefit inequities or perverse incentives.

The Analogous Uncaught Third Strike

The lone genuinely comparable baseball situation involves the uncaught third strike, commonly-but-inaccurately called the "dropped" third strike.

A batter is out on strikes if either a "third strike is legally caught by the catcher," meaning the ball remains in the catcher's glove before touching the ground, or a "third strike is not caught by the catcher when first base is occupied before two are out."[1] The latter provision covers all situations with less than two out and a force-out in effect on at least one base—first base only, first-and-third, and the two infield-fly situations of first-and-second and bases loaded. If the third strike is not caught when first base is unoccupied or when two are out, the batter is not out; he becomes a baserunner and must be tagged or put out at first base.[2]

Consider the following situation. Bases-loaded/none-out. The batter swings and misses at strike three. The catcher intentionally does not catch the pitch; he allows the ball to pop out of his glove and land at his feet by home plate, as the batter and the three baserunners watch.

Under current rules, the batter is out, as first base is occupied before two are out. He never becomes a runner and the three baserunners are not forced to advance. Although they can run, as on any pitch, they likely will not on this play, as the ball did not roll far from the catcher. If they do run, it is not a force-out and they must be tagged.

But imagine that the ordinary rule of "three strikes, you're out"[3] applies to this uncaught third strike. The batter becomes a runner, obligated to run to first. This forces the baserunners to advance, creating force-outs at every base. The catcher can pick the ball laying at his feet and step on home plate, forcing out the runner on third base for the first out. He then could throw to third base, forcing out the runner on second for the second out. The third baseman has two options for gaining the third out—he could throw to second to force-out the runner on first or he could throw across the diamond to first to put out the batter. The result is an inning-ending triple play—on strike three. This occurs without the infielders having to tag any runner. And it occurs before the baserunners—standing on or near the bases, not running on the pitch, and not planning to advance on a ball that was not put in play and did not bounce far from the catcher—could figure out what is going on, much less run 90 feet in enough time to beat any of these throws or otherwise counter this play.

This was the rule and prevailing result prior to 1887.[4] Under my framework, this play stands on all fours with the infield-fly situation. Consider what happens under pre–1887 rules.

(1) In not catching the third strike, the catcher intentionally fails to perform the expected athletic skill or to achieve excellence in the athletic virtue he is expected to perform and ordinarily wants to perform—catch a ball thrown by the pitcher. A catch is generally necessary to complete an out on any play, including a strikeout. And catching the pitch allows the catcher to better control the ball if the baserunners attempt to advance.

(2) The fielding team becomes substantially better off by the catcher intentionally not catching the third strike than by catching it, gaining a

similar overwhelming, inequitable, and one-sided cost-benefit advantage. By not catching strike three, the defense gets two (possibly three) outs and perhaps gets out of the inning; by catching strike three, the defense gets one out on the batter on the strikeout and leaves the batting team with the prime scoring opportunity of bases-loaded/one-out. The defense incurs no costs in making this play, so long as the catcher controls where the ball lands and everyone makes quick and accurate throws. The batting team experiences all of this as high costs—multiple outs instead of one, loss of one or more baserunners and baserunners in scoring position, perhaps the end of its turn at bat and opportunity to score runs—while gaining no benefits on the play.

(3) The defense controls the play and the offense is unable to counter or influence the outcome. The catcher can choose at the last instant whether to catch the ball; he can let the ball hit his glove or pop out of the pocket and fall to the ground in front of him, then pick it up, step on home (if there is a runner on third), and throw to his teammates covering the bases. As on the infield fly, the baserunners are up a tree. They cannot run if the catcher holds the ball; they easily would be thrown or tagged out, especially the runner on third heading home. If they wait until the ball drops from the catcher's mitt, it will be too late to run—again, especially the runner on third heading home. The baserunners could run on the pitch, but risk being caught stealing if the catcher catches the pitch and makes an accurate throw—again, especially the runner on third attempting to steal home. And because the batter would have to run on the third strike, the runners are forced to advance, so the defense puts the baserunners out without a tag. The baserunners' only hope is for the ball to skitter far from the catcher or for the fielders to make inaccurate throws, neither of which it influences.

(4) The combination of (2) and (3) creates the perverse incentive for (1)—the catcher always will intentionally not catch the third strike when this situation arises. The defense always will take additional outs, fewer base runners, and possibly the end of the inning, especially when this play carries little risk. And making the non-catch on the pitch is simple, increasing the incentive.

The strikeout rules in effect since 1887 eliminate this strategic option for the defense, via a limiting rule in § 5.05(a)(2) that functions on the same terms as the Infield Fly Rule. The rule demonstrates that the Infield Fly Rule is not an anomalous or random relic; it reflects a consistent response to particularly unbalanced game situations that trigger perverse incentives to unwanted on-field action.

Rather than prohibiting catchers from dropping the third strike (it is not clear how a rule could do that), the limiting rule disincentivizes them from doing so. The rule imposes an outcome on the play—one out on the batter on the strikeout, baserunners not forced to advance—as if the catcher made the expected athletic move and caught the third strike. By imposing that outcome, the rule eliminates any perverse incentive for a catcher to intentionally fail to perform the expected athletic skill in the expected manner by eliminating the extraordinary cost-benefit advantage. Because the catcher gains no additional outs by not catching the third strike (barring unwise decisions by the baserunners), he has no incentive not to catch the pitch.

This framework also demonstrates that, like the Infield Fly Rule, the third-strike rule has the appropriate scope, reaching only those plays likely to produce extreme cost-benefit disparities and perverse incentives and leaving untouched plays unlikely to produce extreme cost-benefit disparities or perverse incentives.

The batter is not out on strikes and does become a baserunner if first base is empty or if there are two outs. With two outs, the defense has no incentive to seek a double play; it only needs one out to end the inning and the easiest way to gain that out is to catch the third strike to put out the batter. The catcher has no reason or desire to force himself to make the more difficult play to get one out, so the rules need not remove any incentive. With first base empty, the baserunners are not forced to advance or to run into a double play when the batter becomes a runner. The runners control when and whether to run. And since the catcher cannot trigger force-outs on the baserunners through a non-catch, his only guaranteed option is one out on the batter, again leaving no reason or incentive to make a more difficult play to get one out.

With either first base empty or with two out, the need to protect the offense against inequitable force-outs also disappears. The focus shifts to the adverse consequences to the defense of unintentional non-catches. Those consequences are clear in baseball's most infamous uncaught third strike—Brooklyn Dodgers catcher Mickey Owen missed the third strike on what would have been the final out in Game 4 of the 1941 World Series against the Yankees, after which the Yankees scored four runs in the ninth to win the game and ultimately the Series.[5]

As with an uncaught infield fly, an uncaught third strike remains alive, even if the batter is declared out. Other double-play combinations thus remain possible. A runner may run at his own risk if the third strike bounces away from the catcher. In trying to advance that runner might be thrown out to complete an unusual strike-out/throw-out double play. But teams share control and influence over this play—any double play results from the runner's voluntary decision to run, rather than a force, and an even exchange of strategic moves. The play on the advancing runner would be a tag play, a more-difficult play for the defense and one reflecting choice by the offense. Like the Infield Fly Rule, the uncaught-third-strike rule cures an inequitable cost-benefit imbalance which the offense cannot meaningfully counter when the runners are forced to advance. But the rules do not protect teams from unwise voluntary baserunning choices.

Critics of the Infield Fly Rule must account for the uncaught third strike, given the identical structure and logic of the rules. If an infielder should be allowed to intentionally not catch an easily playable fair fly ball in search of a double play, a catcher should be allowed to intentionally not catch a third strike in search of a double play. One early critic of the Infield Fly Rule predicted confusion over that new rule by comparing baserunner confusion over the third-strike rule, which was less than ten years old at the time.[6] Otherwise, critics must identify a meaningful and reasonable distinction between intentionally not catching a fly ball to produce a force-out double play and intentionally not catching a third strike to produce a force-out double play.

One possible distinction is that an infield fly triggers an exciting play. Infielders demonstrate strategy and skill in executing the non-catch double play and baserunners can test those skills through aggressive base running, all triggered by a high fly ball that takes time to develop and gives players on both teams time to react and strategize.[7] Dropping a third strike is a simple move involving little skill, performed before anyone has a chance to respond, with little planning or strategy, and without time to develop as a larger play.

Not catching strike three in a way that triggers a double play may be easier than not catching a fly ball in a way that triggers a double play. But both entail identical interplay among fielders picking an intentionally uncaught ball off the ground and making throws for force-out double plays and baserunners attempting the near-impossible task of beating those throws. The plays are the same aesthetically and strategically. While it may be easier for a catcher to control an uncaught pitch than for an infielder to control an uncaught fly ball, the differences are marginal, especially for practiced, skilled fielders.

A second distinction involves how each rule operates. Baseball's rule-makers addressed the problem of the uncaught-third-strike double play by broadening the definition of when a batter is out on strikes and narrowing the circumstances in which he becomes a batter-runner to be put out at first; that change eliminated any situation in which a third strike could force a baserunner to run into a non-tag double play. But the rule operates in the background. Unless first base is open or there are two outs, the batter is simply declared out on strikes, with no special announcement that a controlling rule (again, other than "three strikes, you're out") is in effect. The umpire also does not influence this play the same way. The umpire need only decide that first base is occupied, less than two are out, there were two strikes on the batter, and the pitch was a strike; only the last fact requires judgment. The umpire need not judge the catcher's intent in not catching the ball or determine whether the catcher could have caught that third strike with ordinary effort. The umpire need not invoke the rule and observers are not even aware that a limiting rule is affecting the play.

The Infield Fly Rule introduced to the game a new concept and a series of new umpiring judgments. It operates in the foreground and is highly visible when in effect. The umpire must affirmatively invoke the Rule by determining that a batted ball is a non-line-drive, non-bunt, fair fly ball that can be handled by an infielder with ordinary effort, then immediately declaring that fact and calling the batter out through a hand signal (a raised right arm while the ball is in the air). The call entails multiple judgments—whether the ball had sufficient arc to be a fly ball, whether it was playable by an infielder with "ordinary effort," whether the infielder was settled comfortably underneath the ball, and when that had become apparent. Players, coaches, commentators, and fans are aware of and can second-guess those judgments.

That affirmative declaration notifies and instructs both sides of their obligations and what can or must happen next. Most umpire calls resolve one binary question—ball or strike, safe or out—based on what the umpire observed the players having done on the field, resembling the type of decision generally understood as judicial. Invoking (or not invoking) the Infield Fly Rule has a broader regulatory effect, dictating to players what they must do or not do next. Some critics reject the Rule for that reason—it strips power from the players and places it with a man in a blue suit, "waving his arms and bringing a halt to all the fun."[8]

The Infield Fly Rule thus offers a richer target for fan criticism and for calls for repeal, as it is more familiar to fans and a more obvious and visible part of baseball's fabric.

The third argument is that a catch should not matter to the strikeout and the batter should be out on the third strike regardless of what the catcher does. If the pitcher throws an unhittable low-and-outside slider that the batter misses by six inches, the batter should be out on strikes, regardless of whether the catcher holds the ball.[9] (A pitcher is credited with a strikeout, even if the batter still must be put out on the tag or at first or even if the batter reaches base).[10] The pitcher has done his "job," so his team should not suffer (and the offense should not benefit) because the catcher failed to do his, whether intentionally or unintentionally.

But the default throughout baseball's rules is that the last fielder involved in a play must legally catch the ball to complete an out; the failure of that final player to catch the ball negates the out, regardless of what previous defensive players did on the play or how well they did it. Every player involved on a play must "do his job" to get the out; that one fielder does his job when another does not is not sufficient to create an out. A batter-runner is not out if the shortstop makes a great stop and throw but the first baseman drops the ball; the first baseman must catch the throw from the shortstop to complete the groundout, regardless of how great the throw. Similarly, the catcher must catch the pitch from the pitcher to complete a strikeout, regardless of how great the pitch.

Responding to Unintended Consequences and Unexpected Perverse Incentives

Rule problems might arise not from the text of a rule, but from interpretations of existing rules creating unintended consequences, compelling a reversal or adjustment to rules or interpretations. Such a controversy arose in 2014, when a new interpretation of what constitutes a catch triggered potential problems under this framework. Rulemakers responded with a revised interpretation that removed cost-benefit disparities and perverse incentives.

The rules define a catch as "the act of a fielder in getting secure possession in his hand or glove of a ball in flight and firmly holding it." But the fielder must "hold the ball long enough to prove he has complete control of the ball and that his release of the ball is voluntary and intentional. If the fielder has made the catch and drops the ball while in the act of making a throw following the catch, the ball shall be adjudged to have been caught."[11]

Prior to the 2014 season, MLB attempted to clarify the distinction between when a fielder had not caught a ball and when he had caught it and dropped it in the act of removing it from the glove to make a throw. The clarification targeted middle infielders' practice of "flipping" the ball from the glove to the throwing hand when turning a double play at second base. Under the new interpretation, it was no longer a legal catch if the infielder flipped the ball from his glove but lost possession without having secured it in his throwing hand. The interpretive change made sense as applied to its target. The best middle infielders receive the ball and take it out of the glove for the throw in virtually a single motion, making it difficult for "umpires to determine in real time whether a ball was dropped on the catch or on the transfer," because they occur nearly simultaneously. The new interpretation triggered immediate controversies in the first month of the season, prompting arguments and video challenges to plays around second base.[12]

But the interpretation created an unexpected problem for a play that was not the rule's target. Several umpires applied the new interpretation to outfielders who dropped the ball while taking it out of the glove to throw it back to the infield, sometimes several seconds after securing the ball in the glove or after taking several steps with the ball in the glove. Although outfielders were not performing the single-motion quick-flip-and-throw as middle infielders, umpires applied the same scrutiny to the transfer from glove to hand.

One commentator realized that applying this new interpretation to outfield fly balls unexpectedly and unintentionally produced the situation the Infield Fly Rule was designed to eliminate. On fly balls hit well into the outfield, baserunners on first and second typically lead toward the next base, sometimes as far as halfway, depending on where the ball is hit; this gives them enough of a lead that they can advance if the ball is not caught while remaining close enough to retreat if the ball is caught. Baserunners use the ball entering the glove as the relevant event dictating what to do next—once the ball enters the glove, they retreat. But under the new interpretation, the relevant event became not the ball entering and remaining in the glove, but the outfielder successfully moving the ball from glove to throwing hand; if he dropped the ball at any point before throwing it back to the infield, it was not a catch, even with a delay of several seconds or steps between the two actions.[13]

This created the following possible play. With first-and-second/one-out, the batter hits a line drive on which the left fielder makes a diving catch. Seeing the ball enter the glove, both runners, waiting halfway, retreat to their current bases. Seeing that, the outfielder stands up, removes the ball from his glove, and intentionally drops it from his throwing hand, negating the catch. The ball is now in play, the batter is not out and becomes a runner, and the baserunners are forced to advance. The left fielder can throw the ball to second for the tag-the-retreating-runner/step-on-the-base double play or throw to third to begin a third-to-second force-out double play. Alternatively, if the runners do not retreat but remain halfway to the next bases, anticipating the drop on the transfer, the outfielder can retain control of the ball for the catch and out on the batter, then quickly throw behind the lead baserunner to double him off.

This play readily fits the framework. By dropping the ball on the transfer, the outfielder intentionally acts contrary to ordinary athletic expectations by doing something he ordinarily does not want to do. Dropping the ball creates an extraordinary and inequitable cost-benefit advantage for the defense, turning a one-out play into a two-out play, without corresponding costs on the defense. The baserunners are up a tree and unable to counter the play, for the same reasons baserunners are up a tree on an infield fly. And while the distance required for the throws perhaps makes this double play less certain than on a ball hit on the infield grass, the possibility is sufficiently high, given baserunner confusion, to give outfielders a perverse incentive to intentionally drop the ball.

No outfielder attempted this move in the first month of 2014. Perhaps recognizing the potential problem, and certainly in combination with the genuine confusion and controversy on plays around second base, MLB revised its interpretation less than a month into the season. The revision, which took effect immediately, stated that a catch occurs if the fielder gains complete control over the ball in his glove, even if he drops the ball after intentionally opening his glove for the transfer. There is "no requirement that the fielder successfully remove the ball from his glove in order for it to be ruled a catch" if the fielder drops the ball while attempting to move it from the glove to his hand to make a throw.[14]

This is not the typical limiting rule in the sense of a new rule enacted to close a textual gap that players were exploiting in search of cost-benefit advantage. But the interpretive change functions as a limiting rule. It removes from the game the potential for an inequitable force-out double play on multiple baserunners on an intentionally uncaught fair fly ball. Dropping the ball on the transfer no longer negates the catch. Baserunners can return to their common practice of reacting to the ball entering the outfielder's glove; they retreat if the outfielder holds the ball, without fear of the catch morphing into a non-catch on the transfer. The interpretive change eliminates the defense's opportunity for the inequitable and one-sided cost-benefit advantage. And with no cost-benefit advantage to be gained, an outfielder no longer has perverse incentive to intentionally drop the ball after removing it from his glove.

The interpretive change reveals that MLB is consistent in its response to game situations that fall within this framework. Having identified a game situation unexpectedly presenting all four defining characteristics as a result of its own interpretation of existing rules, MLB reinterpreted, establishing new rules to limit players' strategic options, thereby eliminating inequitable cost-benefit disparities and the perverse incentive to seek them.

Non-Comparable Baseball Situations

The most common move for critics of the Infield Fly Rule is to compare the infield-fly situation to numerous other baseball situations, plays, and strategies—none subject to infield-fly-type limiting rules and all left to ordinary rules, ethics, practices, and strategies. Critics insist that if these game situations are not subject to limiting rules and if players remain free to seek cost-benefit advantages through ordinary strategic options, the infield-fly situation should not be subject to a limiting rule and players should be left to a full range of strategic option in search of cost-benefit advantage.

But the framework and the four characteristics show why that argument fails. No other play in baseball is comparable to the infield fly or to the uncaught-third-strike, the two paradigms of baseball plays commanding limiting rules. Every other play offered to critique or question the Infield Fly Rule lacks one or more of the defining characteristics. As such, a limiting rule is unnecessary and inappropriate, every play properly left to the game's ordinary rules, ethics, practices, and strategies. And MLB's failure to subject these plays to limiting rules does not undermine the Infield Fly Rule.

In exploring these close-but-not-comparable plays, several patterns emerge. Some plays entail relatively equitable cost-benefit exchanges, in which each team incurs some costs and gains some benefits. Other plays leave neither team helpless or up a tree, each having an opportunity to control and influence the play and to respond to the other's strategic efforts. Other plays produce a highly inequitable cost-benefit exchange, but one achieved only because the team gaining the benefit performs the expected athletic skills and executes the athletic virtues in the expected manner, rather than by intentionally acting contrary to athletic expectations. Others provide a cost-benefit advantage to one team, but a smaller and less inequitable one, which minimizes the perverse incentive for players to act contrary to ordinary athletic expectations. And others exemplify ordinary gamesmanship within the rules and the fight for an edge, involving none of the four defining characteristics.

Close examination of these plays reveals where each fits within the framework and which characteristic (or characteristics) the play lacks. But they share a common conclusion—no limiting rule is warranted as to any of them and the absence of a limiting rule on them says nothing about the need for a special rule on infield flies.

Groundball Double Play

The problem with the infield fly cannot be the simple fact of the defense getting two outs on the play, even two outs by force-out. Baseball accepts, and even celebrates, the defense getting a double play with two force-outs on a groundball. Baseball reveres the "twin killing" that is the "pitcher's best friend."[15] Poetry has been dedicated to it, memorializing "Tinker to Evers to Chance,"[16] the infield of the early 20th-century Chicago

Cubs that famously keyed the franchise's only two World Series titles prior to 2016.

A groundball typically produces a different double play than the uncaught infield fly, involving a force out on one baserunner (usually at second base) and the batter, rather than on two baserunners. But, the argument goes, it produces just as overwhelming and inequitable a cost-benefit disparity. The advantage to the defense (and disadvantage to the offense) is the same—two outs, potentially the end of the inning, certainly killing a rally by removing runners from the base paths and from scoring position. It has been argued that a groundball double play with bases loaded (an infield-fly situation) is statistically the worst thing a batter can do offensively.[17] Numbers from 2016 bear this out. An inning-ending double play with bases-loaded/one-out cost the batting team an average of more than 1.5 runs in the inning. A double play from bases-loaded/none-out had a greater effect. A home-to-first double play (where the defense forces the lead runner out at home, then throws the batter out at first, leaving the batting team with second-and-third/two-out) decreased the batting team's run expectancy from more than 2.27 runs to less than 0.6 runs, a cost of more than 1.6 runs. And even if the defense turned a 6–4–3 double play at second and first and allowed the lead runner to score, that single run reflected less than the batting team's run expectancy from the original situation (2.2715 runs, down to .1028 runs).[18]

But cost-benefit disparity, even substantial, does not end the inquiry. An extraordinary one-sided cost-benefit imbalance becomes problematic, and a limiting rule necessary and proper, only when that disparity is accompanied by the other defining characteristics, all of which are absent on a groundball.

Infielders cannot complete a groundball double play by intentionally failing to perform the expected athletic skills in the expected manner by intentionally dropping or failing to catch the groundball. Quite the opposite. The double play is possible only if the infielder catches the ball cleanly and if he and his teammates make good, accurate throws. This double play—and the inequitable cost-benefit advantage—requires the infielders to successfully execute the athletic virtues and both teams to behave according to the game's ordinary rules, ethics, practices, and strategies. If the shortstop misses the ball, it rolls through the infield and into the outfield, preventing the defense from getting any out. If the shortstop drops or bobbles the ground ball, even if he recovers it, the time added to the play makes the double play more difficult and less likely.

We might think of this in a different way. A double play is a natural and expected consequence of certain ground balls with at least a runner on first, accounted for in the positioning of infielders at "double-play depth," the distance between the bases, the speed of the batted ball, and the speed of runners. A double play is in the DNA of that groundball—if infielders successfully field and throw the ball, two outs are a natural result of the play. If the infielder drops the groundball, however, those considerations all work against the double play. On the other hand, the natural and expected consequence of a fair fly ball—its DNA—is one out on the batter from the infielder catching the ball, not a force-out double (or triple) play on multiple baserunners.

The groundball double play also lacks the same disparity in control over the play, because the runners are not trapped, powerless, and up that tree. The key to the double play on an infield fly is that the baserunners cannot move immediately on the fly ball. They must wait close to their current bases to see whether the infielder catches the fly ball. And it then becomes impossible to advance safely when the ball hits the ground.

But baserunners move immediately on a groundball, giving them a running start and greater speed heading to the next base. The runner can break on the pitch, putting him far enough toward the next base to beat the play at second. And if moving on the pitch, he can keep running once the batted ball touches the ground (rather than having to stop and watch to see if a fly ball is caught); teams often start runners on the pitch to avoid groundball double plays. The lead baserunner might reach the next base in time, depending on where the ball is hit. He might at least be able to disrupt the double play with a hard slide. The batter (who is the second out in the typical groundball double play) can thwart the twin-killing by hustling up the line to beat the relay throw. The offense has some realistic opportunity to influence the play and avoid the double play within the game's ordinary rules, practices, and strategies, an opportunity missing from the infield-fly and uncaught-third-strike situations.

It may not work all or even much of the time. There is a reason we speak of "routine" double plays and the pervasiveness of double plays shows the difficult task for the offense in avoiding it. The point is that the batting team can do more to avoid the groundball double play than it can to avoid the infield-fly double play. And that extra bit of control makes the difference under this framework.

Deep Foul Fly Ball

Critics commonly offer this play as the infield-fly analogue, because it entails the defense intentionally not catching a fly ball.

Imagine the following situation. The tying or go-ahead run is on third base with less than two outs in the top of the ninth inning. The batter hits a foul fly ball down the right-field line, deep enough or in a spot on the field where the baserunner will tag-up and score if the outfielder catches the ball. The throw home may be too far, given how deep the ball is hit. Or the throw might be too difficult. Many retro ballparks contain odd nooks and features along the foul lines, designed to recall early ballparks built into early 20th-century urban blocks. Baltimore's Orioles Park at Camden Yards houses the ground-crew shed in an alcove in foul territory just in front of the right-field foul pole, hidden behind the grandstand. An outfielder who catches a foul ball in that alcove would have to throw the ball over the grandstand or run around the grandstand to throw home. Knowing that the runner will score from third on this play, a smart outfielder might intentionally drop the ball or let it fall untouched to the ground in foul territory. The defense loses a sure out, but the runner cannot advance to score on a ball that lands in foul territory.[19]

Three characteristics are present on this play, making it tempting to compare it with the uncaught fair fly ball under the Infield Fly Rule.

By intentionally not catching a playable batted ball, the outfielder intentionally fails to perform the expected athletic skill as he ordinarily would and as the game ordinarily expects. The outfielder has a strong incentive not to catch this ball to prevent the tying or go-ahead run from scoring. And the defense wields exclusive control over the play; the outfielder chooses whether to catch the ball and everything else on the play—namely, the baserunner's opportunity to advance—flows from that choice. The offense only reacts to the outfielder's decision and is helpless to otherwise affect the outcome of the play.

The critical difference is that the fly ball is foul, not fair. As a result, and unlike either an infield fly or uncaught third strike, the play does not produce an extraordinarily inequitable and one-sided cost-benefit advantage for the defense or disadvantage for the offense. The play instead produces an equitable two-way cost-benefit exchange, with each team gaining something and surrendering something. The defense loses an out by not catching the foul fly ball (a cost), but does not surrender an important run (a benefit); the offense loses a probable run (a cost), but does not give up the out (a benefit).

The intentional non-catch ends with both teams in the same position as before the foul ball—same batter, same base-out situation, same count (if the foul ball comes with two strikes) or one more strike (if the foul ball comes with less than two strikes), and the same prime scoring opportunity of (at least) runner on third with fewer than two outs. The cost-benefit exchange on the foul fly ball itself is even; who benefits more in the exchange depends on what happens on subsequent plays, particularly what the batter does with his now-extended at-bat.

Rundown to Let Teammate Score

This is the batting team's version of the above play—a baserunner on first wanders from the base to draw a throw, gets caught in a rundown, and prolongs the rundown long enough to allow his teammate on third base to break for home and score. If two are out, the goal is to ensure that his teammate scores before being tagged out in the rundown.[20] This play can take many forms. It may involve a batter hitting a long single and taking an intentionally wide turn around first to draw the throw and begin the rundown, allowing his teammate (who went from first to third on the single), to score while the defense focuses on the runner on first. It may involve a double steal from a first-and-third situation, in which the runner on first breaks for second to draw a throw, then lengthens the play to allow the runner on third to score. The most extreme version of this is the "Skunk in the Outfield"—in a first-and-third situation, the runner on first takes his lead 15–20 feet onto the outfield grass, hoping to induce a balk or to lull the defense into chasing him in the outfield, allowing his teammate to score from third.[21]

Regardless of form, the play requires a baserunner to intentionally do what he ordinarily does not want to do—get caught in a rundown or tagged out, often while declining to run hard so as to draw the throw. But if the move works and his teammate scores it produces a run on a play that ordinarily would not produce a run. That unexpected benefit offers a baserunner some perverse incentive to attempt this seemingly unhelpful move in search of benefits for his teammate.

But any form of the play lacks a disparity in control over the play. The defense has several responses and counters that might prevent the run. It might break-off the rundown and throw out the baserunner trying to score from third. With two out, it might execute the rundown quickly and efficiently so the infielder can tag that runner for the third out before the other runner crosses the plate. The response to the skunk in the outfield is not to chase the runner on first, thereby depriving the runner on third the time or space to run home. The defense may succeed in these counter-moves or not—all require sharp execution by the fielders, with accurate throws and good tags. The point is that the defense has a realistic opportunity to execute a strategy to prevent the run from scoring and to avoid the cost on the play.

Even if the rundown produces an out, the cost-benefit exchange is not one-sided, as each team incurs both costs and benefits on the play. The offense gains a run but surrenders an out, while the defense gains an out but surrenders a run. Whether the exchange is equally helpful to both teams depends on the score, inning, and other circumstances of the play—perhaps the run is worth more to the offense than the out or the out more to the defense than the run. Both teams might be satisfied with the exchange. The point remains that because both teams exercise choice and control over the play, both remain free to pursue basic strategy and to exchange risks, costs, and benefits in search of an advantage. Neither team enjoys a structural advantage and nothing in the situation deprives either side of influence.

Intentional Walks and Semi-Intentional Walks

Sometimes a pitcher does not try to throw strikes or get the batter out, instead throwing four pitches outside of the strike zone for a base on balls.

This may be intentional. Historically, an intentional walk occurred when the pitcher obviously and openly threw four pitches well wide of home plate and outside the catcher's box, with the catcher standing up and stepping outside the box to receive the ball once it left the pitcher's hand.[22] Or it is what we might call a semi-intentional walk, with the pitcher "pitching around" the batter. The catcher is stationed in his usual position and the pitcher throws the ball near home plate; he pitches close enough to the strike zone that the batter might swing, but outside the zone, such that the pitch will be called a ball if the batter does not swing. The pitcher intentionally does not give the batter "anything good to hit," hoping to induce him to swing at a bad pitch, but happy to put him on base if he does not.

We might collectively label these plays "not-unintentional walks." While formally distinct, they share two characteristics. As with all pitcher-batter encounters, the pitcher wields first-mover advantage in the initial decision of how to pitch the batter, leaving the batter in a reactive posture. (Baseball is unique among sports in that the defense begins each play with possession of the ball.) The pitcher does not perform the expected athletic skill in the expected manner. He is not trying to throw the ball in (and, on an intentional walk, anywhere near) the strike zone and is not primarily interested in getting the batter out. The defense does not expect the batter to swing and is intentionally allowing, or at least enabling, him to reach base. The difference between intentional and semi-intentional walks is obviousness and intent. In the former, the pitcher has surrendered and is doing nothing but allowing the batter to reach base. In the latter, the pitcher's primary intent is to put the batter on base, although a secondary effect is that the batter might get himself out by chasing bad pitches.

But not-unintentional walks represent baseball's paradigmatic equitable, two-way cost-benefit. Each team makes a less-than-optimal move, accepting some costs and granting the other side some benefits in exchange for other benefits for itself. The defense allows a runner to reach base (a cost to the defense and benefit to the offense) in exchange for several possible benefits.

One benefit is to create a more-favorable base-out situation. Facing runner-on-second/one-out, the defense might intentionally walk a batter to set-up first-and-second/one-out, setting up a possible inning-ending groundball double play, as well as a possible infield-fly call.

Another benefit is the chance to face a weaker hitter. In National League games played without a designated hitter, teams may not-unintentionally walk the eighth-spot hitter (often the weakest-hitting position player) to face the pitcher, who is almost always a worse hitter than even the least-productive position player. The rise of advanced metrics and statistical analysis has prompted teams to intentionally walk truly great hitters in all situations, willingly taking a chance with "merely good" hitters. In a 13-inning game against the Cubs in 2016, Washington Nationals outfielder Bryce Harper, a great hitter enjoying an early-season hot streak, walked six times, three intentionally; the player behind him, first baseman Adam Zimmerman, went 1-for-7, stranding 14 baserunners.[23] In 2002, at the height of his late-career offensive power surge, San Francisco Giants outfielder Barry Bonds (a Hall-of-Famer but for suspicions of using performance-enhancing drugs[24]) walked 198 times, including 68 intentionally, records he broke two years later.[25]

The offense benefits from not-unintentional walks, gaining an additional baserunner and an additional opportunity to score a run without surrendering an out. That benefit reflects the central *Moneyball* insight—more baserunners, no matter how they reach base, and fewer outs equal more opportunities to score runs, which is the batting team's goal.[26] This is not to say that the walk is the optimal outcome for the offense; it may even represent a cost. The 2002 Giants would rather have had Bonds hitting and the 2016 Nationals would rather have had Harper hitting. And almost every team would rather have its weakest position player batting than the pitcher. But because the batting team receives some benefit, this reflects more than a one-sided exchange.

The batting team also is not helpless in the face of this strategy, but has opportunities to counter the move. A batter determined to get a hit can refuse the free pass by swinging at bad pitches that are close enough to the strike zone. The pitcher might make a mistake, throwing the intentional ball too close to the plate and allowing the batter to tee-off on a slow pitch.

To the extent those offensive efforts fail and the batter gets out—surrendering the small benefit the defense offered—he exercises control and influence over the play. A batter's unwise strategic actions impose the costs on that play, not the structures of the game or manipulations by the opposing team; again, the rules do not and need not protect players from their bad decisions. The offense also might benefit from the pitcher losing control of an intentional ball, producing a wild pitch allowing the baserunners to advance and even score.

One might contest the strategic wisdom of not-unintentional walks, particularly in many of the situations in which they are employed. But the strategy's supposed lack of wisdom highlights the equity of the exchange, both in terms of control and cost-benefit balance. The offense benefits from the defense pursuing bad strategy; the offense should reject a limiting rule that might protect the opponent from its own silly strategy.

A balanced strategic exchange remains. The occasional mistake by the pitcher produces a hit or wild pitch, providing extra benefits to the offense beyond the extra baserunner. The defense benefits through the occasional pitching deception or batter complacency. In Game 3 of the 1972 World Series between the Oakland A's and Cincinnati Reds, A's pitcher Rollie Fingers had a full count on the Reds' Johnny Bench. The A's set-up to intentionally throw ball four, with the catcher standing as if ready to receive ball four outside the catcher's box. But Fingers threw the pitch over the outside corner and the catcher jumped back into the box to catch it for strike three.[27]

This analysis is in flux with respect to intentional walks. Prior to the 2017 season, MLB eliminated the requirement that the pitcher throw four balls for an intentional walk, awarding the batter first base on a signal from the dugout. The stated purpose was to speed the game by removing what seemed a time-consuming-but-pointless ritual of throwing four pitches wide of the strike zone, although the relative rarity of intentional walks and the little time needed to throw four pitches outside the zone meant the rule would save, on average, 16 seconds per game.[28]

The new process for intentional walks reintroduces a third characteristic. The batting team no longer has an opportunity to respond or counter the intentional-walk strategy, because the defense no longer must perform even minimal athletic skills. The batting team also cannot reap extra benefits from the occasional pitching mistake. But the exchange remains equitable and two-sided—the batting team gets the benefit of an additional baserunner without surrendering an out, while the fielding team gets the benefit of facing a weaker hitter or a more-favorable base-out situation. It therefore does not call for a limiting rule and can be left to the teams' competing strategic options.

Productive Outs

The batting team's version of the not-unintentional walk is the "productive" out, encompassing many plays in which the batter willingly foregoes a complete effort to reach base in exchange for a run or for moving a teammate into better scoring position. These include sacrifice flies[29]; squeeze bunts with a runner on third base (either safety, in which the runner does not break until the ball is bunted in play, or suicide, in which the runner breaks on the pitch[30]); sacrifice bunts designed to advance runners from first or second[31]; hit-and-run plays,[32] in which the runner on first breaks on the pitch, although not looking to steal, and the batter tries to put the ball in play and on the ground (with the goal of avoiding a groundball double play); and hitting to the right side to advance a runner from second to third with less than two outs.

On each of these plays, the batter intentionally fails to perform (at least primarily) the expected skills in the expected manner. He is not trying to get a hit by hitting the ball hard, far, or in a place where a fielder cannot catch it. Getting on base has become his secondary goal, at best; instead, he seeks to hit the ball in a way more likely to produce an out. He bunts rather than swings, and may telegraph to the defense that he is doing so. He tries to hit the ball to a spot on the field where it is likely to be fielded for an out. He swings at pitches outside the strike zone to protect the breaking runner. If the pitcher throws a pitchout[33] on an expected suicide squeeze, the batter may literally throw his bat at a ball well out of the strike zone, trying to foul the pitch off to protect the breaking runner. And he approaches the overall at-bat differently than if he were trying to get on base, making different choices about hitting strategy and how and when to swing.

As with not-unintentional walks, two characteristics are absent. The offense does not exercise exclusive control over the play, because the defense can counter or thwart the strategy. The pitcher can throw high pitches or pitches out of the strike zone that will be difficult to bunt or put in play, especially on the ground. He can throw pitches that will be more difficult to hit to the right side to move a runner along (for example, low-and-away to a left-handed batter). He can throw a pitch-out against an anticipated hit-and-run or suicide squeeze, providing an easy pitch for the catcher to handle and tag or throw out the breaking runner. Infielders can try to catch a bad bunt on a fly (recall that the Infield Fly Rule does not apply to bunts, although the intentional drop rule does, making possible a double play on the non-catch). Infielders can try to throw out the lead runner (often on a force-out) rather than taking the sure out at first on the batter willingly giving himself up. These counters involve their own risks for the defense. But having responsive options means the defense is not helpless in the face of the offensive strategy. These plays reflect baseball's typical move/counter-move balance, with the outcome depending on how well each team performs the expected skills involved in the play.

Like not-unintentional walks, productive outs involve an equitable, two-way exchange of costs and benefits. Each team accepts a sub-optimal result to gain some benefit and surrender some cost. The offense accepts the cost of an out in exchange for a run or for moving runners into better scoring position; the defense incurs the cost of the run or runner advancing in exchange for the benefit of an additional out that brings it closer to the end of the inning. Who prevails on this balanced exchange depends on what happens on subsequent plays.

As with not-unintentional walks, many believe productive outs, particularly sacrifice bunts, constitute bad strategy—that it is unwise for a team to sacrifice one of its 27 precious outs for a relatively small gain in advancing a baserunner.[34] This critique highlights the equity of the exchange. If the offense wants to adopt bad strategy, the defense should welcome it, not seek a limiting rule to save the offense from its own unwise choices.

"Let's Get This Over With": Intentionally Ending an Inning and Moving the Game Along

Baseball is famously untimed. As Annie Savoy says near the end of *Bull Durham*, baseball is not linear, but is a spatial, non-time-connected game.[35] The goal in baseball is to score the most runs possible while securing the 27 outs on the other team needed to end a nine-inning game. Baseball also guarantees both teams an equal opportunity to score by providing each its full complement of 27 outs (except where a home team leads after the visiting team has used its full complement, where the home team does not need the additional opportunity). One team cannot prevent the other from moving to offense and having a chance to score.

The best one team can do is delay the other's turn at bat by extending its own. A batting team therefore seeks to maximize the runs its scores and minimize the outs it surrenders. Even when intentionally surrendering an out through a productive out, it does so believing (rightly or wrongly) that the play enhances its chance to score runs and to prolong the at-bat.

While it is difficult to imagine a batting team not wanting to score runs where possible, there are some exceptions. In the late innings of a blow-out, the leading team, secure in the number of runs it has scored, wants to bring the game to an end, which it only can do by ending its at-bat and allowing the opponent to bat. Batters may swing at bad pitches, not try to hit the ball as hard or far, not run as hard to first base on batted balls, and otherwise not exert full effort to reach base safely. The goal is to end its half inning and allow the opponent to use its final outs.

Another exception arises when rain threatens to suspend a game. An MLB game becomes official after five innings have been completed, four-and-a-half if the home team leads.[36] A batting team with a lead when rain threatens to cancel the game might similarly forego additional runs, with the goal of ensuring that the other team bats and that enough innings are completed to establish a regulation game.

Cricket codifies this strategy through Law 14's "Declaration and Forfeiture." A team captain can declare an innings closed at any time during that innings or he can forfeit an entire innings prior to it beginning.[37] The captain does this believing his team has scored enough runs, incentivized by a desire to ensure sufficient time to complete the game. Rather than going through the motions of batting without real effort or desire, as in baseball, a cricket team declares its opportunity to score over and allows the opponent its turn. These formal rules do require strategic decision-making in wielding the strategy—a team must not declare so early that it has not given itself enough of a cushion or so late that the opponent cannot complete its turn and the game cannot be completed.

Imagine a game between Team W (winning) and Team L (losing), in which Team W wishes to move the game along to ensure its completion. Team W acts contrary to the game's ordinary expectations by intentionally batting without any desire or effort to score runs to get the inning over with.

But the other defining characteristics are absent. This situation produces another equitable, two-way cost-benefit exchange. In fact, this strategy does not involve any exchange, but one team unilaterally granting benefits to its opponent, believing that it also benefits. Team L receives only benefits and incurs no costs by Team W's strategy. Team W gives Team L what it wants—the opportunity to bat and score runs while no longer having to worry about Team W scoring. And because it now comes to bat, Team L is not helpless—it can (and hopes to) score runs, taking the lead or tying the game, thereby complicating Team W's efforts to end (or win) the game quickly. The possibility of Team L scoring represents Team W's risk in surrendering its scoring opportunity. But Team W benefits from Team L batting to ensure completion of the game, provided it can keep Team L from scoring. The result is an even exchange, with each team attempting to perform the competing athletic skills in the expected manner during Team L's subsequent at-bat—Team L attempts to get hits and score runs, while Team W attempts to prevent Team L from doing so.

The perverse incentive to employ this move does not arise very often. It requires an extremely lopsided game, with a deficit that statistics and experience suggest Team L cannot overcome. Or it requires the looming threat of rain severe enough not only to delay the game for a short time, but to force the umpires to call the game off. Rain delays are rare enough; a storm that will require cancellation of the game midway through reflects a still-smaller class of rain delays. It also is impossible for a team to know in advance what might happen if it does rain. Without some certainty, Team W will not invoke this strategy. The incentive may arise more frequently in cricket, where play must stop at a designated time and matches may be halted by darkness. Even there, however, a team never can be certain how many runs is enough.

The need for any limiting rule to be administrable prevents baseball from halting this practice, because it is difficult to image any workable rule. While baseball includes some rules requiring umpires to determine player intent (notably the intentional-drop rule), it would be impossible to legislate or enforce a regulation on how hard a player must run to first base on a ground ball or whether the lack of hustle reflects an intent to not reach base or a desire to move the game along.

Nor are players alone in wanting to push the game to its conclusion. Umpires also have an incentive to move a one-sided or weather-threatened game to completion and might expand the strike zone or call close plays with an eye towards moving the game along.

* * *

This chapter applied the four-characteristic framework throughout baseball. It revealed three things. The one genuinely analogous situation— the uncaught third strike—is subject to a logically and functionally identical limiting rule. Faced with an existing rule that unexpectedly created a risk of an extraordinary inequitable cost-benefit disparity, baseball adjusted the rules to eliminate the risk. And every other imaginable baseball situation is different from the infield-fly situation around one or more of those characteristics, leaving all free of limiting rules and subject to the game's ordinary rules, practices, ethics, and strategies.

In the next chapter, I carry this framework beyond baseball and into other sports, producing identical results. Some plays and situations in other sports possess the four defining characteristics; those that do are subject to limiting rules that, like the Infield Fly Rule, prohibit or disincentivize players from intentionally acting contrary to athletic expectations in search of cost-benefit advantage. Other plays and situations in other sports lack one or more characteristics; those are properly not subject to limiting rules.

Chapter 4

Infield Fly Rule
in Other Sports

Critics of the Infield Fly Rule argue two analogies.

They first point to a host of baseball plays and game situations purportedly comparable to the infield-fly situation, but lacking a similar limiting rule. If these situations do not get special rules, they argue, neither should the infield fly. Chapter 3 used this framework to show why that argument fails. The few genuinely comparable situations—those featuring four defining characteristics—are subject to limiting rules reflecting the structure and logic of the Infield Fly Rule. All other, unregulated situations are not genuinely comparable, lacking one or more characteristics and rendering limiting rules unnecessary.

Critics next move beyond baseball to argue that purportedly comparable plays and game situations in other sports remain free of infield-fly-type limiting rules, thereby undermining the logic of the Infield Fly Rule in baseball. Chapter 4 addresses that second argument.

My framework can measure, analyze, and explain any game situation in any sport in light of the four defining characteristics—players intentionally acting contrary to ordinary athletic expectations, players seeking an inequitable and one-sided cost-benefit advantage, one team exclusively controlling the play and the other lacking any influence, and a perverse incentive to intentionally act contrary to ordinary expectations. As in baseball, the presence of all four suggests the need for a limiting rule that either prohibits or disincentivizes teams from acting contrary to expectations. As in baseball, the absence of one or more characteristics in a situation eliminates the need for any limiting rule.

Extending the framework to other sports demonstrates the universality of these four characteristics to define game situations and to analyze when limiting rules are appropriate. It rebuts the charge of cherry-picking some characteristics unique to the infield-fly situation, while ignoring other features not unique to that baseball play. All sports are as susceptible to plays producing inequitable cost-benefit disparities and perverse incentives to fail to perform the game's athletic virtues in the expected manner. As in baseball, most plays in other sports lack one or more characteristics and are properly left free of any limiting rule. Some possess all four and are or can be subject to limiting rules akin to the Infield Fly Rule.

It would be impossible to catalogue every play in every sport at every level. I look at three team sports—football, basketball, and soccer—and a few plays in each that are either common occurrences or have arisen as points of rules discussions in recent years. I also examine the rules for starts in track and swimming races.

One preliminary point is in order. The framework must account for differences among the details, strategies, and goals of different sports. This is especially important in considering the first characteristic—whether players and teams act consistent with a game's ordinary expectations and strategies and whether they execute the expected athletic skills and virtues in the expected manner.

What qualifies as acting consistent with those expectations and virtues varies by sport. And the significant variant among sports, which may affect athletic expectations and virtues, is time.

As discussed in Chapter 3, baseball is untimed and guarantees each team the same number of scoring opportunities (nine at-bats, 27 outs). With the rare exception of looming rain or darkness, teams never forego the opportunity to score runs. Otherwise, baseball is unconcerned with time. We have no sense, or interest, in how long those 27 outs take, except among those who worry about how it affects TV ratings and attendance from younger fans who believe games are too long (hence efforts in the mid–2010s to speed the game).[1] The defense's goal is to get outs and the offense's goal is to score runs, which becomes easier when it puts men on base. This explains why an infielder intentionally failing to catch an easily playable fair fly ball in the infield-fly situation seems so outside baseball's ordinary expectations and athletic virtues—it represents the only play on which a team regularly and easily places itself in a substantially better situation by intentionally not catching a batted ball in fair territory.

But a clock alters the strategic calculus for players, teams, and the game. In timed sports, the framework's first prong—players intentionally failing to do what is ordinarily expected on the field or intentionally doing what they ordinarily do not want to do—accounts for the clock and how time affects what players want or expect to do. Many strategies that produce timing benefits are worth pursuing, even if contrary to the team's interests in accumulating or preventing points. The goal of a timed sport is not to score as many points as possible, only to score more points than the opponent when time expires. A team thus might exchange possession of the ball or an opportunity to score for time. This, in turn, affects both how we understand when a team is performing the expected athletic skills and athletic virtues in the expected manner and what constitutes an equitable two-way cost-benefit exchange on a play.

For example, a football team leading late in the game and in possession of the ball may run a series of low-risk plays—running the ball into the middle of the line of scrimmage, with the runner holding the ball with two hands, running into the pile and going down easily, and seeking only short yardage. In the NFL, the clock continues to run between plays unless the ball (or the player holding the ball) goes out of bounds or a forward pass is incomplete.[2] By not throwing a pass and by running the ball in the middle of the field, the offense avoids both risks, guaranteeing the clock runs unless the defense calls one of its three timeouts in the half.[3] By staying low and holding the ball with two hands, the runner reduces the risk of fumbling. Although this play likely will not lead to a score or gain much yardage, the offense acts consistent with the game's ordinary expectations—it maintains possession of the ball and keeps the clock running, both of which are more important than scoring or gaining substantial yardage. Any costs resulting from failing to gain points or yardage are offset by the benefits in time lapse. Conversely, the defense gains the benefit of preventing a score or gain of big yardage, but at the cost of lost time. The result is a two-way cost-benefit exchange, although one that works more in one team's favor than the other.

Basketball teams employ similar strategies, where a team leading and with the ball in the final minutes might elect not to shoot or to wait until the end of the shot clock before shooting. A shot with time running out might be more difficult, decreasing the team's chances of scoring. But the benefit of time off the clock outweighs, or at least balances against, the cost of it being more difficult to score points. And the benefit to the trailing team of getting the ball back on the missed difficult shot is offset by the cost of having less time to score points of its own.

The question in both sports is where and how a leading offensive team strikes that balance. Basketball teams that begin "milking" the clock too early take themselves out of their offense, have a more difficult time scoring because taking more difficult shots, and leave too much time for the opponent to come back when it gets the ball back, putting too much pressure on its own defense. Teams that wait too long extend the game, giving the opponent the ball back too many times with too much time to score points and close the deficit. But that is a strategic question, built on the understanding that ceding points, possession, or yardage in exchange for time is consistent with the game's ordinary expectations.

With that caveat, we turn to non-baseball sports in search of game situations that feature the four defining characteristics and that demand limiting rules, as well as those that lack one or more characteristics and should be left free from limiting rules.

Fouling in Basketball

The ordinary goal for the defense in basketball seems straight-forward enough: Stop the offense from scoring by forcing a missed or difficult shot (and rebounding that miss) or a turnover. In doing this, defenders inevitably commit fouls, an unintended-but-unavoidable product of closely guarding the opposing players. But the defense generally does not intend to foul, as fouls benefit the offense and hurt the defense. Sometimes the offensive player shoots free throws for easy points—when the foul occurs as the offensive player is in the act of shooting or, in the NBA, on all fouls subsequent to the fourth foul of the first ten minutes of a quarter or all fouls subsequent to the first foul in the final two minutes of a quarter.[4] If the player with the ball was not shooting and the fouling team has not accumulated the requisite number of fouls, the offense retains possession of the ball and has a new period of at least 14 seconds to shoot.[5] Fouls accumulate on an individual player, who is disqualified from the game upon committing his sixth foul.

But defensive incentives with respect to fouling change in some situations, compelling a team not only to accept fouling as an inevitable mistake, but to foul as an intentional strategy. Fouling might appear to be basketball's analogue to not catching an easily playable fair fly ball—it is unavoidable that a player will do it unintentionally on occasion, but a player acts contrary to ordinary athletic expectations by doing it intentionally. That basketball does not have a limiting rule to disincentivize or prohibit intentional fouls frequently is offered to suggest that the Infield Fly Rule is unnecessary to disincentive intentional non-catches.

Basketball's structure incentivizes intentional fouling in three situations. First is late-game intentional fouling, where Team L (losing the game) intentionally fouls a player from Team W (winning the game) to stop the clock in the closing minutes, forcing Team W to shoot free throws and giving Team L a chance to get the ball back. Second is intentionally fouling to prevent a game-tying three-point shot—Team W, leading by three in the closing seconds, intentionally fouls a player from Team L before he can shoot a three that would tie the game. Third is "hacking," or "Hack-a-Shaq," intentionally fouling a bad free-throw shooter at any time and place.

Late-Game Fouling When Trailing

Defensive incentives change when Team L, on defense, trails in the closing minutes or seconds of the game. At this point, it is not enough to stop Team W from scoring so it can get the ball back. Team L must stop Team W quickly, without too much time elapsing, so it has sufficient time and possessions to score the points necessary to come back. At the same time, Team W no longer has incentive to shoot or otherwise surrender possession of the ball; it is content to hold or pass the ball around and milk as much time as it can—surrendering the opportunity to score (because it does not need more points) in exchange for time. Even good defense by Team L may not succeed in getting the ball back, at least with sufficient time to score.

The answer for Team L is to intentionally foul the player holding the ball. Although the Team L defender will at times try to make it appear that he is attempting to steal the ball, everyone, particularly the officials, knows what is going on. The foul stops the clock. And once Team L has committed enough team fouls, Team W must shoot free throws, meaning it cannot hold the ball, as it would prefer. This might appear to run contrary to the game's ordinary expectations, where fouling and allowing the other team to shoot free throws and score easy points is contrary to the defending team's interests. But clock considerations alter ordinary strategies. Team L's real goal in this situation is to get the ball back with sufficient time remaining to give it an opportunity to score. Fouling, even if it means Team W scoring one or two points, is the only means to that end. Fouling therefore is consistent with Team L's strategic goals in this situation.

Late-game fouling lacks two characteristics, providing an equitable two-sided exchange on a play that both teams influence and control. Who comes out ahead on the exchange depends on how each team executes and what happens on subsequent plays. Team W incurs the cost of not being able to run time off the clock or retain possession of the ball, but gains the benefit of being able to score two easy points by making the free throws. Team L incurs several costs—two potential points allowed, additional personal fouls on the fouling player, and additional team fouls. But it gains multiple benefits—the clock stops, the shooter might miss one or both free throws, and it gets the ball back, either following the made free throw or by rebounding the miss. Team L gains an additional potential benefit from the existence of the three-point shot, which allows it to score more points on its possession than it allows on the free throws—even if Team W makes two free throws every time, Team L closes the deficit by hitting three-pointers. If repeated enough times, a trailing team could close a two- or three-point gap even when both teams score on every late-game possession.

Team W is not helpless, unable to counter the strategy, or unable to avoid the costs imposed. It defeats the intentional foul in three ways. Most obviously and easily, it can make the free throws. It can rebound any missed free throw to regain possession of the ball (with the rebounder likely getting fouled again and given a chance to shoot more free throws). And, when Team L gets the ball back, Team W can play good defense to stop it from scoring, thereby preventing it from obtaining the benefits of its strategy.

Fouling does raise aesthetic concerns. It is not fun to watch a game in which play and the clock continually stop for intentional fouls. And repeated fouling can cause the final three minutes of game time to last 20 minutes or more in real time.[6] Rulemakers must consider aesthetics in deciding whether to allow or eliminate a strategic practice. Baseball's main limiting rules—the Infield Fly Rule and the uncaught-third-strike rule—reflect, in part, aesthetic choices not to incentivize fielders to intentionally fail to catch batted or thrown balls. But aesthetics alone do not compel limiting rules to eliminate strategies that, although perhaps visually unappealing, do not produce overwhelming cost-benefit inequities and otherwise fit within accepted game strategy.

Late-game fouling presents a further problem for rulemakers—eliminating the practice would alter basketball in a one-sided and inequitable fashion by making it impossible for Team L to overcome a late-game deficit. With Team W content to hold the ball, not shoot, and run time down in 24-second chunks, Team L could not get enough possessions with enough time to come back if it did not have some way to stop the clock and get the ball back.[7] At some point, considering time and score, it would become mathematically impossible for Team L to make up the deficit. (This is an important distinction with the infield-fly situation—the limiting rule does not leave the fielding team in an impossible situation if unable to turn a double play through the intentional non-catch, because it is guaranteed one out on the catch or the call.) Even if inclined to stop the practice, there is no obvious solution. The rules could not prohibit "intentional" fouls, as by awarding Team W the free throws and allowing it to retain possession. It would be too difficult for officials to distinguish an intentional foul from a foul on which the defender genuinely tries for a steal, at least if the defender makes a play on the ball. Either no fouls could be identified as intentional, rendering the rule meaningless, or officials, knowing the late-game incentives at work, call everything intentional, eliminating Team L's opportunity to come back.

At best, rulemakers can address aesthetic concerns by increasing the cost to Team L and the potential benefit to Team W, thereby disincentivizing overuse of the strategy. To move from the NBA to college basketball for a moment, the evolution of the NCAA's rules on team fouls and the free-throw bonus reflects these concerns.

Prior to 1990, non-shooting fouls after the sixth team foul of a half placed the fouled team in the bonus, shooting a "one-and-one"—the player shot one free throw, but got a second "bonus" free throw only if he made the first. This made it easier for the losing team to come back, since it increased the likelihood the winning team would score no points on a possession—if Team W missed the first free throw, it never shot the second. This incentivized teams to intentionally foul earlier, extending the game and leaving Team L more time to force Team W to shoot free throws, to get the ball back, and to score points. North Carolina State won the 1983 Men's Basketball National Championship against a heavily favored University of Houston team through such strategic fouling.[8]

In 1990, the NCAA addressed the aesthetic objections to the practice by establishing two bonus levels. From the seventh to the ninth foul of a half, the offense shoots one-and-one. Beginning on the tenth foul, teams move to the "double bonus" and all fouls result in two shots (as in the NBA).[9] The change sought to limit (although not eliminate) late-game fouling. Team W gains an additional benefit—it is more likely to come away with some points on the possession, since the fouled player gets to shoot (and perhaps make) the second free throw if he misses the first. That additional benefit to Team W perhaps disincentivizes Team L from fouling, at least as early—by fouling too soon, Team L quickly places the opponent in the double bonus to shoot two free throws on every foul. But it does not prohibit late-game fouling, retaining it as the only way that Team L can come back in the closing minutes or seconds of the game.

Nick Elam, a former middle-school principal and now professor of educational leadership, offered a more radical solution to late-game fouling in 2017. Under Elam's proposal, the game clock (although not the shot clock) would be turned off with three minutes remaining in regulation (four minutes in college) and the teams would play until one team reached a target score, set at +7 of the leading team's score when the clock was turned off. For example, if Team W leads 99–91 at the 3:00 mark, the teams play until one team reaches 106 points. The Basketball Tournament—a $2 million, 64-team semi-professional tournament comprised of teams of former college and professional players—used these rules for early-round games in 2017 and 2018.[10]

Elam's proposal eliminates intentional late-game fouling by removing the time concerns that incentivize the intentional-fouling strategy. Team L has no incentive to foul for two reasons. Team L need not stop the clock to preserve time, since there is no game clock to stop. And Team W still must score seven more points, so it retains an incentive to run its ordinary offense and shoot the ball; it no longer wins by holding the ball without shooting until the shot clock expires and time runs out in the game. Team L can get possession, and give itself a chance to score and come back, by playing good defense and rebounding Team W's missed shots; it is guaranteed more possessions and more opportunities to score, without worrying about time expiring. Fouling returns to being contrary to Team L's ordinary athletic expectations, goals and virtues.

Late-Game Fouling and the Three-Point Shot

Leading by three points on what is likely the final possession of the game (typically with approximately four or fewer seconds remaining), Team W might foul the Team L player with the ball before he can attempt a game-tying three-point shot. If fouled before the shot, Team L gets the ball out of bounds or shoots two free throws (or perhaps only one-and-one in college), depending on how many team fouls Team L had accumulated to that point. But those two free throws cannot tie the game. If Team L makes both free throws, Team W gets the ball back, still leading by one, with only a few ticks on the clock. Team L, back on defense and down one, is back to the incentives described in the previous section—it needs a steal or must intentionally foul and hope Team W misses free throws. And even then, with fewer than four seconds left, there may not be time for Team L to score even if it gets the ball back following the free throws.

Team L has a counter to the intentional foul—make the first free throw (cutting the deficit to two), intentionally miss the second free throw, and try to get the offensive rebound and put-back to tie the score. Teams design and practice this play, and it occasionally works.[11] Team W then has its own counter to the counter—rebound the intentionally missed free throw or defend the put-back shot.

This situation lacks the third characteristic of disparity in influence over the play and the inability of one team to avoid potential costs. Each team can respond to the opponent's strategy with its own counter-strategy, exchanging costs in search of benefits and hoping to emerge with an advantage once the situation plays out. Who prevails in the exchange depends on who better executes their respective strategic moves. Which is what we expect in any game situation and what ordinary rules should allow.

The strategic wisdom of fouling when up three has been studied at both the college and professional levels. The question is whether the likelihood of a game-tying three-pointer by Team L is greater than the likelihood of an offensive rebound and game-tying put-back if Team L intentionally misses the second free throw. No consensus has emerged, amid some sense that any difference is not statistically significant.[12]

But as with sacrifice bunts and intentional walks, the wisdom of a game strategy is irrelevant to whether limiting rules should prohibit or deter it. Because each team can influence this play in search of a cost-benefit advantage, each should be left to those choices. No limiting rule is necessary or appropriate to control this strategic exchange.

Hacking

Hacking, or "Hack-a-Shaq," is a fouling strategy to which time and score are irrelevant. Team D (on defense) intentionally grabs an especially poor free-throw shooter from Team O (on offense), away from the ball and away from the play, forcing that poor shooter to shoot free throws. The strategy originated, and drew its moniker, in the early 2000s around Hall-of-Fame Center Shaquille O'Neal, a dominant offensive player but notoriously poor free-throw shooter (his career free-throw shooting percentage was 52.7 percent, with seven seasons shooting below 50 percent).[13] What began as a strategy to foul O'Neal as soon as he caught the ball but before he could shoot (preventing him from scoring in the low post) morphed into fouling him anywhere on the floor, even when he did not have the ball and was uninvolved in the play. By the mid–2010s, the strategy had spread throughout the league, targeting particularly poor shooters on numerous teams.[14]

Team D benefits from this strategy in several respects. It can get the ball back quickly by rebounding the (likely) missed second free throw. It renders Team O's offense less effective. If the hacked shooter shoots 43 percent from the free-throw line, Team O scores .86 expected points on that possession when the poor shooter gets two free throws. But if Team O's regular offense scores 1.12 points per possession, Team D is statistically better off letting the poor shooter take free throws than allowing Team O to run its offense.[15] And if the fouling becomes frequent enough, the hacking target consistently misses the free throws, and its offense stalls, Team O may have to remove the target player from the game. That deprives it of the benefits from the things that player does well (targets of hacking tend to be big men who are good defenders, rebounders, and screeners).

An entire strategic machinery developed around hacking. Teams would foul the hacking target while he was standing out of bounds. In the final two minutes of the game, when all away-from-the-ball fouls result in one free throw by any Team O player in the game (not necessarily the fouled player) and Team O retaining possession,[16] Team D's fouling player would jump on the target's back during a free throw, a loose-ball foul to which the free-throw-and-possession rule did not apply.[17] According to one study, the number of non-shooting intentional fouls jumped between 2011 and 2016, with the largest increase in fouls drawn by poor-shooting big men likely to be hacking targets.[18]

The nadir of hacking occurred in a January 2016 game between the Houston Rockets and Detroit Pistons. Pistons Center Andre Drummond was a 35 percent free-throw shooter and a regular hacking target. In the first two-and-a-half minutes of the third quarter, the Rockets hacked Drummond away from the ball on 12 consecutive plays, all as soon as the ball was inbounded. The first four fouls were committed in nine seconds by a bench player inserted into the game solely to commit those fouls. Drummond went to the line following the fifth foul, committed seconds later, and on the seven subsequent Pistons possessions. In all, Drummond went to the line eight times and shot 16 free throws, making just five. The Rockets cut a nine-point deficit to one in that time, at which point the Pistons removed Drummond from the game.[19]

How does hacking fair under this framework?

Intentional fouling runs contrary to basketball's ordinary athletic expectations and the athletic virtues players ordinarily want to execute. Especially because the hacked player does not have the ball and is not involved in the play, this cannot be disguised as the incidental effect of good defense or a failed attempt to steal the ball. Nor is this akin to late-game fouling as an exchange of potential points for time and possession, which is consistent with ordinary athletic expectations given the overall game situation and the time-sensitive structure of basketball. Here, Team D is intentionally doing something it ordinarily does not want to do.

But like the other intentional-foul situations, hacking offers an equitable two-sided cost-benefit exchange rather than an extraordinarily imbalanced and one-sided one. Team D trades the cost of two free throws and the statistical risk the hacked player might make them for the benefits of making Team O less likely to score and making it more likely Team D will get the ball back following the missed free throws. Team O bears the cost of not being able to run its offense as it chooses and of having an unreasonably poor shooter taking free throw after free throw, although with the possible benefit that the hacked player will score one or two points by making the shots.

The hacking exchange is analogous to baseball's strategy of intentionally (or semi-intentionally) walking a great hitter, regardless of situation, to face the less-great hitter behind him in the lineup. The batting team gets an additional baserunner and the possibility that the less-great hitter might get a hit, even if his chances are less than the superior hitter. Similarly, Team O gets an opportunity to score points on free throws from the hacked player, even if the chances are less than if the team ran its offense and gave the ball to its better offensive players with an opportunity to score. A hacking Team D incurs an additional cost from the additional personal fouls incurred by individual players and the additional team fouls in the quarter. This explains why the Rockets inserted a non-rotation player to commit the rapid-fire hacking fouls—they did not want one of their key players accumulating personal fouls.

Hacking is subject to an organic temporal limitation—it works only after the fourth foul of a quarter puts the hacking team in the penalty; prior to that, non-shooting fouls, even intentional hacking fouls, do not result in free throws.[20] Barring a repeat of the Rockets' strategy, if a team plays good defense and the game is not called unusually tightly, it may be six or seven minutes into a quarter before a team records enough fouls in the flow of the game to begin hacking.

Hacking also lacks the third characteristic of one team being helpless or unable to counter the strategy and avoid the costs. As with late-game fouling, the hacked team has an obvious response—make the free throws, even if it means getting unreasonably bad free throw shooters to shoot better. A second counter is for the offense to rebound the missed free throw and score on the put-back; one study of the hacking strategy found that the Los Angeles Clippers were uniquely effective at rebounding missed free throws by their hacking target.[21]

The problem with hacking is not overwhelming cost-benefit imbalance or disparity in control over the play, the characteristics that trigger limiting rules. Rather, the problem remains aesthetics. Players, coaches, fans, and commentators all complain about hacking not being "basketball" (perhaps it has become the bladderball to which William Stevens compared baseball without the Infield Fly Rule[22]). It is unpleasant to watch a game consisting of intentional fouls on players entirely uninvolved in the play (including one player jumping on another's back) and badly missed free throws by poor shooters. In explaining his decision not to employ Hack-a-Shaq against O'Neal in the 2004 NBA Finals, then-Pistons Coach Larry Brown insisted he would not make a "farce of the game" through such techniques.[23] Most coaches are not so strident, however, as the prevalence of hacking suggests.[24] Gregg Popovich, a five-team NBA champion and coach of the 2020 Olympic team, hacked O'Neal immediately following the opening tip of a 2008 game, then exchanged a laugh with his coaches and with O'Neal.[25]

By summer 2016, hacking had become sufficiently ridiculous to trigger efforts to restrict, if not eliminate, the practice. Aesthetic concerns became strong enough to compel a limiting rule targeting the strategy, even if not strictly warranted under my framework, given the missing characteristics. The point of debate became what that limiting rule should be.

Prior to summer 2016, all fouls away from the ball (whether intentional hacks or fouls within the flow of the game) in the final two minutes of the fourth quarter and overtime were punishable by one free throw, shot by any Team O player in the game, and continued possession for Team O.[26] The simplest approach to hacking would extend that rule to the entire game. But that would be over-inclusive, imposing the same onerous sanction for non-hacking unintentional off-the-ball fouls, such as on a defender attempting to run around a pick. That extension would disincentivize good defense, to the game's overall detriment. And the loose-ball, jump-on-the-back workaround that teams discovered for the final two minutes would become the workaround for the entire game, undermining the rule change.

The NBA's solution, effective in July 2016, was to extend the off-ball foul rule to the final two minutes of every quarter.[27] This removed the incentive to hack during eight minutes of game time, plus additional minutes in overtime. It also could reduce hacking outside those two-minute windows. The same temporal limitations on fourth-quarter hacking now extend to the entire game. The strategy becomes effective only after four team fouls in a quarter allow the opponent to shoot free throws on all fouls, which may not happen for six or seven minutes of the quarter. That shortens the window for hacking to about three or four minutes each quarter—from the point a team enters the penalty (for example, with five minutes in the quarter) until the 2:00 mark, at which point the anti-hacking off-ball foul rule takes effect. Hacking targets also will be on the bench for scheduled rest for some portion of the penalty situation, further reducing use of the strategy.

The league also eliminated the jump-on-the-back, loose-ball workaround, declaring the play a potential flagrant foul.[28] The fouled team retains possession following any free throws, with the fouling player subject to ejection or subsequent sanctions.[29] This destroys any incentive to employ the workaround, because the hacking team does not get its necessary sought-after benefit of possession after the missed free throw, in addition to losing the fouling player.

Football

In defining when a team acts consistent with ordinary athletic expectations and virtues in football, two additional strategic considerations come into play, in addition to the timing concerns discussed at the beginning of the chapter.

The first involves field position. Team O has four downs to score a touchdown or to gain ten yards and a new set of four downs.[30] If it fails to gain the necessary yardage after four plays, it loses possession of the ball. Rather than run a play on fourth down and risk losing the ball on downs, Team O usually punts the ball to the opponent. The goal is for the punter to kick the ball downfield and for the coverage team to tackle the returner soon after he receives it. Team O trades possession (and the opportunity to score) for field position. From its standpoint, it is more advantageous to give Team D the ball at the far end of the field, needing to traverse greater distance and needing more time to score. The alternative is for Team O to maintain possession and run another play to gain a first down, at the risk of failing to gain the necessary yards on fourth down and surrendering possession closer to its end zone, leaving Team D with a "short field" to score. For example, facing fourth-and-10 on its own 30-yard line, Team O is better off punting the ball 45 yards downfield, giving Team D possession at its own 25-yard line (75 yards from a score). The alternative is to risk the fourth down play, lose the ball on downs, and give Team D the ball 30 yards from scoring.

The choice becomes trickier as Team O moves the ball farther down the field. Studies suggest teams should be more willing to run plays rather than punt on fourth-and-short-yardage near midfield, where there is less field-position benefit from the punt compared with the probability of picking up the first down and retaining possession.[31] One Arkansas high school football coach takes this debate to the extreme by never punting, believing in the better odds of converting the fourth down or stopping the opponent even on a short field.[32] Other studies have explored when Team O should "take the points" by kicking a short field goal deep in Team D's territory or when it should run a play from scrimmage to try for a first down or a touchdown. The touchdown yields more points. Failing to convert means losing possession, but with Team D needing to go nearly the length of the field to score.

A full analysis of the various choices is beyond this book. The point is to recognize the cost-benefit exchanges at work. Team O incurs the costs of losing points, yardage, possession, and the opportunity to score in exchange for the benefits of time and field position; Team D gains the benefits of possession, but at the cost of field position. This reflects another relatively equitable two-sided cost-benefit exchange, with the ultimate beneficiary depending on subsequent events.

Second, football enforces rules by imposing penalties for infractions, measured in yardage gained or lost by the fouling team. The severity of a penalty is calibrated to the severity of the infraction, imposing sufficient penalty yardage to deter the misconduct—an offensive lineman flinching an instant before the snap merits a loss of five yards,[33] an offensive lineman holding a rushing defender and illegally preventing him from sacking the quarterback merits a ten-yard penalty,[34] and a defensive back illegally preventing a receiver from catching a pass downfield merits the ball on the spot of the foul.[35]

Many of the football situations that might trigger limiting rules involve one team intentionally committing fouls and other infractions, trading the yardage costs of the penalty for other benefits. It is easy to say that the first characteristic in the framework—intentionally acting contrary to athletic expectations by intentionally doing something that teams ordinarily do not want to do—is present, because teams ordinarily do not want to commit infractions or incur yardage penalties. But considerations of time and field position sometimes alter those incentives and what teams are expected or want to do on the field. In examining possible limiting rules and the sanction associated with them, rulemakers must account for unique game situations in which a team benefits from committing a foul and will intentionally do so in search of another benefit that outweighs the yardage cost.

Football is a complicated game, with many moving pieces and a complicated set of interacting rules. It would be impossible to catalogue the strategic choices and cost-benefit exchanges in every play or decision, including the decision to commit a foul or infraction. This section applies the framework to isolate several plays from recent NFL seasons that exposed game situations producing extraordinary one-sided cost-benefit disparities triggering perverse incentives to intentionally commit infractions—game situations that, under the framework, might call for limiting rules.

These examples reveal two similarities between football and baseball. Where a play features all four characteristics, the NFL has responded with limiting rules that operate on the same logic and structure as the Infield Fly Rule. And the situations that have not been subject to limiting rules lack one or more of those characteristics.

Running Time Through Intentional Infractions

In Super Bowl XLVI (played in January 2012), the New York Giants led the New England Patriots 21–17 with :17 remaining in the game. The

Patriots had the ball at their own 44-yard line, needing a touchdown to win the game. The Patriots ran a play resulting in an incomplete pass, running eight seconds off the clock. But the Giants were called for having too many players on the field. The incomplete pass became a nonplay and the Giants were penalized five yards for the infraction,[36] advancing the ball to the Patriots' 49-yard line. But those eight seconds remained off the clock. Thus, the Patriots were five yards closer to the winning touchdown, but with only :09 remaining. This left time for one more play, a long pass that fell incomplete, and the Giants won the game and the championship.[37]

There was no indication the Giants intentionally placed too many players on the field. Overhead photographs showed the twelfth player at the top of the field running toward the far sideline and trying to leave the field prior to the snap. He was nowhere near the action and not involved in or able to influence the play. Nevertheless, the Giants gained a cost-benefit advantage. The eight seconds off the clock benefited the Giants more than the five yards cost them, while the eight seconds cost the Patriots more than the five yards benefited them.

The play demonstrates the unexpected strategic wisdom and benefit of intentionally taking a too-many-players infraction in the right situation: Team D leads by more than three points, such that Team O must score a touchdown to tie or win; the game is in the waning seconds; and Team O is sufficiently far from the end zone (the necessary distance is inversely correlated to the time remaining—the less time remaining, the closer the infraction can occur). In such a case, Team D gladly surrenders five yards in exchange for running half the remaining time off the clock.

Former NFL coach Buddy Ryan, the architect of the dominating defense that helped the Chicago Bears win Super Bowl XVI in 1986,[38] designed what he called his "Polish Goalline" defense for this situation.

Facing a goalline situation (Team O inside the ten-yard line), Ryan placed as many as three extra defenders on the field, making it more likely his 14-person defense would stop whatever play the 11-person offense would run, with some time lapsing off the clock. Ryan accepted the lost yardage on the too-many-players infraction (inside the ten-yard line, the ball moves half the distance to the goal[39]) in exchange for the time lapsed, confident that his defense could stop one play in the shortened time.[40] Although Ryan designed the play for goalline situations, the Giants demonstrated that the strategy works anywhere on the field, so long as sufficiently little time remained.

An intentional too-many-players infraction features all four defining characteristics, making it a situation that, under the framework, should be subject to an Infield-Fly-style limiting rule.

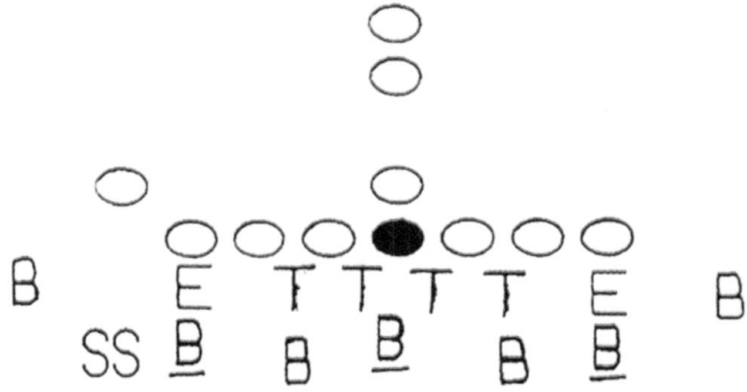

***THREE EXTRA LINEBACKERS GO INTO THE GAME.

SITUATION: THE OPPONENT IS INSIDE THE 5 YARD LINE GOING IN TO SCORE. THERE IS LESS THAN 15 SECONDS LEFT. WE WANT TO STOP THEIR OFFENSE FROM SCORING AND IN THE PROCESS, WE WANT TO RUN THE CLOCK DOWN TO WHERE THEY HAVE ENOUGH TIME FOR JUST ONE PLAY. SO, WE WILL STOP THEM, GET PENALIZED HALF THE DISTANCE TO THE GOAL, BUT LEAVE THEM WITH ENOUGH TIME TO RUN ONE PLAY. WE WILL THEN GO BACK TO OUR REGULAR GOALLINE DEFENSE AND STOP THEM TO WIN THE GAME.

Dom Consentino, *Buddy Ryan's "Polish Goal Line" Defense Was Against the Rules, and That Was the Point*, DEADSPIN (Oct. 19, 2011).

(1) The defense intentionally violates the rules by intentionally placing extra defenders on the field, in a situation in which the infraction is the point. That is the opposite of what teams ordinarily want or intend to do in a game. And it is not reflective of the athletic virtues that players ordinarily seek to perform.

(2) The intentional infraction produces an inequitable one-sided cost-benefit disparity in favor of Team D with the lead. From Team D's standpoint, the play runs time off the clock, while the extra defenders increase the likelihood of stopping Team O on the play. It incurs the cost of the five-yard penalty. But that represents a minimal (to the point of meaningless) cost in this situation, because Team O still has a long distance to travel for the go-ahead touchdown (the Patriots had to travel half the field) and less time to do it. From Team O's standpoint, it incurs high costs offset by minimal benefits—the extra yards do not help much, given the long distance still to travel for the touchdown in a shorter period of time.

This cost-benefit exchange is not entirely one-sided, as with the infield fly or the uncaught third strike. Each team incurs a cost and gains a benefit—Team D runs time but surrenders yardage, while Team O gains yardage but surrenders time. This perhaps better resembles the many plays in baseball and basketball involving equitable two-way cost-benefit exchanges. The difference is that the yardage gained (the cost to the defense and benefit to the offense) is meaningless, given the specific game situation; with only a few seconds remaining and the offense positioned near mid-field and needing a touchdown, five yards does not help the offense or hurt the defense in any meaningful sense. Back to Super Bowl XLVI: Gaining 51 yards for a touchdown (what the Patriots needed following the yardage penalty) is not significantly easier than gaining 56 yards for a touchdown (what the Patriots needed had the prior play stood) in :09. The same is true for the situation Ryan was scheming for. Going three yards on one final play in the shadow of the end zone (following the infraction) is not significantly easier than going six yards on one final play in the shadow of the end zone (without the infraction). A cost-benefit exchange where one side gains a meaningless benefit is not different from an entirely one-sided exchange that provides that side no benefit. At the very least, rulemakers could rationally view such an exchange as sufficiently disparate to reflect the same inequity.

(3) There is a substantial disparity in control over the situation, with the defense free to manipulate the play and the offense relatively helpless to counter or avoid the costs. Team D makes the initial choice to place extra players on the field, providing an obvious overwhelming advantage in stopping whatever play the offense runs. Team O can do nothing but run its play, which is unlikely (or at least less likely) to succeed against a defense of 12 or more players. And the play involves little risk for Team D, given its increased opportunity to stop Team O's play with extra defenders.

(4) The combination of (2) and (3) creates perverse incentives for Team D to attempt (1) whenever the appropriate game situation arises. The likely benefits of stopping the play with extra defenders and running significant seconds off the clock incentivizes the intentional infraction, substantially outweighing the minimal five-yard cost, given the time and distance.

The presence of all four defining characteristics in this situation makes a limiting rule appropriate to disincentivize Team D from intentionally employing this strategy in search of the cost-benefit disparity. With the just-completed Super Bowl XLVI in mind, the NFL implemented a new too-many-players infraction for the 2012 regular season. If the defense has more than 11 players in formation—on the field and ready to be involved in a play—when the snap is imminent, the play is whistled dead prior to the snap, stopping the clock and assessing five yards against the defense.[41]

This is a limiting rule operating on the same logic as the Infield Fly

Rule. It removes the possible benefit for Team D from intentionally acting contrary to athletic expectations, thereby removing the perverse incentive to do so. Because no time lapses on the play, Team D does not gain the sought-after time benefits from the infraction, incurring only the yardage cost. Team D therefore lacks any perverse incentive to intentionally place extra men in formation.

Like the Infield Fly Rule, this limiting rule is arguably over-inclusive. It applies whenever the defense has too many players in formation, even if unintentional and even in a situation in which time and score suggest the defense has no incentive to intentionally commit the infraction. For example, this is unwise strategy if Team D leads by three or fewer points and a field goal by Team O ties or wins the game. That five-yard penalty represents a more meaningful cost to the defense and benefit to the offense, because slicing five yards off a field goal attempt creates an easier kick. Team D also will not intentionally make this move if too much time remains, such that Team O may have time to run more than one or two plays from closer range.

But, as discussed in Chapter 3, most legal rules are over-inclusive. And a rule's over-inclusiveness becomes problematic only if it prohibits conduct that, on balance, is beneficial to the game. There are no circumstances in which football benefits from the defense intentionally placing too many players in formation—no situations in which it is a net positive for the game's logic, ethics, and structures for a team to intentionally commit this infraction or incur this penalty. Football loses nothing as a game by eliminating all plays in which the defense employs excess defenders in formation, even unintentionally.

The NFL did retain the existing live-ball infraction for having too many players on the field but not in formation—that play remains alive and the clock continues to run, with the yardage penalty imposed at the end of the play. The new and old rules co-exist. The dead-ball infraction applies when the defense has too many players in its formation and the snap is imminent. The live-ball infraction applies when the additional players are on the field but not in formation—in other words, the extra player is not involved in the play and likely is running to the sideline, but has not reached it at the snap. The limiting rule is unnecessary in the latter situation, because there is no disparity in control over the situation and likely no cost-benefit inequity. Because the extra defender is uninvolved in the play, the play itself remains 11-on-11, subject to control and influence by both teams. Team D gains no advantage from the extra player, who is not in position to help stop the play; Team O faces no disadvantage in trying to gain yardage, because it runs its play against the expected number of defenders.

Absent that advantage on the play, Team D has no perverse incentive to intentionally place too many players on the field in this way. The infraction only hurts it by nullifying a defensive stop, without benefitting it by adding a player involved in the play. A team still might gain post-play benefits from unintentionally having too many players on the field but not in formation, as appears to be what happened with the Giants in the Super Bowl. But limiting rules are designed to control intentional strategic choices, not unusual circumstances that do not create perverse incentives to intentionally act contrary to athletic expectations. The rules cannot account for all fluke scenarios, only intentional ones.

Saving Time Through Penalties, Intentional and Otherwise

The flip side of an intentional infraction to run time off the clock is a late-game infraction to save time. A welter of rules combine, on the right play, to give a trailing Team D the equivalent of an extra timeout, a cost-benefit advantage, whether through intentional or unintentional misconduct. The penalty allows Team D to extend a game, force Team O to run additional plays, and give itself a chance to get the ball back and score.

Three rules combine to govern clock stoppages. The default rule is that when a team commits a foul, the clock continues as if no foul had occurred once the yardage penalty has been imposed and the ball spotted.[42] That is, if the clock would have continued running without the infraction, the clock restarts as soon as the ball is spotted and ready for the next play; if the clock would have stopped without the foul, the clock restarts on the next snap, as it otherwise would have. The default rule gives way in the final two minutes of the first half and the final five minutes of the second half, with the clock always restarting on the snap, never on placement of the ball.[43] A third rule provides that, in the final minute of each half, teams are prohibited from committing certain acts, including certain intentional infractions, that cause the clock to stop. The penalty for such an act is to override the second rule—the clock restarts when the ball is ready, plus ten seconds are run off the clock.[44]

The second rule is an aesthetics rule, designed to increase excitement by forcing the offense to run more plays, making it harder for Team O with the lead to waste time and easier for a trailing Team O to come back. But in seeking to extend the game and add excitement, this second rule creates mischief. It incentivizes teams to intentionally commit infractions to stop the clock. While the penalty yardage imposed should deter intentional infractions, the clock benefits to be gained might outweigh the yardage costs, especially for a five-yard foul such as defensive encroachment[45] or offensive false start.[46]

The third rule qualifies as a limiting rule to address that perverse incentive. It prevents intentional fouls in the final minute of each half, when time becomes sufficiently important that intentional infractions might be worthwhile. It imposes a result on the play, leaving teams in the same position as if the intentional act (the foul) had not occurred—the clock restarts when the ball is placed and the ten-second runoff puts the clock roughly where it would have been had no foul been called and the clock ran as the players and officials moved to the new spot of the ball. The limiting rule removes any time benefit on the intentional infraction—not only does the clock restart, but the runoff reflects the time that would have lapsed without the whistle stoppage. By imposing the same outcome on the play, the rule eliminates any benefit from the team acting contrary to athletic expectations, thereby eliminating any perverse incentive to do so.

This limiting rule may not go far enough, because it does not apply until the final minute of the half, although the incentive for a trailing team to seek time benefits through intentional infractions begins at least one or two minutes earlier, depending on the score. Perhaps the limiting rule should cover a period closer to the second rule—final two minutes of the first half, five minutes of the second—when time incentives are in play.

But the second rule, standing alone, creates another bit of mischief by enabling a trailing defensive team to obtain similar incidental extraordinary time benefits on unintentional, although undesirable (from the game's standpoint), conduct. The primary example involves the infraction of defensive holding[47] committed in certain precise late-game circumstances. Two plays illustrate the problem.

In November 2013, the New Orleans Saints led the Atlanta Falcons 17–13 with just over 2:00 in the game, with possession. The Saints gained 18 yards and a first down on a play on which the Falcons committed defensive holding, an infraction penalized by five yards and an automatic first down.[48] Because the play produced more yards and a first down, the Saints declined the penalty and accepted the result of the play. Had there been no foul on the play, the clock would have continued to run as the ball was spotted and the players moved to the line of scrimmage. But the holding infraction stopped the clock. And because there were fewer than five minutes remaining in the second half, the second rule controlled—the clock restarted on the snap rather than placement. The Saints had to run several additional plays; the Falcons got the ball back with :05, not enough time to do anything, and the Saints won the game.[49] But the Saints would not have had to run some of those plays had the clock continued following the 18-yard gain and those five seconds would not have remained had the clock not stopped on the infraction.

This combination of rules contributed to a closing-minute parade of horribles that cost the New York Giants a 2015 win over the Dallas Cowboys. The Giants led 23–20 with possession. They completed a pass on third down to produce first-and-goal from the four-yard line with 1:54 on the clock. As in the previous example, the Cowboys were called for defensive holding, the Giants declined the penalty and accepted the result of the play because it gained more yardage and a first down, and the clock remained stopped, pursuant to the second clock rule.

The twist was that the Cowboys had tried to call timeout following the play, which would have left them with one. But following the penalty, and the clock stoppage for the penalty, the timeout was returned, leaving them with two.[50]

Unfortunately for the Giants, the quarterback did not realize what had happened; he recognized that the clock stopped, but believed it was due to the Cowboys timeout. On first down, the Giants called a running play, but the quarterback told the back not to score in favor of taking more time off the clock; the play gained two yards and the Cowboys called timeout with 1:50, leaving them with one (although the quarterback believed it was their last). On second down, the Giants again called a running play and the quarterback again told the back not to score; the play gained one yard, putting the ball at the one-yard line with 1:43, as the Cowboys called their final timeout. This was the timeout the Giants players did not believe the Cowboys had; they expected the clock to continue running. On third down, the Giants threw an incomplete pass, stopping the clock. The Giants kicked a field goal on fourth down, giving them a six-point lead.

But the Cowboys got the ball back with 1:34, and they quickly moved down the field, scoring the winning touchdown with :07.[51] Had the clock not stopped on the infraction, saving the Cowboys that timeout, the Giants could have bled approximately 40 more seconds between second and third down. (The Giants could have lapsed additional time by not throwing an incomplete pass and stopping the clock on third down, but that was a separate mistake.) Even had things played the same otherwise, the Cowboys would have had less time (and likely not sufficient time) for the winning touchdown drive.

Holding fouls in this situation produce a significant inequitable one-sided cost-benefit disparity. Trailing Team D acts contrary to the game's ordinary expectations by committing an infraction, something teams generally do not want to do. The infraction benefits Team D and costs Team O—it stops the clock; it saves Team D time and a timeout, when it otherwise would have been unable to stop the clock without calling one; it requires Team O to run additional plays; and it may allow Team D to get the ball back with additional time remaining. The infraction also does not cost Team D yardage; Team O declines the penalty yardage, at least when its play gains more than five yards. Team D exclusively controls the play by fouling; Team O can do nothing to prevent the foul, prevent the clock from stopping, or avoid having to run additional plays.

Cost-benefit and control disparities aside, this play lacks two characteristics warranting a true limiting rule—Team D intentionally acting contrary to ordinary athletic expectations and the creation of perverse incentives to that intentional action. Neither the Falcons nor Cowboys intentionally held. It appears impossible for a team to manipulate this situation by intentionally committing defensive holding in a way that produces clock benefits it otherwise would not have gained. Team D only gains these time benefits if Team O otherwise gains a first down on the play, such that it will decline the penalty yardage while the clock stops. If Team O does not convert a first down on the play, the holding penalty gives it one,[52] nullifying a successful defensive play. Moreover, Team D cannot know at the point it might commit the holding infraction the outcome of the play, leaving no meaningful opportunity to intentionally commit the foul. The result is a situation that produces a substantially inequitable one-sided cost-benefit advantage for trailing Team D, but only from unintentional acts that Team D has no perverse incentive to attempt and that a limiting rule cannot disincentivize.

Although the framework does not compel a limiting rule, rulemakers might consider whether the cost-benefit disparity is sufficiently inequitable, even if the result of unintentional misconduct, to warrant a limiting rule.

Two rule changes address the problem. One is to eliminate the second clock rule and apply the default rule throughout the game—the clock always restarts as it would without the infraction when the ball is placed. Under this rule, the Falcons and Cowboys would not have gained the clock benefits following the (likely unintentional) defensive-holding infractions—either the clock would have resumed running once the ball was spotted or they would have had to use timeouts. A milder solution would amend the second rule—in the closing minutes the clock restarts on the placement of the ball (not the snap) if a foul is called but the penalty is declined. This eliminates the time benefits for Team D from the holding fouls, since Team O will decline the penalty on a defensive-holding infraction if it gains the first down on its own. And if Team O does not gain the first down, then the infraction provides the first down, imposing a different cost on Team D. Either solution obviates the need for the third clock rule.

Intentional Scores and Intentional Nonscores

The statistics-and-probability approach to football that has developed over the previous decade[53] has sharpened the balance between points and time. Teams increasingly prefer time benefits to point benefits—scoring or preventing points is viewed as sub-optimal when it carries adverse clock effects. In a close game, Team D wants Team O to score quickly, allowing it to get the ball back and score in response; Team O wants to delay scoring in favor of running time off the clock, limiting the time remaining when Team D gets the ball back following the score. This applies regardless of who is winning or losing in a close game. Team O may delay scoring the go-ahead points and Team D may allow a quick go-ahead score, at least so long as the game remains within a single score of some kind.

The conflict between these incentives was on display during the Giants' winning scoring drive in Super Bowl XLVI, the drive immediately preceding the Patriots possession on which the Giants benefited from the too-many-players infraction.

With 1:04 remaining and trailing 17–15, the Giants had the ball on second-and-goal at the Patriots' six-yard line. The Giants were highly likely to score the go-ahead points. Statistics from 2013 showed that a team had a 68 percent chance of scoring a touchdown when it had the ball on the opponent's six.[54] A field goal was even more likely. The ball on the six meant a 24-yard field goal (a field goal is kicked from eight yards behind the line of scrimmage and the goalposts are in the back of the end zone, ten yards beyond the goal line); during the 2013 season, teams converted 231 of 239 attempts from 20–29 yards. Advancing the ball to the one-yard line would have given the Giants an 19-yard field goal, on which teams converted all 15 attempts that season.[55]

Recognizing this, the Patriots' incentive to prevent the Giants from scoring disappeared. It was better for the Patriots that the Giants score quickly, leaving the Patriots more time when they got the ball back following that inevitable score. The solution was to allow the Giants back to run untouched into the end zone on the next play, giving them the ball with :57, trailing by five (assuming the Giants converted the point-after), with one timeout remaining.[56]

Had the Patriots stopped the Giants from scoring the touchdown, the Giants could have run one more play, forced the Patriots to use their final timeout, and run the clock to about :30 before kicking that easy go-ahead field goal. The Patriots would have gotten the ball back with approximately half-a-minute and no timeouts, although only needing a field goal to win, meaning they only had to move the ball far enough to enter field-goal range, roughly around the Giants 40-yard line.

The Giants had competing incentives. They were better-off not scoring, at least right away. Their optimal action was to hold the ball, run plays to drain as much clock as possible without scoring, and wait to score until the latest moment. The Giants understood this. On second down, running back Ahmad Bradshaw recognized the defense was not trying to tackle him or prevent him from reaching the end zone, so he tried to stop at the one-yard line. Unfortunately, his size and momentum carried him forward and he fell into the end zone for an unintentional Super-Bowl-winning touchdown.

This situation presents a strange picture under the framework. Both teams were simultaneously intentionally failing to perform the expected athletic skills and virtues in the ordinary expected manner—Team O was intentionally trying not to score from six yards away, while Team D was intentionally trying not to stop the offense from scoring. And given the possible clock benefits, both had strong incentives to intentionally fail to perform as expected.

The mutuality of these efforts (or non-efforts) eliminates the third characteristic and the need for a limiting rule. There is no disparity in influence over the play, in which one team acts contrary to expectations and the other is up a tree and helpless to meaningfully respond, counter, or avoid costs on the play. Both offense and defense influence the play through their intentionally unexpected conduct, each attempting to manipulate the play to its advantage. Those competing efforts (or non-efforts) counter and cancel one another out. Team D will not try to tackle the runner or keep him out of the end zone; Team O will instruct its players to stop or fall down before reaching the end zone; Team D might push the reluctant runner into the end zone, giving him points against his will (this was the Patriots' plan).

And each team has additional strategic responses and counters. Had the Giants succeeded in not scoring the touchdown on second and third down, the Patriots still would have had a chance to contest the play on which the Giants finally attempted the go-ahead field goal. However difficult or unlikely, nothing in the game's ordinary rules, practices, ethics, and strategies prevented them from doing so. Alternatively, the Giants could have accepted the quick-and-easy score to seize the lead, then relied on their defense to hold the lead, even with more time on the clock. Which is what happened, as the Giants defense kept the Patriots from moving the ball past mid-field (helped by the fortuitous too-many-players infraction) as the clock struck :00.

This play also produces an equitable two-way cost-benefit exchange, with subsequent plays determining who got the better of the exchange. Each team incurs costs (points surrendered by Team D, points foregone by Team O) in exchange for clock benefits (time saved by Team D, time wasted by Team O). Both teams also bear risks in their strategy. In allowing the Giants to score, the Patriots risked being unable to overcome those points, even with additional time (as proved to be the case). In refusing to accept those points, the Giants risked failing when they finally tried to score.

Finally, it might be inappropriate to describe either team as intentionally failing to perform the expected athletic skills in the expected manner, depending on how we understand the balance between points and time and the purpose of football. If using the clock to one's advantage is as important (at least late in the game) as scoring or preventing points, then these strategies reflect expected skills that the rules accommodate. Teams do not act contrary to ordinary athletic expectations in not scoring or in allowing the score, when those ordinary athletic expectations include timing benefits.

The problem returns to aesthetics. There is a visceral sense that it must run contrary to the ethos of football and the way the game "ought to be played" for the offense to intentionally try not to score or for the defense to intentionally allow a score, especially in the closing moments of the biggest game. As one commentator wrote of Bradshaw flopping into the end zone, "it was not a proud or particularly dignified way to decide the Super Bowl."[57] Presented with the long-dreamed opportunity to score the winning touchdown in the Super Bowl, a running back should not regret that he could not stop himself from crossing the goal line. It is aesthetically unappealing to see that player, on the verge of that touchdown, scoring only because his weight and momentum caused him to flop backward into the end zone.

Even if football rulemakers wanted to eliminate these dueling strategies for aesthetic, if not cost-benefit, reasons, it is not clear what any enforceable limiting rule could look like. It would be impossible for officials to identify when the offense intentionally tries not to score or when the defense intentionally fails to tackle. It also would be too easy for players to hide or fake their intentions. And it is not clear what sanction the rules could impose—must the offense accept the touchdown and points it tried to avoid? The rules may be unable to legislate against some undesirable in-game behavior because any limiting rule would be impossible to formulate or to administer.

Intentional Safety

A safety is a unique play in sports, in that the defense scores points without taking possession of the ball. It occurs in three circumstances—when a ball-carrier is tackled in his end zone, when the offense causes the ball to go out of bounds in its end zone, or when the offense commits certain penalties in its end zone.[58] Team D scores two points and receives possession of the ball, with Team O surrendering possession by making a free kick following a safety, usually by punting the ball, undefended, from its 20-yard line.[59]

Team O also may intentionally accept a safety.

Sometimes this happens in the heat of a play gone wrong. For example, a bad long snap sails over the punter's head and bounces towards his end zone. Facing the prospect that Team D will recover the loose ball in the end zone for a touchdown or deep in Team O's territory with a short field for a score, the punter bats the ball through the end zone and out of bounds. From Team O's standpoint, it is better to give up two points on the safety than seven on a touchdown. And the free kick gives Team D the ball, but, assuming a good kick, at the opposite end of the field. By accepting the safety, Team O incurs the costs of surrendering points, but gains the benefits of surrendering fewer points than it otherwise would and of giving the ball back with better field position to defend.

A safety also could be strategic, planned, and intentional, as seen in the closing seconds of Super Bowl XLVII, played in February 2013. The Baltimore Ravens led the San Francisco 49ers 33–29 with :11 remaining. The Ravens had the ball on fourth down at their own eight-yard line and were about to punt the ball away.

A punt in this situation carried risks for the Ravens. A punter receives the snap 15 feet behind the line of scrimmage, placing him at the back of the end zone, with pressure coming from rushing defenders looking to block the punt. Several bad outcomes might immediately lose the Ravens the game: (1) a blocked punt recovered in the end zone by the 49ers for the winning touchdown; (2) a fumbled snap recovered in the end zone by the 49ers for the winning touchdown; (3) a poor punt under pressure returned for the winning score; or (4) a poor punt under pressure giving the 49ers the ball deep in Ravens territory, needing to travel a short distance for the winning score. The best-case scenario for the Ravens would have given the 49ers the ball around midfield (an average NFL punt travels approximately 46 yards from the line of scrimmage, although the heavy rush in this situation made a below-average punt more likely), with time enough to attempt one or two throws to the end zone. An intermediate result involved a blocked punt or fumbled snap bouncing out of the end zone or recovered in the end zone by the Ravens for a safety, giving the 49ers two points, although not the lead, and the ball back on the free-kick-after-safety.

Faced with these options, the Ravens chose to take the safety intentionally, but in a controlled manner. The punter took the snap and ran around the back of the end zone with the ball for eight seconds before stepping out of bounds ahead of the rush.

The Ravens willingly surrendered two points, making the score 33–31, still having to kick the ball back to the 49ers. But the kick was now a free-kick-after-safety, from the Ravens' 20-yard line, with no rush and no risk of a block or bad snap. More importantly, only :03 remained on the clock. The safety kick traveled 61 yards in the air, far longer than the average punt-under-pressure from scrimmage and further down the field than if kicked from the end zone. The 49ers returner fielded the punt around his 20-yard line and returned it to mid-field as time expired. Even if the game had not ended on the return, the Niners would have had time to run only one more play from scrimmage, from worse field position.

Clock aside, the Ravens intentionally acted contrary to football expectations and strategies. The punter made no effort to perform the ordinary and expected athletic virtue of punting the ball; he caught the snap and ran around with the ball for several seconds before intentionally stepping out of bounds in his end zone. The offensive linemen blocked only to give the punter more time to run around in the end zone. The Ravens' plan from the beginning of the play was to surrender two points, distinguishing this from one player's snap decision to accept the safety in the midst of a play gone wrong.

The play produced costs and benefits for both teams. The Ravens incurred the cost of giving up two points and surrendering possession of the ball. But they were about to lose possession anyway, and two points were not significant in the waning seconds of a four-point game. On the other hand, they gained substantial benefits by running eight seconds off the clock and obtaining better field position by kicking the ball from the 20-yard line without pressure. The 49ers incurred significant costs from getting the ball back in substantially worse field position with less time remaining, while gaining the small benefit of two points and possession (that they were about to gain anyway). Although the cost-benefit exchange ran two ways, it was overwhelmingly weighted towards the Ravens, since the benefits to them were greater than the minimal benefit to the 49ers. The uneven weight of this exchange offers a team similarly situated to the Ravens the perverse incentive to make this strategic move in this game situation.

What is again missing is that third characteristic—disparity in control and influence over the play. The 49ers were not up a tree, helpless, or unable to influence the play or counter the Ravens' strategy. They could have limited the time that elapsed on the safety, thereby limiting the cost incurred, by tackling the punter or forcing him out of bounds more quickly, rather than allowing 75 percent of the remaining time to lapse, seemingly unprepared for the play. Had the 49ers rush gotten to the punter and forced the safety more quickly, they would have regained possession with more time on the clock and more of an opportunity to take advantage of the play.

More importantly, the 49ers had several options when they regained possession following the safety, trailing by two and needing only a field goal to win the game. The returner might have taken the free kick for a touchdown. The returner could have signaled for a fair catch on the safety kick,[60] leaving them time to attempt a game-winning play from scrimmage, albeit from long distance and with time for only one play (again, because they allowed so much time to elapse on the safety). Most intriguing for a book about esoteric sports rules, the fair catch might have set-up a fair-catch kick. This is a field goal (which would have won the game) attempted without a rush from the spot of the fair catch.[61] This is a vestigial rule, a throwback to football's original rugby elements and the "goal from mark" play.[62] This would not have been an option in this game, given how far the safety kick traveled, but it might have been feasible on a shorter kick. When not under pressure and especially indoors, an NFL kicker could make a 75-yard field goal—meaning a ball kicked from the opposite 35-yard line.

It is sufficient that football's basic rules provide potential opportunities to counter the intentional safety, however improbable success might be. The 49ers had more options available to them than would a team trying to run a play against 14 defenders. And each of those options is less optimal than the opportunity to block the punt in the end zone or to return a live punt kicked under pressure. That reflects the Ravens' cost-benefit strategy. Taking the intentional safety granted them greater benefits with fewer risks than the punt, while imposing greater burdens on the opponent. But a limiting rule is inappropriate and unnecessary where costs and benefits flow in both directions, even if not equally, and when the disadvantaged team retains some opportunities to counter the strategy and avoid the cost-benefit disadvantage under the game's ordinary rules and practices.

The safety in Super Bowl XLVII contained an additional wrinkle. Part of why the 49ers took so long to reach the punter on the safety, and the Ravens ran so much time off the clock, was that the Ravens' offensive line committed multiple, blatant holding infractions in the end zone, none of which was called. The 49ers had an important counter to the intentional safety—a strong rush on the punter that would force him out of bounds more quickly, leaving more time on the clock for when they got the ball back. The uncalled holds denied them that counter, in a way that violated football's rules. This arguably did create an extraordinarily inequitable cost-benefit imbalance, as the Ravens intentionally took actions that not only ran counter to athletic expectations, but were themselves prohibited by the rules.

The rules attempt to restore this balance because offensive holding in the end zone results in a safety.[63] The result on the play—safety, two points for the 49ers, Ravens safety kick—would have been the same had the infractions been called. This ordinarily eliminates the perverse incentive to commit holding in this situation—there is no reason to commit the infraction if it results in a safety.

But clock considerations created different incentives. Holding is a live-ball infraction, meaning play continues and the clock runs until the play ends. Even had those holds been called, the play would have continued until the punter stepped out of bounds, with those eight seconds still lapsing on the non-play. Given the Ravens' goal of prolonging the play as long as possible before taking the safety, as opposed to avoiding the safety, that rule would not limit the cost-benefit inequity or the perverse incentive for the offense to hold. Some further limiting rule is necessary to eliminate the time benefits from the holding foul.

One possibility is to make holding in the end zone a dead-ball infraction—as soon as an official recognizes the hold, the whistle blows the play dead and stops the clock. This change removes the additional timing benefits to Team O from the infraction, while giving Team D a more equitable opportunity to contest the play and avoid the loss of time. But this creates serious player-safety concerns. It is difficult to stop the action mid-play (as opposed to immediately before or after the snap)—players may be running at full speed and may not hear the whistle, a recipe for someone getting hurt. Given the player-health and safety problems facing football, a play with such built-in risks is a bad idea.

A safer and more workable limiting rule would impose a time penalty for the infraction by restoring the clock to where it stood at the start of the contested play. In the Super Bowl, the clock would have reset to :11 for the safety kick, giving the 49ers more time once they regained possession. By eliminating the time benefits from the holding foul, the rule eliminates the perverse incentive to intentionally hold to prolong the play. In fact, the opposite becomes true. If the play would have lasted four seconds without holding (leaving :07 on the clock) but the hold resets the clock to :11, the offense places itself in a worse position by the infraction. Which is as it should be.

Either time penalty would be easy to administer. Football already imposes time penalties by running time off this clock, as with an intentional foul in the final minute; this would go in reverse and restore time, but the point is the same. And given football's regular use of video replay to resolve factual disputes, including for clock determinations, officials have the tools for deciding when the infraction occurred and how much time to return to the clock.

This timing rule could be limited only to the moments in the game when the extra seconds lost or saved on an end-zone holding infraction become strategically significant, such that the offense has a genuine incentive to commit holding infractions to waste time. A team might take an intentional safety in the middle of the third quarter to avoid surrendering a touchdown or to improve field position, but it would not also have incentive to waste time on the play. The late-game intentional-safety (for example, in the final two minutes of the game) is sufficiently unique that the limiting rule would not become overinclusive.

The Ravens perfected this end-of-game gambit in a 2016 regular-season game, sparking new controversy. The Ravens led the Cincinnati Bengals 19–12 with :11 remaining, facing fourth down at their own 22-yard line. The punter took the snap at the 10-yard line and gradually drifted backwards into and through the end zone as the seconds ticked down. Once again, his linemen committed multiple, even-more blatant holds to keep the rushers at bay. Eventually the punter stepped out of the back of the end zone for a safety.

This safety differed from the one in the Super Bowl in two respects. Time expired before the punter stepped out of bounds. And officials threw penalty flags when they recognized the holding fouls. After conferring, the referee announced, "There were multiple fouls on the play against the offense for holding. The result of the play is a safety. That two points will count. And by rule there is no extension, so the game is over."

This play sits at the intersection of several rules, exposing another gap and perhaps requiring a new limiting rule to fill it. Current rules limit when a period can be extended for one untimed down. A "natural" safety resulting from an offensive player being tackled or stepping out of bounds in his end zone does not extend a period. Nor does offensive holding. But "[i]f a safety results from a foul during the last play of a half," the score counts and a safety kick is made if requested by the receiving team.[64]

The question for this game is why the safety was scored. If because the punter stepped out of bounds in the end zone, then the game properly ended. If because of holding fouls, then the Bengals should have been given the option of receiving an untimed safety kick and trying to return it for a touchdown (because the Bengals trailed by five after the safety, a fair catch followed by a fair-catch kick was not an option). Although not entirely clear, it appears the officials awarded a natural safety on the punter stepping out of bounds. The called holds all occurred outside the end zone, so they did not cause the safety.

But that makes both the official penalty announcement and the post-game media conversation surrounding the play confusing. The referee need not have mentioned the holding fouls in his announcement of the call, since they did not affect the outcome of the play. And much of the post-game media conversation erroneously focused on offensive fouls (including holding) not providing grounds for extending a period,[65] which should have been beside the point, given that the officials awarded the natural safety. The called holds on this play were no different than the uncalled holds in the Super Bowl, other than allowing the Ravens to bleed more clock; none caused the safety, which is why this was not a safety that could, under current rules, extend the game.

The necessary limiting rule is obvious—a "natural" safety should be grounds for extending a period, with the receiving team having the option to receive a safety kick and either return it for a touchdown or attempt a fair catch/fair-catch kick. While neither is likely to succeed, they offer enough of a counter to the intentional safety as to ease the disparity in control over the play and to limit the perverse incentive to take an intentional safety. Teams attempt point-after plays when a period, even the game, ends on a touchdown.[66] It would be internally consistent to also extend time for the automatic follow-up play when the final play is a point-creating safety.

NFL rules contain one additional provision that might function as a limiting rule in this situation—the prohibition on a "palpably unfair act," a catch-all unsportsmanlike-conduct infraction. Officials wield broad discretion to penalize such acts, including disqualifying the offending player, awarding an "equitable" yardage penalty, or awarding a score.[67] A half can be extended for a palpably unfair act by the offense.[68] Officials in the Ravens-Bengals game could have deemed the multiple, blatant holding infractions a palpably unfair act, extending the game for an untimed down for the safety kick. Following the game, the NFL announced that mass holdings do not constitute palpably unfair acts, although doing so on consecutive plays might have qualified.[69]

The NFL recognized intentional holding fouls as a problem and imposed a limiting rule. Beginning with the 2017 season, the rules banned the commission of "multiple fouls during the same down in an attempt to manipulate the game clock," imposing a penalty of a loss of 15 yards, resetting the game clock to where it was at the snap, and allowing an additional untimed play.[70] This rule would not have changed the result on either the Super Bowl safety or the 2016 safety, both of which were "natural" and not caused by holding infractions. But the change should deter similar intentional fouling in the future.

Sideline Interference

The potential for unexpected strategy involving intentional misconduct in Super Bowl XLVII between the Ravens and 49ers did not end with that intentional safety. As the teams prepared for the subsequent safety kick, Ravens quarterback Joe Flacco was recorded on the sideline talking with teammates about running from the sideline onto the field to tackle the 49ers' returner if he broke free and was about to score a touchdown. Although Flacco stated that he did not know the penalty for doing this, he believed it was worth it, given that the worst that could happen would be officials awarding the touchdown anyway.[71] The returner never broke free and was tackled near midfield, so the situation never presented itself.

This hypothetical play contains all four defining characteristics. Flacco would have intentionally acted contrary to ordinary athletic expectations, doing something players ordinarily do not want to do. The returner could do nothing to counter or respond to the play; having beaten 11 would-be tacklers, he was not prepared to beat a twelfth defender unlawfully jumping into the play from the sideline. Nor could the other 49ers players, having helped to free their teammate, protect him against a rogue player jumping in from nowhere. The benefits to the Ravens—stopping a Super-Bowl-winning touchdown—are obvious, overwhelming, and inequitable, incentivizing the strategic move in that circumstance.

Even if successful in stopping the touchdown, the play would not be costless for the Ravens. A game cannot end on a foul by the team not in possession of the ball.[72] The 49ers would have gotten one untimed play from scrimmage or an attempt at a game-winning field goal following any yardage penalty. But the benefits to Flacco and the Ravens outweighed the costs, at least at the unique stage of the end of the championship game. A player in Flacco's situation would rather prevent a certain, imminent score and take his chances that his defensive teammates stop one untimed play from scrimmage or that the 49ers miss the field goal. Conversely, the cost to the 49ers of losing a certain game-winning score far outweighs the benefits of being able to run one for-the-game play or field-goal attempt against a set defense.

We might label this an "earn-it" infraction—one team breaks the rules to stop a certain score, forcing the opponent to "earn" the points another way. Earn-it infractions arise in many sports. In basketball, the defense will foul a shooter about to score an easy lay-up or dunk, forcing him to "earn" the two points by making two free throws; the "playoff foul" has become a staple of aggressive post-season basketball in which defenses refuse to surrender easy scores.[73] In soccer, defenders commit the "foul-in-the-box," an infraction inside the penalty area to prevent a certain goal and to force the player to convert a penalty kick for the score.[74] An infamous example arose in a 2010 World Cup match between Ghana and Uruguay. An Uruguayan defender committed a blatant handball while standing on the goal line, an "instinctive" play that stopped a Ghanaian player, who had beaten the Uruguayan goalkeeper, from scoring a certain winning goal from point-blank range in the final minute of play. The play succeeded when the Ghanaian player could not earn it—he missed the penalty kick and Uruguay prevailed in extra time.[75]

The NFL's rule against palpably unfair acts prohibits this type of "earn-it" infraction. A player running from the sideline to tackle a ball-carrier on his way to score a touchdown almost certainly would have been regarded as a palpably unfair act and the officials almost certainly would have awarded the 49ers the otherwise-inevitable touchdown. At worst, the 49ers would have gotten a substantial yardage penalty and a chance to kick a short game-winning field goal.

The palpably-unfair-act rule combines both types of limiting rules— a prohibition on conduct and a disincentive on conduct. The rule prohibits the offending conduct of running onto the field. It then imposes the outcome—the game-winning touchdown—that would have resulted had the player not acted contrary to the game's ordinary expectations by violating the rule. By imposing that outcome, the rule eliminates the remaining perverse incentive to ignore not only ordinary expectations, but an express prohibitory rule.

The sanction for palpably unfair conduct is discretionary—the official "may" award a score, meaning he may enforce the infraction another way, such as a yardage penalty. The rule thus may not eliminate the perverse incentive, depending on how it is enforced on a given play. Flacco still might run onto the field, hoping for a lenient exercise of discretion. Infield flies offer something similar—infielders may intentionally not catch the fly ball even in the face of the Infield Fly Rule, hoping to fool the umpire into not judging a ball playable with ordinary effort and not invoking the Rule, leaving the defense the opportunity for the force-out double play.

This demonstrates a fundamental point—eliminating perverse incentives depends not only on the limiting rule that rulemakers create, but on how game officials exercise their judgment and discretion in applying and enforcing that limiting rule. If football officials do not vigorously punish palpably unfair conduct, especially on the biggest play in the biggest game, the perverse incentive to interfere from the sideline—and to make the offense "earn it"—remains. If umpires do not scrupulously invoke the infield fly where appropriate (as through a presumption of invoking on a close play), the perverse incentive to intentionally not catch the fly ball in search of an inequitable double play remains. Recall the triple play the Orioles turned against the Red Sox in 2017 when the umpire failed to invoke on a close ball or the double play the Angels turned against the Twins in 2013 (both discussed in Chapter 1).

Soccer: Law 11, Offside

Soccer's Law 11, Offside,[76] represents that sport's iconic counterpart to the Infield Fly Rule. Both are incomprehensible to non-fans, although easily understood on closer examination. Fans do not understand either as well as they believe they do. Both depend on official judgment that often creates controversy and anger among managers, coaches, players, fans, and media. And both function as entrée to the game—just as a person understands baseball if she can explain the Infield Fly Rule, a person understands soccer if she can explain Offside.

Despite their shared iconic status in their respective sports, the rules serve different purposes and rest on different rationales. Unlike the Infield Fly Rule and other sports rules discussed in this book, Offside does not constitute a limiting rule under this framework and does not respond to an extreme cost-benefit inequity creating perverse incentives. It is a purely aesthetic rule, necessary to make soccer the game its rulemakers want to create or to keep it from becoming a game they do not want to create.

Law 11 establishes two concepts—Offside Position and Offside Offense. A player is in offside position if he is in the opponent's half of the field and his head, feet, or body is closer to the opponent's goal line than both the ball and the second-to-last defender (which can include the goalkeeper, if he comes far out of the net). Being in offside position is not, by itself, a violation. That requires an offside offense. A player commits an offside offense if he is in offside position at the moment the ball is played or touched by a teammate and he becomes "involved in active play" by touching or playing a ball passed or touched by a teammate, interfering with an opponent seeking to play the ball, or gaining an advantage for playing a rebound off a missed or saved shot.[77]

Offside is an anti-cherry-picking rule. It prevents a team from camping one (or several) players near the opposing goal and passing long balls over the top of the defense to create one-on-one situations against the goalkeeper, which would offer easy scoring opportunities. Law 11 eliminates the incentive for a team to hold a player in offside position and to kick long balls to him by removing the benefit to be gained from having him there—he will be unable to become involved in active play on any long ball that comes his way, so there is no reason to camp there.

The offense would enjoy a steep cost-benefit advantage without Law 11—one offensive player, alone and one-on-one against a goalkeeper, has a good chance to score. But this play lacks the first and third characteristics. The offensive player does not intentionally act contrary to athletic expectations by standing behind the defense. By being in offside position, the offensive player tries to succeed as expected by putting himself into the best position to control the ball and score. The play also lacks an overwhelming disparity in control and influence. The defense is not helpless against this strategy; it counters by keeping one (or several) defenders back with those offensive players, ensuring no one gets behind the defense and challenging any long balls. From a cost-benefit perspective, no special rule is necessary to avoid this play.

The problem is the aesthetics that the defensive response creates. Each team would load the end of the pitch with players (offensive players on one side, defensive players on the other), leaving no players or action in the middle. Offside ensures that the game does not devolve into a "ping-pong match" of long over-the-top balls, back and forth across the pitch, directed to multiple guarded offensive players camped near the opposing goal. The Offside Law forces teams into short passes among players stationed across the pitch, with players running up and through the middle. Long balls demand skill and timing, as both the run and pass must be timed to keep the lead offensive player in onside position. Law 11 is not about eliminating perverse incentives or extraordinary one-sided cost-benefit disparities, all of which can be prevented by changing defensive strategy. It is only about ensuring the game is played the "right" way.

Racing False Starts

A final example involves rules governing "false starts" in racing sports such as swimming and running. Swimming defines a false start as "starting before the starting signal has been given."[78] Track defines it as when a runner "commences his start" after assuming a full and starting position but before the report of the gun.[79]

Different sports impose different rules against false starts. International swimming disqualifies any swimmer who starts before the starting signal.[80] Horse racing does not recognize false starts, but resets the starting gates if a horse breaks through before the starting bell. Over the past two decades, international track has struggled to craft the appropriate rule for sprinting, cycling through three rules since 2003. These efforts, and the evolution of the false-start rule, illustrate the operation of this framework and the difficulty of calibrating limiting rules in response to situations defined by the four characteristics.

Prior to 2003, each racer could false start one time without consequence, facing disqualification only on his second false start. Races often included multiple false starts. An eight-person race theoretically could have eight false starts by eight different runners with no disqualifications. Critics complained that this slowed the action, bored fans, and caused television broadcasts to run long, hurting the "entertainment spectacle" that should be part of track competition.[81]

A 2003 rule change provided one false start to the field, with the next false start resulting in disqualification of that false-starter, even if a different person had been responsible for the initial false start.[82] Rulemakers believed this would speed the action, as there would be only one false start for the race, by anyone in the field, before disqualifications began.

While resolving the problem of a parade of false starts delaying the race, the new rule created an unexpected problem. One runner might intentionally false-start, using the field's lone freebie, in exchange for two benefits. His false start triggered disqualification of any runner who subsequently false-started. And it caused faster starters and faster runners to be more cautious breaking off the blocks, knowing that a false start would disqualify them, despite not being responsible for the initial false-start. This benefited slower starters and runners, whether by disqualifying competitors from the race or by reducing their speed disadvantage by slowing other runners off the blocks.

Under this framework, the 2003 rule created a situation featuring all four defining characteristics and demanding a limiting rule.

(1) By false-starting, Runner S (slower runner) intentionally acted contrary to ordinary athletic expectations and failed to perform the athletic virtues in the expected manner. Runners typically do not want to false start, since false starts are prohibited by the rules and make it impossible to commence and complete a race. A false-starting runner cannot run or win a race, which is the purpose of the competition and the athletic skills to be performed. (That false-starting is contrary to athletic expectations should not be subject to dispute, while one might hint intentional non-catches in baseball are not contrary to expectations.)

(2) Runner S gained extraordinary benefits from his false start. He moved every competitor closer to disqualification. He limited his own competitive deficit by either triggering those disqualifications or slowing faster runners off the blocks. The other runners in the field gained no benefits

from Runner S's false start, only steep costs—the risk of disqualification should they next false-start and the need to adjust their strategy to avoid that risk.

(3) Runner F (a faster runner in the field who did not commit the initial false start) could not counter this move or avoid the costs. He was pushed closer to disqualification through no action of his own and could do nothing to prevent runners from intentionally false-starting. The only counter was for Runner F to take care to ensure a fair start and avoid the disqualification by slowing his start off the blocks—precisely what Runner S wanted to achieve with his intentional false start. Unlike hacking or late-game fouling in basketball—where the offense defeats the strategy by making free throws—the only counter for Runner F was to give Runner S the very benefit he sought in intentionally acting contrary to athletic expectations.

(4) The combination of (2) and (3) created the perverse incentive for Runner S to commit (1)—the benefits to be gained and exclusive control over the situation created a perverse incentive for him to intentionally false start for the field. If Runner S's false start forced Runner F out of the race on the latter's subsequent false start or to be slow off the blocks to avoid that false start, then Runner S had every incentive to do this intentionally.

Although there was no evidence this occurred or worked in high-level racing, the incentives and risks were obvious. A limiting rule was necessary to eliminate the perverse incentive for Runner S to intentionally act contrary to athletic expectations, thereby eliminating the inequitable one-sided cost-benefit disparities.

In 2010, the IAAF adopted the current provision, mimicking swimming's rule with what some label a "zero tolerance" rule—one runner is disqualified on his own false start,[83] with no single freebie for an individual or for the field. This change reflects a quintessential limiting rule. It eliminates the cost-benefit advantage to Runner S from intentionally false-starting, thereby eliminating the perverse incentive for him to do so. Runner S has no incentive to intentionally false start, because his false start produces only the cost of his disqualification, not the benefit of slowing down or disqualifying competitors. While Runner F must be cautious to avoid a false start, that caution does not come from Runner S's actions; nothing Runner S does affects Runner F. By eliminating the perverse incentive to intentionally false-start, the new rule prevents the extraordinary inequitable cost-benefit disparity.

Recognizing that a limiting rule is necessary does not always answer what the limiting rule should look like. That the 2003 rule was unworkable did not dictate the content of the rule change. A zero-tolerance rule was not the only option available to avoid the inequities and perverse incentives. A second option was to return to the pre–2003 regime of allowing each runner his own free false start. If the point was merely eliminating perverse incentives to act contrary to athletic expectations in search of extraordinary benefits, either rule sufficed. Under the original rule, Runner S had no perverse incentive to intentionally false start and no opportunity to gain extraordinary benefits, because his false start did not affect Runner F or move Runner F closer to disqualification.

Given the choice between two limiting rules, aesthetics entered as an additional consideration. Returning to the pre–2003 rule would have eliminated the perverse incentives, but reproduced the aesthetic problems of multiple false starts—delays, fan boredom, television overruns, and loss of entertainment value. The zero-tolerance alternative became the only workable option.

The zero-tolerance rule creates its own, different aesthetic problem—some see it as unfair, harsh, and unforgiving.[84] And it risks disqualifying star runners from important races. The 2016 Rio Summer Games featured multiple televised false-start disqualifications, although none involved track's superstars. The most significant zero-tolerance disqualification—and for many the paradigm of the rule's unnecessary harshness—involved world-record-holder (and greatest sprinter of all time) Usain Bolt of Jamaica in the 100 meters at the 2011 World Championships.[85]

Dueling aesthetic concerns created a conundrum for rulemakers—the ugliness of multiple false starts or the ugliness of disqualifying star runners and perceived harshness and unfairness. Track resolved the conundrum in favor of risking the loss of a top runner in a single race in exchange for better, cleaner, more efficient, and more watchable competitions. One might quarrel with the choice. The point is that it was an aesthetic, rather than cost-benefit, choice. Interestingly, no one has lobbed similar complaints at swimming's identical zero-tolerance rule, perhaps because that sport has been consistent and worked under one rule for longer.

The 2010 amendment eased some of the harshness and aesthetic concerns by narrowing the definition of false start. A runner now false-starts only if one or both feet leave the starting blocks or if one or both hands leave the ground before the gun. Other movements, leans, twitches, or flinches no longer count if the runner otherwise holds set position and maintains contact with the ground and blocks.[86] The limiting rule applies only to the worst and most obvious abuses, not to small infractions.

Nevertheless, it still may result in a runner working for years to get to the Olympics, only to be deprived of the opportunity to compete by one false move. But when the alternative is a rule that incentivizes intentionally unwanted and prohibited athletic conduct in search of one-sided cost-benefit inequities, rulemakers must be willing to take the chance on a limiting rule, however harsh.

*　*　*

The goal of this chapter has been to show that the analytical framework applies across sports and to show that the logic of the Infield Fly Rule, in its proper justification, is not limited to baseball. This discussion reveals three things. Situations entailing all four characteristics arise in other sports—and when they do, that sport's rulemakers respond with limiting rules structured and operating like the Infield Fly Rule. Many more situations in other sports lack one or more defining characteristics—and every sport properly leaves them without limiting rules, subject to the game's ordinary strategies and efforts. Finally, aesthetics plays an important, although distinct, role in creating and modifying the rules of any sport.

Chapter 5

An Empirical Assessment
of the Infield Fly Rule

The discussion to this point has focused on the Infield Fly Rule and other limiting rules as policy—their design, structure, purpose, and operation within baseball and other sports. Baseball's rulemakers created the Infield Fly Rule out of a desire to avoid inequitable double plays on intentionally uncaught easily playable fly balls to an infielder. My framework, grounded on four defining characteristics, offers a detailed model for understanding and justifying that rule and its current scope and application, as well as the lack of similar rules for most other baseball situations. That analytical framework carried to other sports, showing when those other sports do and should establish similar rules in comparable situations, as well as when they face non-comparable situations for which no limiting rule is necessary.

This chapter returns to an exclusive focus on baseball and the Infield Fly Rule, shifting away from legal and policy analysis. Accepting my framework and the conclusion that eliminating the inequitable double play is a worthy policy goal in the abstract, this chapter addresses a series of empirical questions. Does the reality of baseball on the field demand an Infield Fly Rule? Does the Infield Fly Rule achieve its stated purpose of avoiding extraordinary cost-benefit inequities in favor of the fielding team and against the batting team? Does the Infield Fly Rule achieve that purpose sufficiently often to justify its presence in the game? And does the Infield Fly Rule in its present scope work in light of the on-field reality? Or, on the other hand, is the Infield Fly Rule a century-old solution in search of a problem, resolving an abstract policy injustice that in practice is infrequent (perhaps even non-existent) and trivial.

The goal of this chapter is to test the policy-based justifications for the Infield Fly Rule against evidence from the playing field, exploring the effects on the game under current rules and in a counterfactual baseball world without an Infield Fly Rule.

This chapter presents collected data on the Rule, seeking to answer distinct questions.

First is the frequency of infield-fly calls. This considers how often batters come to the plate in infield-fly situations—every situation in which the Rule might be put in effect on an appropriate batted ball and on which umpires signal among themselves prior to the pitch that the Rule might be put in effect—and how often batters hit fair fly balls playable by an infielder with ordinary effort on which umpires invoke the Rule. If the inequitable double play would not occur very often, perhaps no limiting rule is needed to prevent that inequitable double play.

The second question considers the quantitative likelihood of the evil the Infield Fly Rule seeks to prevent—the force-out double play on multiple trapped baserunners off an intentionally uncaught fair fly ball. This measures the likelihood of the defense turning a double play on an intentionally uncaught fly ball and the strength of the infielders' perverse incentive to intentionally not catch the fair fly ball in pursuit of that double play. In other words, on the batted balls identified in response to the first question, would infielders, freed of the strategic limitations imposed by the Infield Fly Rule, intentionally not catch these easily playable fair fly balls in search of the force-out double play. And if so, how likely would they be to complete it?

The obvious way to answer this second question would be to compare what happens in baseball games played without the Infield Fly Rule and how often infielders try, and succeed, at this move. Unfortunately, no such control group exists. The Infield Fly Rule is part of organized baseball at all levels, even American Little League (where the concept of playable with ordinary effort becomes murkier, given infielders' skill level)[1] and Japanese high schools.[2] The best alternative is to construct a counterfactual, speculating how a past baseball game might have proceeded played without the Rule and with infielders free to act on perverse incentives in search of force-out double plays.

The third question considers the practical effect that absence or repeal of the Infield Fly Rule might have on individual plays, innings, games, and seasons. Looking at what happened on the field in a game played with the Rule, we can speculate how the defense and offense might have acted in that situation played without the Rule and with the possibility of a double play. We then can measure how that choice might have affected the remainder of the game.

Counterfactual inquiries are inherently imprecise.[3] So, too, with baseball counterfactuals. It is impossible to determine what might have been on any past play, to say nothing of how a change in one play might have affected everything that followed in that inning, game, and season. Nevertheless, when mixed with empirical data, it offers a useful thought experiment.

This chapter attempts to answer those questions through a comprehensive study of eight seasons of Major League Baseball, covering 2010–2017, looking at every instance in which the Infield Fly Rule was actually or potentially placed in effect.

Before proceeding, I add one disclaimer: Any debate over the Infield Fly Rule cannot be resolved quantitatively. As with other disputed concepts, resort to underlying qualitative or normative judgments in evaluating quantitative evidence is inevitable. The policy conclusions one draws about the Infield Fly Rule by looking to the empirical record depend on where one begins—supporters and critics of the Infield Fly Rule may find confirmation in the numbers that follow. The data are worth examining, if only to describe and visualize a hypothetical baseball world without the Infield Fly Rule, to compare it to the real, known baseball world, and to assess possible effects of repeal. The numbers shed light on the realities of baseball's unique play and how its famous rule operates as part of the game's fabric, even if they do not resolve the policy debate.

Methodology

Major League Baseball does not record infield-fly calls as an official statistic. Under the Rule, the batter is out when infield fly is declared; the play is recorded as a pop-out and a put-out for the infielder who catches the ball, or, if the ball is not caught, to the infielder who would have caught it.[4] That Infield Fly was called is not reflected on a play-by-play report or box score where the infielder caught the ball. Different play-by-play reports follow different rules where the ball was not caught.

Consider, for example, different recordings of the infamous infield-fly call in the 2012 NLWC. ESPN's entry read "A Simmons popped out to shortstop, D Uggla to third, D Ross to second."[5] Data site Baseball Reference's entry read "Popfly SS; Uggla to 3B; Ross to 2B."[6] The data site Retrosheet offered the basic statement "Simmons popped to shortstop [Uggla to third, Ross to second]."[7] None referenced the out being on the infield-fly call and none mentioned that the infielder did not catch the ball. Retrosheet provided fuller information about the call and the play, including exacting detail about what happened and how the Braves and their fans responded:

> SS Peter Kozma ran out into shallow LF and stopped under the fly ball; when he turned and put his hands out to call off LF Matt Holliday, LF umpire Sam Holbrook called it an infield fly; the signal was repeated by 3B umpire Jeff Nelson;

Kozma then moved away and the ball dropped onto the field; when the Braves realized that Simmons was out, manager Fredi Gonzalez ran out to argue with Holbrook; fans started throwing trash onto the field, some of it in the direction of the umpires; the Carinals [sic] left the field while a crew picked up the debris; the Braves protested the ruling, which was denied shortly after the game concluded, based on the fact that an infield fly is a judgment call and not subject to a protest; the delay lasted 19 minutes.[8]

But this was a unique play in a uniquely high-profile game that produced a unique reaction, deserving of greater elaboration. Most game reports are not, and need not be, so detailed.

Unable to review statistics, I organized the study in several steps.

At the first stage, we (myself and a rotating group of baseball-obsessed law students) reviewed narrative play-by-play reports for every MLB game, including post-season, for these eight seasons. We identified every plate appearance in an infield-fly situation, broken into each of the four situations:

- first-and-second/none-out
- first-and-second/one-out
- bases loaded/none-out
- bases loaded/one-out.

We counted only plate appearances that began and ended in an infield-fly situation, but not where the situation changed during the appearance. For example, a batter came to the plate with first-and-second/one-out, an infield-fly situation, and the first pitch was a wild pitch on which both baserunners advanced. The batter remained at the plate, but now with second-and-third/one-out, no longer an infield-fly situation, so not counted as a plate appearance in this study. Or the runner on second was picked-off, leaving the batter at the plate with runner-on-first/two-out, no longer an infield-fly situation, so not counted as a plate appearance in this study.

Having identified plate appearances in each infield-fly situation, we identified every play recorded in the play-by-play reports as a fly ball to an infielder. This provided raw numbers on how often each infield-fly situation arose and raw numbers of potential plays on which the Rule might have been invoked in each situation.

We then cross-referenced the narrative play-by-play reports with Retrosheet's coded play-by-play reports. Written not as narratives but as a series of alpha-numeric codes, these reports detail everything about a plate appearance, including whether infield fly was invoked. For example, Retrosheet's coded report of the 2012 NLWC read as follows: "play, 8,1, simma001,32,SBFBBX,6/P/IF.2–3;1–2."

This indicates the Infield Fly Rule was invoked ("IF") on a popfly ("P") to shortstop ("6"), with the runner on second advancing to third (2–3) and the runner on first advancing to second (1–2). This cross-reference established a preliminary count of plays on which the Rule was invoked, as well as a narrower set of plays for review.

In the second stage, I watched video (accessed through MLBTV and its online media center[9]) of every potential infield-fly call—every play identified in the first stage as a fair fly ball caught by an infielder in one of the four infield-fly situations. I watched all possible plays from the narrative reports, whether or not identified as infield-fly calls in the coded Retrosheet reports.

Video review revealed two things.

One is a complete count of infield-fly calls and probable infield-fly calls. The count revealed reportable numbers of plate appearances in infield-fly situations, actual infield-fly calls, and percentage of plate appearances resulting in the Infield Fly Rule going into effect. I encountered some identification problems at this stage. At times, video clearly established that infield fly was invoked, because the umpire could be seen signaling the play (raising his right arm to signal the batter out while the ball remained in the air, the signal depicted on the cover) or because the announcer reported the Rule as being in effect, or both. I coded a play as an infield fly call if Retrosheet identified it as a call or if video established that the Rule was invoked. At other times, video was inconclusive—it showed what appeared to be a fair fly ball playable by an infielder with ordinary effort, but the umpire was not visible and the announcers did not say anything. If Retrosheet recorded such a play as an infield-fly call, I coded it as such. If Retrosheet did not record the call and video was inconclusive, I did not code it as an infield-fly call. This suggests that the figures in this study underreport the frequency with which the Infield Fly Rule is invoked—it may occur more often than the raw numbers suggest.

Video also revealed where on the field the ball was caught, dropped, or fell to the ground on every play on which the Rule was or could have been invoked. Charting location offered a sense of whether, without the Infield Fly Rule, an intentional drop might have produced a double play, given the location of the ball and the actions and positioning of the infielder near the ball, his teammates covering the bases, and the baserunners.

This information about numbers and location of infield-fly calls allowed exploration of each of the empirical questions identified at the outset of this chapter.

Before proceeding, it is important to identify several limitations on this piece of the study.

It is impossible to test the counterfactual of whether the defense would have turned a double play had infielders intentionally failed to catch the fair fly balls. We cannot know how the ball might have bounced once it hit the ground, how the infielders might have fielded and thrown the ball, and what the baserunners might have done. Of the small handful (fewer than 25) fair fly balls that were not caught in eight seasons, only five can readily be defined as intentional.

It also is impossible to know how skilled infielders and teams would become at the new, heretofore unnecessary, skill of intentionally not catching fly balls and turning them into double plays, a skill that becomes relevant without an Infield Fly Rule. Whatever happened on these actual plays might have played differently under a different set of rules. Finally, it is impossible to know how baserunners would respond to a world in which they might be forced to run (or not) on these plays. Absent the Infield Fly Rule, the default option of staying safely at the current base would be eliminated.

In their critique of the Infield Fly Rule, Guilford and Mallord argue that those questions demonstrate why the Rule should be repealed—it would add tension and excitement to the game, creating a cat-and-mouse game between the fielders and baserunners.[10] At the very least, the uncertainty confounds our efforts to reimagine past plays and games under new rules.

Empirical Question # 1: Frequency

The foundational empirical question is the frequency of invocation of the Infield Fly Rule. Whether the Rule is necessary depends on the frequency of the game situation that creates the extraordinary cost-benefit inequity and the perverse incentives that the Rule seeks to eliminate. If the situation does not arise often enough to create a problem worth addressing, perhaps the limiting rule is unwarranted.

Table 5.1 offers three pieces of information. The eight seasons run down the left column and each of the four infield-fly situations runs across the top. Within each situation within each season, the first row shows the number of plate appearances in that situation, the second row shows the number of Infield Fly calls, and the third row shows the percentage of calls out of total plate appearances. The column on the far right shows totals for each season across the four game situations, and the bottom row shows totals for each situation across the eight seasons. The box in the bottom-right corner shows totals for the full sample.

What do these numbers reveal? Over eight seasons, the Infield Fly Rule was unquestionably invoked 1,912 times in slightly fewer than 73,600 possible plate appearances, representing an average of 239 calls in 9,200

TABLE 5.1 TOTAL INFIELD FLY CALLS

Infield Fly		1st & 2d-0	1st & 2d-1	Bases Loaded-0	Bases Loaded-1	Totals
2010	PA	2658	4566	721	1771	9716
	IFR	65	132	21	42	260
	%	2.2	2.2	2.2	2.2	2.6
2011	PA	2373	4532	662	1677	9244
	IFR	58	106	24	59	247
	%	2.4	2.3	3.6	3.5	2.7
2012	PA	2403	4275	637	1534	8849
	IFR	52	106	19	57	234
	%	2.2	2.5	3	3.7	2.6
2013	PA	2464	4399	620	1602	9085
	IFR	51	115	17	51	234
	%	2.1	2.6	2.7	3.2	2.6
2014	PA	2657	4550	662	1580	9449
	IFR	59	121	20	53	253
	%	2.2	2.7	3.0	3.4	2.7
2015	PA	2346	4088	637	1405	8476
	IFR	63	105	17	40	225
	%	2.7	2.6	2.7	2.8	2.6
2016	PA	2484	4360	697	1792	9333
	IFR	53	117	18	45	233
	%	2.1	2.7	2.6	2.5	2.5
2017	PA	2591	4513	713	1631	9448
	IFR	57	116	18	35	226
	%	2.20	2.60	2.50	2.10	2.40
Totals	PA	19,976	35,283	5,349	12,992	73,600
	IFR	458	918	154	382	1912
	%	2.3	2.6	2.9	2.9	2.6

plate appearances per season and medians of 234 calls in 9,209 plate appearances. Batters in these game situations hit fair fly balls playable by an infielder with ordinary effort 2.6 percent of the time.

The 2010 season represents the high-water mark in the study, with 260 Infield Fly calls in just over 9,700 plate appearances. The 2015 season is the low-water mark, with only 225 calls in just under 8,500 plate appearances. Numbers in most categories were down compared with the other five seasons, including a substantial decrease in total situational plate appearances. The 2017 season had just one more call at 226, but in more than 9,400 situational plate appearances (one of the highest figures in the study). While the 2015 low represented a call in 2.6 percent of possible plays (the same as the overall sample), the 2017 figured represented a call in 2.4 percent of possible plays.

The numbers break along game situation. In every season and in the study totals, the greatest number of plate appearances and infield-fly calls came with first-and-second/one-out. Over eight seasons, there were 918 calls in 35,283 plate appearances in that situation; that accounts for approximately 48 percent of all calls in the study and is nearly twice the next highest figure of 458 calls in first-and-second/none-out. By contrast, the most frequent calls per capita came in bases-loaded situations, with the Rule invoked 2.9 percent of the time in both situations. Bases-loaded/one-out also produced the highest per capita season in 2012, when the Rule was invoked 3.7 percent of the time in that game situation.

For first-and-second/none-out, 2010 was the high season with 65 calls, while 2013 was the low at 51. For first-and-second/one out, 2010 was the high season with 132, while 2015 was low at 105. For bases-loaded/none-out, 2011 had 24 calls, while 2013 and 2015 had 17. For bases-loaded/one-out, 2011 was high with 59, while 2017 was low with 35.

There is an interesting statistical connection between bases-loaded/one-out and first-and-second/none-out. These situations alternated for second-highest total in the study—the former saw more calls in 2011 and 2012, the latter more in the remaining seasons. Over eight seasons, there were 76 more Infield Fly calls with first-and-second/none-out—458 to 382, approximately 9 more per season; but this is a small difference compared with the gap between these two situations and the most- and least-frequent situations.

The close numbers of infield-fly calls in these two situations arose within a wide disparity of infield-fly opportunities. There were more than six times as many plate appearances in first-and-second/none-out than bases-loaded/one-out. That is, batters came to the plate substantially more frequently in the former than the latter situation, but hit fly balls triggering the Infield Fly Rule in similar numbers.

What might account for the disparity? One explanation is that first-and-second/none-out is a common sacrifice bunt situation—in 2016, all MLB teams executed 162 successful sacrifice bunts in that situation and attempted 260[11] (a figure that does not account for times in which an initial bunt attempt failed and the batter switched strategy to swing away). This means those 63 infield-fly calls in 2015 came around more plate appearances in which the batter was bunting and therefore unlikely to do anything to trigger the Infield Fly Rule—either because the goal is to keep the bunt on the ground or because the Rule does not apply on an unintentionally popped-up bunt. A converse explanation is that bases-loaded/one-out situations, although less frequent, prompt the batter to try to hit the ball in the air, as a fly ball to the outfield is likely to score the runner retouching from third base for a sacrifice fly. In trying to hit the ball in the air, the batter is more likely to get too under the ball and pop it to an infielder, triggering an infield-fly call.

To the extent the numbers in Table 5.1 are off, they undercount Infield Fly calls. These totals do not include approximately 100 plays over eight seasons in which I could not determine from video or Retrosheet's coded reports whether the Rule had been invoked. I did not code it as an infield fly even if a reasonable person could watch the video and see the signs umpires look for when invoking the Rule—the ball was higher than a line drive, had sufficient arc, the infielder had settled under the ball and was waiting for it to fall to him, and he caught it easily. Absent a definitive call, I did not include it in the totals. Thus, 1,912 calls reflects the minimum number of infield-fly calls in Major League Baseball from 2010–2017; there may have been more. This is consistent with the instinct of umpire educator Brent Rice that the Rule is over-called more than under-called.

The question is the normative conclusions to draw from these numbers. Again, the answer depends on one's starting opinion about the Infield Fly Rule.

A critic of the Rule may find her preferences confirmed. Accepting the risk of an inequitable double play on an intentionally uncaught fly ball and the cost-benefit disparity it produces and accepting that such a disparity is normatively bad, these numbers show that the problem is *de minimis*. It arose just more than 1,900 times in eight seasons, fewer than 240 times per season, and less than 3 percent of the times it might. Even if the double play represents some baseball injustice (again, at least a debatable point), the injustice does not occur sufficiently frequently to justify a limiting rule that upsets the game's ordinary strategies and practices and that strips control from the player's hands and places it with the umpires.[12] An additional 240 double plays each season from intentionally uncaught infield fly balls is not intolerable within the game's structure, especially if one believes those potential double plays add excitement to the game.

The relative infrequency also suggests that the perverse incentive to intentionally not catch the ball is less present than the Rule's supporters might suggest. The small increase in double plays is unlikely to affect many innings, games, or seasons (a point I explore below). And the relative infrequency means infielders may not be tempted by the potential cost-benefit advantage, preferring the simple act of catching the ball for one out to the more difficult and risky act of not catching and trying to throw runners out.

Supporters of the Rule will argue that 240 substantially inequitable outcomes each year are too many. That a problematic situation under this framework will arise, even if on only 3 percent of plays, is sufficient to justify a limiting rule that eliminates the perverse incentive and prevents the cost-benefit disparity. Baseball is a better game without such imbalances resulting from players intentionally acting contrary to athletic expectations, even if those imbalances occur infrequently.

One way to judge whether the Infield Fly Rule is invoked too infrequently to be justified is to compare the numbers of uncaught third strikes—as discussed in Chapter 2, the truly analogous baseball play under my framework in producing inequitable double plays and perverse incentives for fielders to intentionally not catch the ball in similar game situations. The rules governing uncaught third strikes rest on the same policy, logic, and structure as the Infield Fly Rule—eliminating the perverse incentive to intentionally not catch the ball eliminates the extraordinary and one-sided cost-benefit disparity of turning what should be a single out into an inequitable double play. As a policy matter, the two situations must be treated the same. If the rules permit an infielder to seek an overwhelming advantage of a double play by intentionally not catching an easily playable fair fly ball, they also must permit a catcher to do the same by intentionally not catching a third strike. And if the rules prohibit the latter, they should prohibit the former.

But the demand for similar treatment disappears if there is a quantitative difference between the game situations. If the numbers suggest that the double play on the intentionally uncaught third strike creates greater, and more frequent, problems than a double play on an intentionally uncaught infield fly, differential treatment is justified.

Table 5–2 shows strikeouts in each of the four infield-fly situations and is organized in the same way as Table 5–1. The eight seasons run down the left column and the four infield-fly situations run across the top. Within each situation in each season, the first row shows the number of plate appearances (these numbers are the same as the corresponding fields in Table 5–1), the second row shows the number of strikeouts in that situation, and the third row shows the percentage of strikeouts. The column on the far right shows totals for one season across all four situations, while the bottom row shows totals for each situation across all eight seasons. The bottom-right box shows totals for the sample. Because strikeouts are an official statistic, the data could be collected using Baseball Reference's sta-

TABLE 5.2 STRIKEOUTS

Strikeouts		1st & 2d-0	1st & 2d-1	Bases Loaded-0	Bases Loaded-1	Totals
2010	**PA**	2658	4566	721	1771	9716
	K	418	866	109	330	1723
	%	15.7	18.9	15.1	18.6	17.7
2011	**PA**	2373	4532	662	1677	9244
	K	370	792	122	291	1575
	%	15.6	17.5	18.4	17.4	17
2012	**PA**	2403	4275	637	1534	8849
	K	402	817	100	257	1576
	%	16.7	19.1	15.7	16.8	17.8
2013	**PA**	2464	4399	620	1602	9085
	K	421	823	110	301	1655
	%	17.1	18.7	17.7	18.8	18.2
2014	**PA**	2657	4550	662	1580	9449
	K	434	809	123	264	1630
	%	16.3	17.8	18.6	16.7	17.3
2015	**PA**	2346	4088	637	1405	8476
	K	434	823	120	287	1664
	%	18.5	20.1	18.8	20.4	19.6
2016	**PA**	2484	4360	697	1792	9333
	K	429	832	140	334	1735
	%	17.3	19.1	20.1	18.6	18.6
2017	**PA**	2591	4513	713	1631	9448
	K	511	929	141	301	1882
	%	19.7	20.6	19.8	18.5	19.9
Totals	**PA**	19,976	35,283	5,349	12,992	73,600
	IFR	3419	6691	965	2365	13440
	%	17.1	18.9	18.0	18.2	18.3

tistics aggregator, without having to read play-by-play reports or review video of every game for eight Major-League seasons.

Strikeouts occur with far greater frequency than infield fly balls. It follows that, under different rules allowing defenses to seek double plays on uncaught third strikes, the feared cost-benefit disparity would occur with greater frequency. Over eight seasons, there were 13,440 strikeouts in those 73,600 plate appearances, 1,680 per season, representing 18.3 percent of plate appearances. Strikeouts occurred approximately seven times as often as the 1,912 infield fly calls occurring less than 3 percent of the time. In the most common situation of first-and-second/one-out, batters struck out 6,691 times, representing 18.9 percent of situational appearances, and more than seven times the number of infield-fly calls in the same situation.

But these significantly greater numbers do not answer the normative question about appropriate limiting rules, any more than the numbers answer the normative question about the Infield Fly Rule.

One might argue that the substantial numeric disparity between strikeouts and infield flies shows that the situations need not be treated similarly. The inequitable double play from an intentionally uncaught third strike would occur so much more frequently, given the greater frequency of strikeouts, as to have a severe and definitive effect on the game. The greater frequency of strikeouts also highlights the *de minimis* nature of the inequity arising from infield flies. When an inequitable double play is a possibility 18 percent of the time, a limiting rule is necessary, even if it is not necessary when the inequitable double play is a possibility only 3 percent of the time.

On the other hand, even if more frequent than infield fly balls, strikeouts represent only 18 percent of plate appearances, nowhere near a majority or even plurality of plate appearances in the relevant game situations. That the uncaught-third-strike rule is triggered more often than the Infield Fly Rule reveals nothing about the validity or necessity of either rule. Moreover, the Infield Fly Rule and the uncaught-third-strike rule are not in competition with each other, as they cover distinct events arising in similar game situations. In some sense, they work together to strip the defense of both strategies for obtaining extraordinarily inequitable double plays involving multiple forced baserunners in the four game situations. Viewed this way, the rules together prevented the defense from seeking inequitable double plays on more than 15,000 plate appearances, reflecting 20 percent of plays in these game situations in eight seasons.

Question # 2: Likelihood of the Evil to Be Prevented

The Infield Fly Rule is designed to eliminate a specific evil—the extraordinarily inequitable and one-sided benefit to the defense of a double (or triple) play on multiple forced baserunners on an intentionally uncaught fair fly ball. A second way to quantitatively evaluate the Infield Fly Rule is to measure the likelihood of that evil in the absence of the limiting rule. That is, in a game without an Infield Fly Rule, would an intentionally uncaught fair fly ball produce the feared double play and consequent cost-benefit disparity in favor of the defense and against the offense? This involves several distinct but related empirical questions: How likely is the double play absent the Infield Fly Rule, how much of a perverse incentive would the situation create for infielders, and, how often and under what circumstances might players act on that incentive?

Because baseball is always played under the Infield Fly Rule, the perverse incentive to seek the double play is non-existent. Infielders intentionally failed to catch the ball on fewer than ten of the 1,900 batted balls in the study, because they gained nothing by doing so, other than the small chance to fool a baserunner or umpire into a mistake. We only can speculate as to what might have happened in the same game played under different rules allowing for different strategies and different player skills.

But video reveals one important fact—where every infield-fly ball was hit and where on the field it was caught, dropped, or fell to the ground untouched. That fact provides a proxy for likelihood of the double play, which provides a proxy for the infielder's perverse incentive to intentionally not catch the fly ball absent the Infield Fly Rule. This relies on a line of simple, but reasonable, inference. The closer the fly ball is to the infield or to the first target base (the base to which the infielder will throw when he picks the uncaught ball off the ground), the closer the baserunners must remain to their current bases and the shorter and quicker the one or two throws to produce the double play. The shorter the throws and the farther the baserunners must travel, the more likely the defense is to successfully turn the force-out double play on an uncaught fly ball. And the more likely the double play, the greater the perverse incentive to intentionally not catch the easily playable fair fly ball in search of that inequitable cost-benefit advantage.

The figures below show the location of every fly ball on which infield fly was invoked in eight seasons. It also includes approximately 100 plays on which the Rule might have been invoked, but on which video was inconclusive. This provides the location of approximately 2,000 fair fly balls hit in infield-fly situations. Each mark is on the spot where the ball was caught (as almost every ball was), where it landed on the ground untouched, or where the infielder touched the ball before dropping it. For each season, figure (a) records plays with runners on first-and-second, while figure (b) records plays with the bases loaded.

This information allows a simple, if speculative, question: If these same fly balls were hit in these same situations in these same games but there were no Infield Fly Rule, what might have happened? Would infielders have intentionally not caught these fly balls in search of double plays? And what would have happened on the plays following the intentional non-catch?

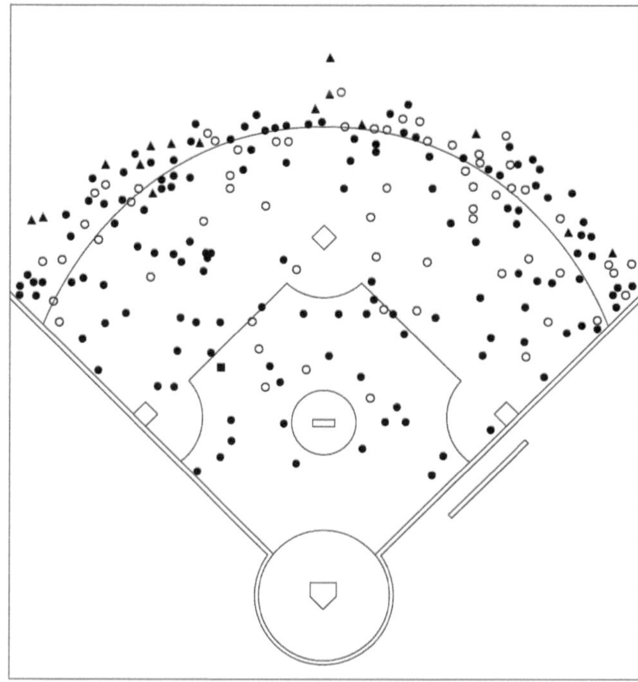

(○) Ball hit with none out

(□) Ball not caught; Infield Fly invoked

(•) Ball hit with one out

(+) Ball not caught; Infield Fly not invoked

(▲) Ball caught; unclear if Infield Fly invoked

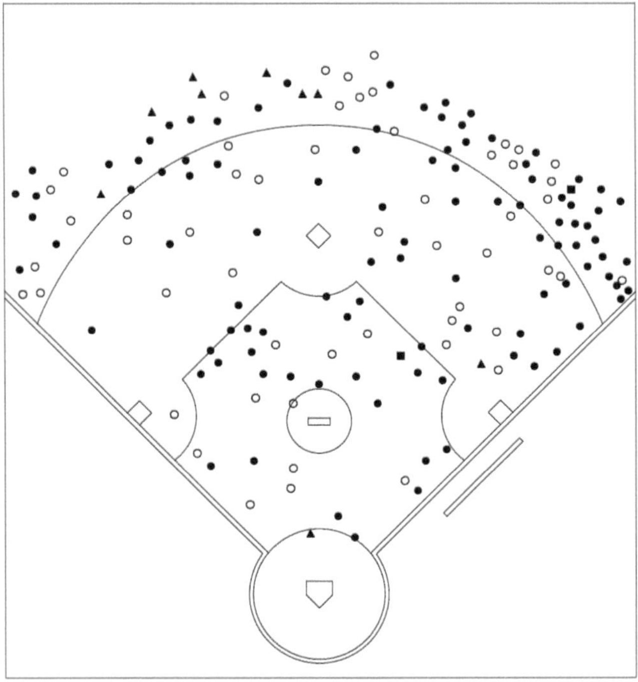

2011(a)

(○) Ball hit with none out
(□) Ball not caught; Infield Fly invoked
(•) Ball hit with one out
(+) Ball not caught; Infield Fly not invoked
(▲) Ball caught; unclear if Infield Fly invoked

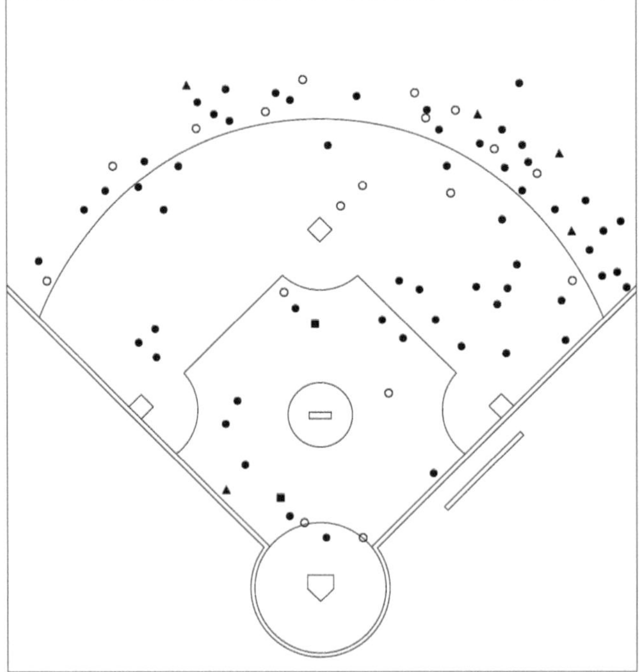

2011(b)

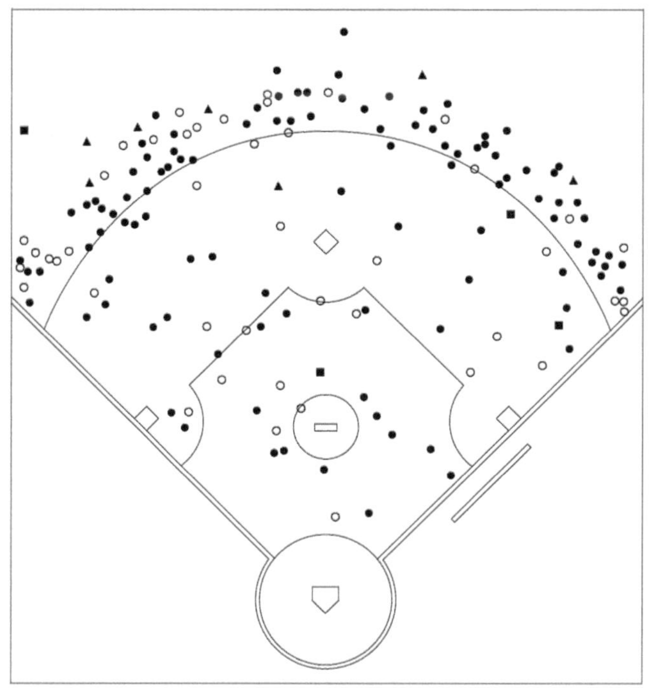
2012(a)

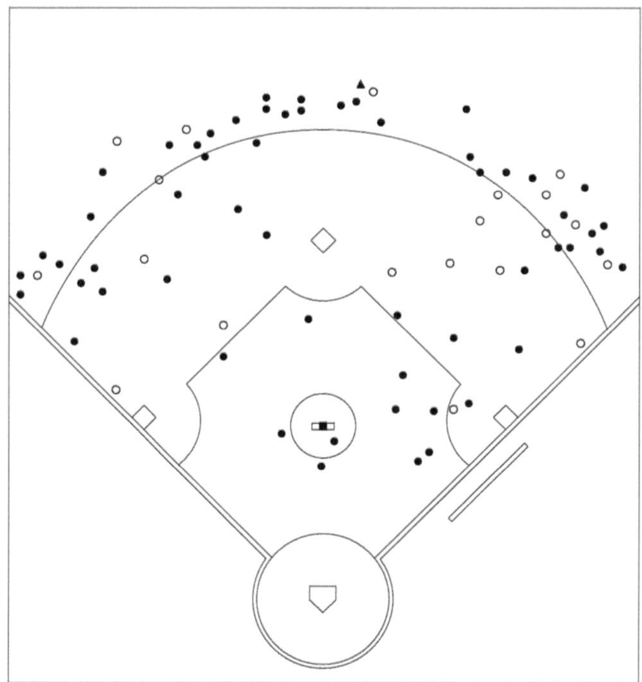
2012(b)

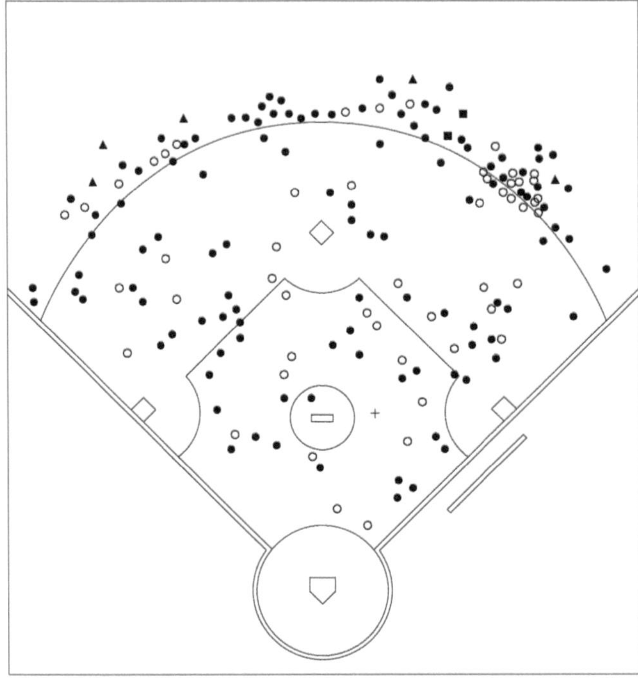

2013(a)

(○) Ball hit with none out

(□) Ball not caught; Infield Fly invoked

(●) Ball hit with one out

(+) Ball not caught; Infield Fly not invoked

(▲) Ball caught; unclear if Infield Fly invoked

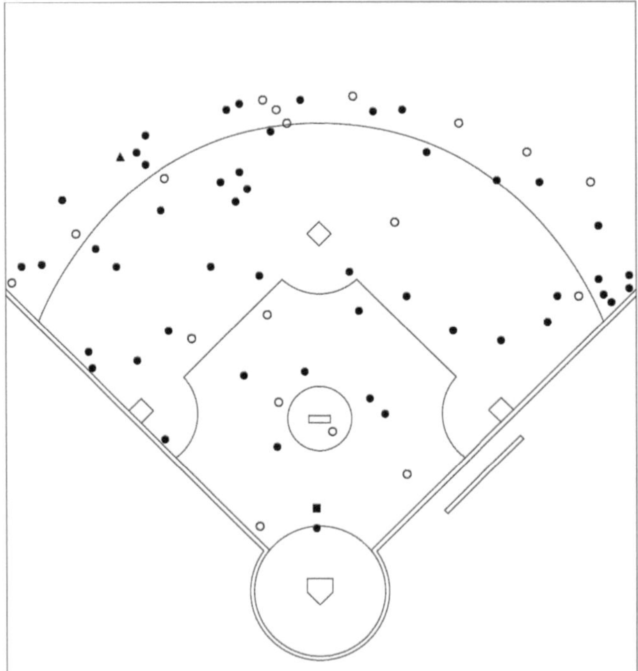

2013(b)

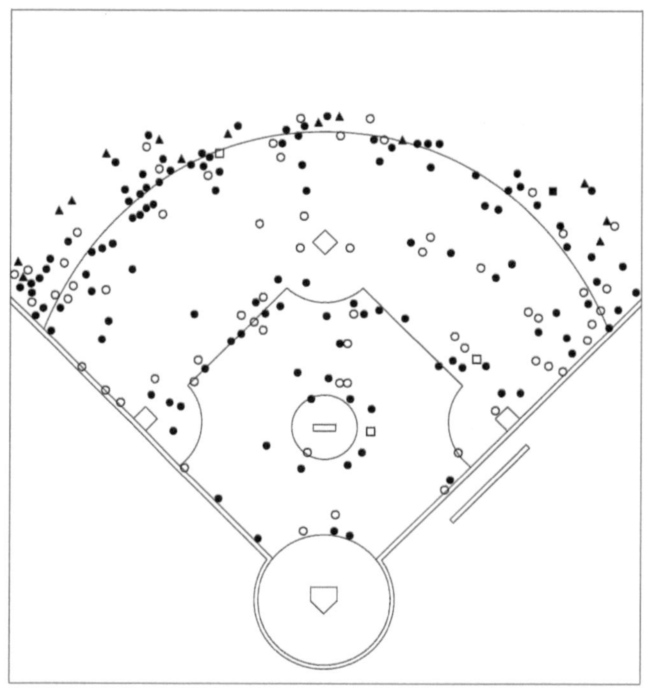

2014(a)

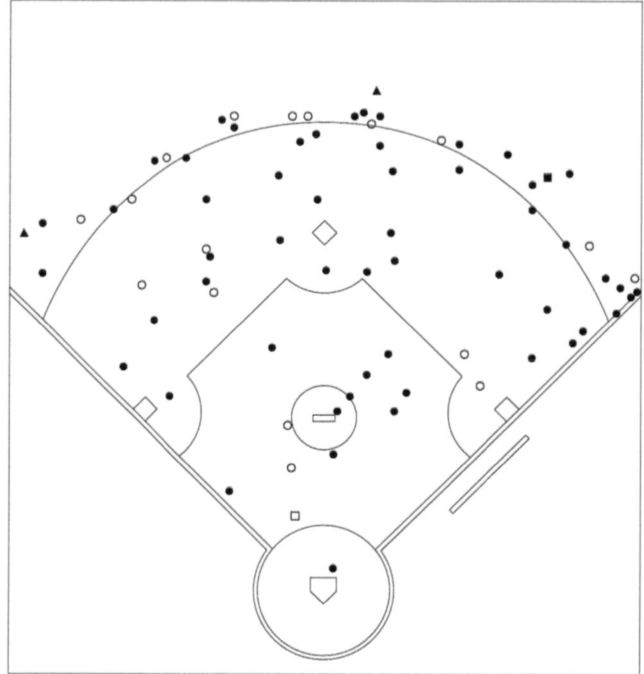

2014(b)

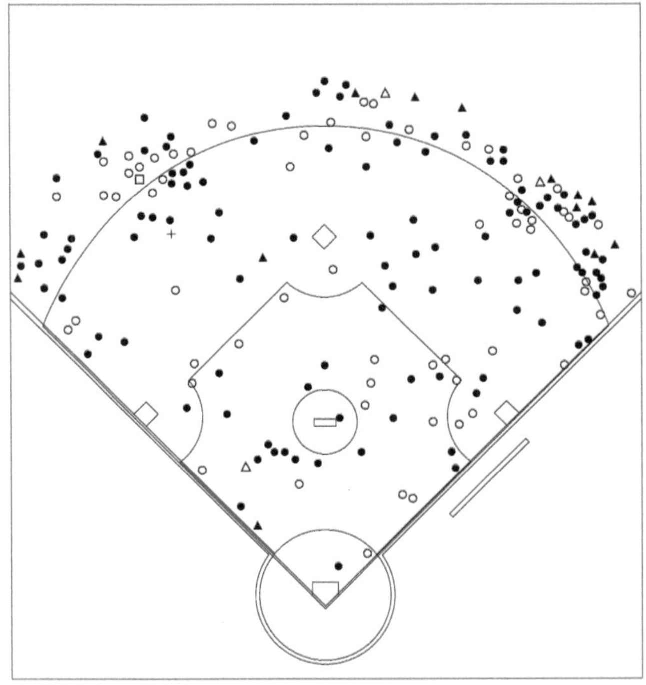

2015(a)

(○) Ball hit with none out

(□) Ball not caught; Infield Fly invoked

(•) Ball hit with one out

(+) Ball not caught; Infield Fly not invoked

(▲) Ball caught; unclear if Infield Fly invoked

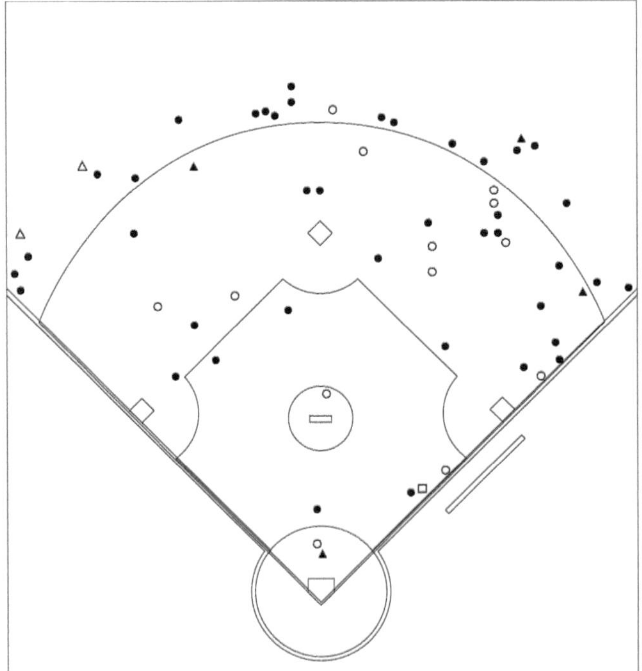

2015(b)

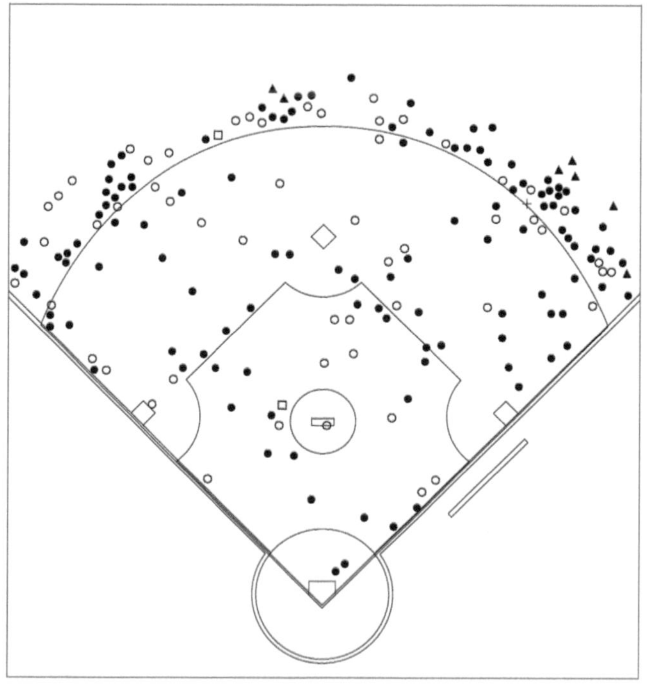

2016(a)

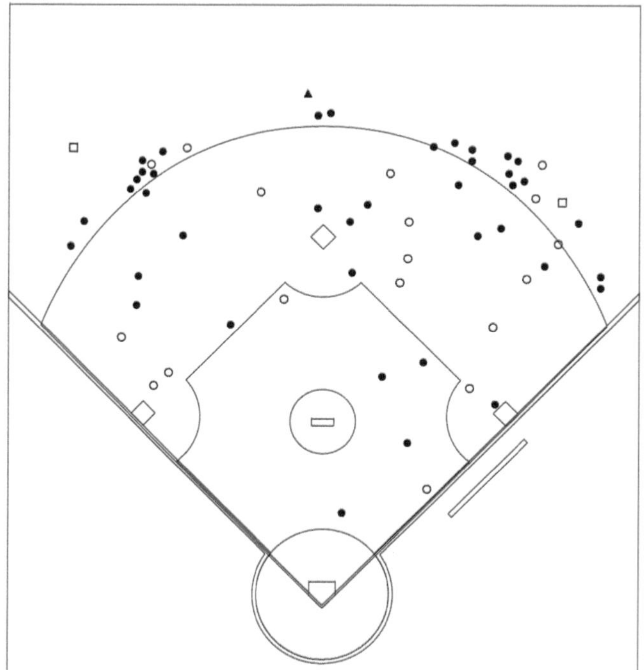

2016(b)

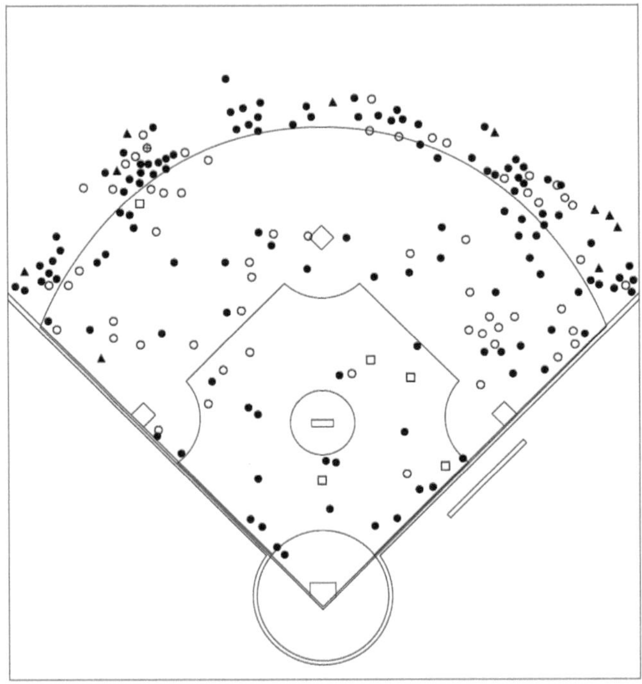

2017(a)

(○) Ball hit with none out

(□) Ball not caught; Infield Fly invoked

(•) Ball hit with one out

(+) Ball not caught; Infield Fly not invoked

(▲) Ball caught; unclear if Infield Fly invoked

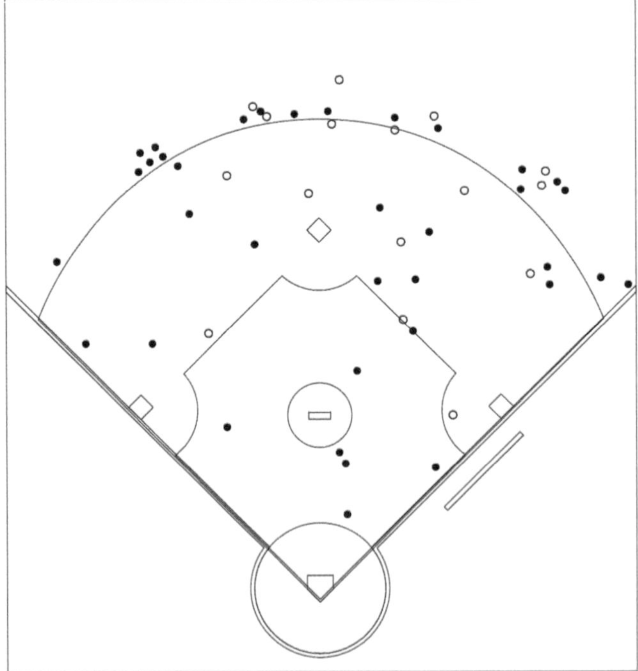

2017(b)

The figures show a wide distribution of balls across the left, middle, and right sides of the field, and across the infield grass, infield dirt, and shallow outfield grass, although bunched in a few places within each area. The distributions are generally consistent across the eight seasons, with a few outliers. Fewer balls were caught on the infield dirt in 2012 and 2016 compared with other seasons (Figure 5–3(a), 5–3(b), 5–7(a), 5–7(b)). More balls were hit into the shallow outfield on the right side in 2011 (Figure 5–2(a)); more were hit into the shallow outfield on the left side, particularly near the foul line, in 2014 (Figures 5–5(a), 5–5(b)). The 2013 season featured a cluster of balls to the area near where the second baseman typically is positioned (Figures 5–4(a), 5–4(b)), with fewer balls behind first base; the 2017 season featured a cluster of balls to the shortstop and behind third base (Figures 5–7(a), 5–7(b)). The 2015 season saw more balls on the right side than the left side overall in first-and-second situations (Figure 5–6(a)), while the reverse was true for other seasons.

Again, most balls were caught. Infielders are trained to do that with batted balls in fair territory by practice and repetition, and the presence of the Infield Fly Rule removes any incentive for them to do otherwise. Only 30 fair fly balls were not caught over eight seasons. And only five of the non-catches appear from video to have been intentional. One occurred in the Twins-Angels game in July 2013, discussed in Chapter 2, where the infielder's intentional non-catch convinced the umpire not to invoke infield fly, resulting in a double play. (This play is marked by a + to the right of the mound in Figure 5–4(a).) On two plays in 2014—one by the shortstop near the second-base bag, the other by the first baseman—the infielder allowed the ball to fall to the ground untouched as the umpire was calling infield fly. Two infielders tried the same move in 2016. The hope was to fool the runner into straying from the bag, although the gambit failed each time. The remaining 25 non-catches involved seemingly unintentional miscues— although, as discussed in Chapter 2, some resulted in double plays because baserunners made bad decisions (or the last in an exchange of mutual bad decisions). Among the unintentional non-catches was the 2017 triple play that the Orioles turned against the Red Sox when the umpire did not declare infield fly on a ball that was not caught in shallow centerfield (this play is marked by a + inside a circle in Figure 5–19).

As with the raw numbers of infield-fly calls, evidence of location is descriptively interesting and illustrative, but normatively ambiguous—it does not resolve policy questions about the wisdom of the Infield Fly Rule without resort to pre-existing value judgments. These charts of fly balls operate as a Rorschach Test—one sees different things based on one's ideas about the Rule.

Fly balls on the infield grass and dirt, which location suggests are more likely to produce double plays, represent a majority of batted balls in most seasons across the survey. Once these balls land on the ground, the defense must make one or two short throws to get force-outs on the two lead runners. And the runners must remain so close to their current bases to avoid being doubled-off on the catch that the single-throw/tag-the-runner-step-on-the-base double play at second-base is especially probable. The same is arguably true for balls hit to the edge of the outfield grass, especially in the middle and left sides of the field; the ball remains close enough to the infield that the infielder has a short initial throw to force the lead baserunner and the runners must remain close to their current bases. (Umpire instructor Brent Rice's suggests umpires are more likely to invoke the rule on balls to the left side of the field.) Balls in these two areas represent a significant number of plays each season covering a large swath of territory on the field from just to the right of second base (where the second baseman ordinarily positions himself) to the left-field line.

By contrast, a double play is less likely on balls hit deeper into the outfield, especially right field, and on balls in the shallow outfield behind first base and along the right-field foul line, for reasons discussed in earlier chapters. There were approximately 20–25 balls in this area each season, other than 2013 (Figures 5–4(a), 5–4(b)), which saw fewer than ten.

Location information validates the critique that the Infield Fly Rule is over-inclusive, as written and as applied. Accepting the inference from location to likelihood of double play to perverse incentive, the Rule perhaps was invoked or might have been invoked on many fly balls on which a double play would have been unlikely, leaving the infielder with no perverse incentive to intentionally not catch the fly ball. Figure 5–3(a) shows how far into the outfield the infamous fly ball in the 2012 NLWC traveled (the solid box in the upper-left-hand corner); given how far the runners had moved, it demonstrates the impossibility of a double play even if the shortstop had intentionally not caught the ball. In each season, triangles (indicating a play on which it could not be determined whether the Rule was invoked, although it might have been) are placed among calls, suggesting some inconsistency about how far into the outfield umpires are willing to invoke.

But location information also suggests that a double play was possible, and even highly likely, on many batted balls. Approximately 200 balls in eight years (an average of around 25 per year) were hit to areas on the field (deep or behind first base) on which the double play appears impossible. That leaves the overwhelming majority—nearly 1,800 fly balls, 225 per season—on the infield grass, infield dirt, and shallow outfield on the left and middle of the field where a double play is more likely and where some perverse incentive would remain in the absence of the limiting rule. This offers a visual display of the guesstimate of former MLB umpire Jim Evans that infielders would succeed in turning a double play on approximately 75 percent of the balls on which the Rule is now invoked.

Despite some over-inclusiveness, in other words, the Infield Fly Rule appears well-calibrated. The question remains how to balance competing sets of plays, which remains a value rather than empirical judgment. Does the risk of 225 inequitable double plays each year without the Rule outweigh granting 25 automatic outs where the targeted evil was absent? A proponent of the Rule would argue that the numbers validate any over-inclusiveness. The overwhelming cost-benefit disparity arises 9 times as often as unnecessary automatic outs, with a higher figure in a season such as 2013, with fewer balls hit in the no-man's-land behind first base (Figure 5–6(a), (b)).

Although not reflected in the figures, video of every actual and potential infield-fly call reveals a second way in which the Rule is applied too broadly—many fly balls were arguably not playable with "ordinary effort" because the wind carried the ball and made it obviously difficult for the infielder to settle under the ball (ordinary effort requires "due consideration" of field and weather conditions). But many were on the infield and close to the target bases, such that the baserunners had to stay close and had too far to run to reach the next base safely when the ball fell to the ground. Most of the 25 unintentionally uncaught fly balls over eight seasons were on the infield or the edge of the outfield. And of the balls on which baserunners attempted to advance on the dropped ball, both runners advanced safely on only four. One runner was put out on the other plays, completing a double play under the Infield Fly Rule with the out on the batter, often after some confusion among the fielders, runners, and announcers (but never the umpires). Even accounting for an infielder's need to scramble after an unintentionally dropped ball that he was not prepared to play off the ground, the field was too short, the runners too trapped, and the ball too close to the target base for the runner to avoid the out.

Question # 3: Practical Effects of the Infield Fly Rule

Recall how the Infield Fly Rule functions. Because the batter is out on the infield-fly call, the baserunners are not forced to advance, even if the ball is not caught. The defense gets one out, either on the catch or the call, and the runners can remain where they are (although they can try to advance at their own risk). Because the outcome is the same, infielders have no incentive to intentionally not catch the ball. Without the Infield Fly Rule, that perverse incentive returns. Because the batter is not out, baserunners are forced to advance, making it possible for the defense to turn a double play by forcing out two baserunners (not the batter, hustling up the line) on some 2,000 fair fly balls in the eight-year study.

With that in mind, we can measure the practical effect of the Rule on specific plate appearances, plays, innings, and games. More precisely, we can measure the practical effect of repealing the Infield Fly Rule and leaving the defense to its full range of strategic options. This requires comparing what happened in the game as played with the Infield Fly Rule with what might have happened in that game played without the Rule, by imagining the consequences of the defense turning a double play through an intentional non-catch of a fair fly ball.

We begin with the batter who hit the fly ball to the infielder in the infield-fly situation. We then imagine that, absent the Infield Fly Rule, this fly ball produced a force-out double play on the baserunners. From there, we can measure the effect on subsequent batters and subsequent plate appearances.

For simplicity, I make three assumptions, reflecting the most likely results on the batted balls. With the Infield Fly Rule, the batter is out and the runners remain where they are; the next batter comes to the plate in the same baserunner situation, but with one additional out. Without the Infield Fly Rule, the defense would turn a force-out double play on the two lead baserunners; the next batter comes to the plate with one less baserunner and two additional outs. This simplifies the analysis, while reflecting the presumptive result on a majority of fair fly balls. If the infield fly occurs with one out, the double play ends the inning and the next batter does not appear at the plate in that inning.

Consider an example. A batter comes to the plate with first-and-second/none-out and hits a fly ball that is catchable by the shortstop with ordinary effort. If the Infield Fly Rule is invoked or the ball is caught and the runners remain at their current bases, the next batter comes to the plate with runners still on first and second, but now one out. If there is no Infield Fly Rule and the infielder intentionally does not catch the fair fly ball and turns a force-out double play on the lead runners, the next batter comes to the plate with a runner on first base only and two outs in the inning.

I use several metrics to evaluate these distinct game situations for the next batter, quantifying the predicted costs to the offense and benefits to the defense from repealing the Infield Fly Rule.

Run Expectancy

Run Expectancy calculates the number of runs, on average, a team scores in an inning from a particular base-out situation until the end of that at-bat.[13] Table 5.3 shows the offense's run expectancy for the batter following the infield fly ball, comparing the resulting base-out situations with and without the Rule.

TABLE 5.3 RUN EXPECTANCY

Run Expectancy		1st & 2d-0	1st & 2d-1	Bases Loaded-0	Bases Loaded-1
2010	**IFR**	0.9032	0.4506	1.5514	0.7211
	No IFR	0.2251	0	0.4506	0
	Diff	0.6781	0.4506	1.1008	0.7211
2011	**IFR**	0.8936	0.4344	1.5344	0.6922
	No IFR	0.2174	0	0.4344	0
	Diff	0.6762	0.4344	1.1	0.6922
2012	**IFR**	0.9025	0.4391	1.5367	0.7012
	No IFR	0.2214	0	0.4391	0
	Diff	0.6811	0.4391	1.0976	0.7012
2013	**IFR**	0.8815	0.42	1.5265	0.6809
	No IFR	0.2064	0	0.42	0
	Diff	0.6751	0.42	1.1065	0.6809
2014	**IFR**	0.8623	0.3985	1.5102	0.6435
	No IFR	0.1946	0	0.3985	0
	Diff	0.6677	0.3985	1.1117	0.6435
2015	**IFR**	0.8919	0.4361	1.5263	0.6971
	No IFR	0.2203	0	0.4361	0
	Diff	0.6716	0.4361	1.0902	0.6971
2016	**IFR**	0.926	0.4345	1.5694	0.6955
	No IFR	0.2199	0	0.4345	0
	Diff	0.0761	0.4345	1.1349	0.6955
2017	**IFR**	0.9448	0.4553	1.5915	0.7299
	No IFR	0.2349	0	0.4553	0
	Diff	0.7099	0.4553	1.1362	0.7299

The four infield-fly situations run across the top, with a different season running down the left side. The numbers show run expectancy for the next batter. For each season in each infield-fly situation, the first row shows run expectancy with the Infield Fly Rule, with the next batter hitting with one more out and the same baserunners. The second row shows run expectancy without the Infield Fly Rule, assuming a double play on the lead runners, with the next batter hitting with two more outs and one less baserunner. The third row shows the difference in run expectancy between the two, reflecting the cost to the offense and benefit to the defense of repealing the Infield Fly Rule.

Over eight seasons, the batting team's run expectancy is always higher, often substantially, when the Infield Fly Rule protects it from a double play. Run expectancy always drops, often substantially, when the defense turns a double play without the Rule. In each season, where the fly ball occurs with none out, a double play costs the offense more than ⅔ of a run with first-and-second (and more than .7 runs in 2016 and 2017) and more than one full run with bases loaded. Consider bases-loaded/none-out in 2017. With the batter out (either on the catch or the Infield Fly call), the next batter hits with bases-loaded/one-out, a run expectancy of 1.5915. With the defense turning a double play without the Rule, the next batter hits with first-and-second/two-outs, a run expectancy of 0.4553. The difference between those—1.1362 runs—represents the cost to the batting team from the rules permitting and incentivizing the defense to turn that double play by intentionally not catching the fair fly ball.

Measuring the run-expectancy effect when the fly ball comes with one out is trickier, because the double play ends the inning and the offense's turn at bat, meaning the next batter does not appear at the plate in that inning. The team's run expectancy falls to zero—the team has no chance to score any more runs in that now-completed turn at bat. With bases loaded, runs lost ranged from just under 0.65 to more than 0.7, with highs of 0.7299 in 2017 and 0.7211 2010. With first-and-second, the range runs over 0.4 runs lost in every season.

Run expectancy can measure the effect of the Rule's absence on three significant plays in the eight-year study: the call in the 2012 NLWC, the non-call in the July 2013 Twins-Angels game that produced a double play, and the non-call in the May 2017 Red Sox-Orioles game that produced a triple play.

Because the non-catches in Twins-Angels and Sox-Orioles produced multiple outs, they demonstrate the cost of the uncaught fly ball. Had the Rule been invoked (as it probably should have been) in Twins-Angels, the batter would have been out and the runners would have remained in place;

the Twins would have had first-and-second/one-out, a 2013 run expectancy of 0.8815. Following the double play, the Twins had runner on third/two-outs, a run expectancy of 0.3527. The double play off the intentional non-catch cost the Twins more than half a run in a one-run ballgame. And had Angels pitcher Ernesto Frieri made the correct move of a force-out double play on the lead baserunners (rather than the batter and one baserunner), the Twins would have faced first-only/two-outs, a run expectancy of 0.2064, a loss of more than ⅔ of a run. Either result shows the significant cost-benefit disparity from a double play that would be routinely available to defenses if the Infield Fly Rule were repealed.

The Orioles triple-play had greater effect on the inning, although less effect on the outcome of the specific game. Had the Rule been invoked, the Red Sox would have first-and-second/one out, a 2017 run expectancy of 0.9448. Because the Rule was not invoked and the Orioles turned a triple play, the Sox turn at bat ended, leaving them with a run expectancy of 0, a loss of almost a full run. Because the Sox were leading 5–2 in the eighth inning and the Orioles did not score in the ninth, the lost runs did not affect the outcome.

The 2012 NLWC was unique in that invocation of the Infield Fly Rule worked to the detriment of the batting team, the side the Rule is designed to protect. Had infield fly not been invoked (as it perhaps should not have been), the Braves would have had bases-loaded/one-out, a run expectancy of 0.7012 runs. Because the baserunners advanced on the uncaught ball, the Braves were left with second-and-third/two-out, a run expectancy of 0.5815, a loss of just over 0.1 runs. That is a smaller loss than if the runners had stayed put (as typically happens when the Rule is invoked), leaving the Braves with first-and-second/two-outs and a run expectancy of 0.4391.

Win Expectancy

Win Expectancy represents the percentage probability that one team will win from one point in a game, considering base-out situation, inning (top or bottom), whether the home or visiting team is winning, and run differential.[14] The figures are based on the results of actual games from a period of years, considering how often the home or visiting team won from that point in the game. Where run expectancy offers a sense of how many runs the offense loses in a generic inning, win expectancy offers a sense of how repealing the Infield Fly Rule and allowing the defense to turn a force-out double play on an intentional non-catch adversely affects the batting team's chances of winning a specific game.

Table 5.4 Win Expectancy (Tie)

Win Expectancy: Tie Game		1st & 2d-0	1st & 2d-1	Bases Loaded-0	Bases Loaded-1
Top 7	IFR	52.39	48.42	62.85	47.84
	No IFR	44.01	39.19	48.42	39.19
	Diff	8.38	9.23	14.43	8.65
Bottom 7	IFR	66.59	61.99	77.66	65.94
	No IFR	55.34	52.19	61.99	52.19
	Diff	11.25	9.8	15.67	13.75
Top 8	IFR	56.71	46.22	71.65	43.1
	No IFR	41.29	37.83	46.22	36.83
	Diff	15.42	8.39	25.43	6.27
Bottom 8	IFR	71.22	63.27	78.51	68.23
	No IFR	57.78	52.12	63.27	52.12
	Diff	13.44	11.15	15.24	16.11
Top 9	IFR	59.3	47.21	70.61	45.59
	No IFR	39.79	34.48	47.21	34.48
	Diff	19.51	12.73	23.4	11.11
Bottom 9	IFR	74.37	62.68	85.93	67.8
	No IFR	57.39	52.22	62.68	52.22
	Diff	16.98	10.46	23.25	15.58

Table 5.5 Win Expectancy (Visitor +1)

Win Expectancy Visitor +1		1st & 2d-0	1st & 2d-1	Bases Loaded-0	Bases Loaded-1
Top 7	IFR	73.5	68.37	78.1	74.17
	No IFR	66.53	64.02	68.37	64.02
	Diff	6.97	4.35	9.73	10.15
Bottom 7	IFR	45.98	33.44	57.89	42.9
	No IFR	29.62	24.58	34.44	24.58
	Diff	16.36	8.86	23.45	18.32
Top 8	IFR	78.05	73.92	83.91	79.06
	No IFR	73.36	70.43	73.92	70.43
	Diff	4.69	3.49	9.99	8.63
Bottom 8	IFR	39.51	28.69	57.06	37.16
	No IFR	22.75	15.13	28.69	15.13
	Diff	16.76	13.56	28.37	22.03
Top 9	IFR	87.87	83.56	89.3	83.21
	No IFR	83.23	81.72	83.56	81.72
	Diff	4.64	1.84	5.74	1.49
Bottom 9	IFR	36.26	16.37	54.91	25.89
	No IFR	8.67	0	16.37	0
	Diff	27.59	16.37	38.54	25.89

TABLE 5.6 WIN EXPECTANCY (HOME +1)

Win Expectancy Home +1		1st & 2d-0	1st & 2d-1	Bases Loaded-0	Bases Loaded-1
Top 7	IFR	36.8	25.36	35.28	30.86
	No IFR	25.57	18	25.36	18
	Diff	11.23	7.36	9.92	12.86
Bottom 7	IFR	84.57	81.51	89.24	82.9
	No IFR	81	77.54	81.51	77.54
	Diff	3.57	3.97	7.73	5.36
Top 8	IFR	30.96	20.54	43.95	25.86
	No IFR	17.23	10.92	20.54	10.92
	Diff	13.73	9.62	23.41	14.94
Bottom 8	IFR	90.63	89.42	93.77	92.13
	No IFR	87.78	86.65	89.42	86.65
	Diff	2.85	2.77	4.35	5.48
Top 9	IFR	28.14	13.06	47.08	22.81
	No IFR	6.42	0	13.06	0
	Diff	21.72	13.06	34.02	22.81
Bottom 9	IFR	N/A	N/A	N/A	N/A
	No IFR	N/A	N/A	N/A	N/A
	Diff	N/A	N/A	N/A	N/A

Win expectancy accounts for inning, which team is winning, and run margin. At some point, a game is so one-sided that a double play's effect on win expectancy will be negligible. Similarly, its effect is negligible early in the game. I limited the study to the final three innings of games within one run either way. Table 5.4 shows games tied at the time of the infield fly, Table 5.5 shows Team V (Visitor) leading by one run at the time of the infield fly, and Table 5.6 shows Team H (Home) leading by one run at the time of the infield fly. These numbers confirm that repealing the Infield Fly Rule would disadvantage batting teams, while capturing the situations most sensitive to differences between outcomes with and without the Rule.

For each table, the four infield-fly situations run across the top, while each of six half innings (top and bottom of the seventh, eighth, and ninth) runs down the left-hand side. For each half inning in each situation, the table shows the batting team's win expectancy (as a percentage) for the batter immediately following the infield fly ball. For each half-inning in each situation, the first row shows the batting team's win expectancy with the Rule, with the batter hitting with one more out and the same baserunners. The second row shows the batting team's win expectancy without the Rule and assuming a double play, with the batter hitting with two more outs and one less baserunner. The third row shows the difference between those figures, reflecting the win-expectancy cost to the offense and benefit to the defense of not having the Rule.

Repealing the Infield Fly Rule (assuming it results in a double play on the fly ball) would have a consistently negative effect on a batting team's win expectancy. The effect is substantial in many situations—a decrease in win expectancy of between 10 and 20 percent. The effect increases as we move later in the game. And the effect remains greater on infield flies hit with bases-loaded than with first-and-second and greater on balls hit with none out than with one out.

Consider bases-loaded/none-out on each chart. In a tie game (Table 5.4), both teams experience a drop of at least 14 percent from the seventh inning on, culminating in a drop of more than 23 percent in the respective halves of the ninth inning. When either team has a one-run lead, the trailing team incurs a loss of more than 20 percent, which grows as the game progresses. The leading team's win expectancy also drops, although by smaller amounts that shrink as the game progresses.

Look specifically at bases-loaded/none-out with Team V leading by one run (Table 5.5). Team V's win expectancy drops by about 10 percent in the seventh and eighth, but only about 6 percent in the ninth inning, as its win expectancy exceeds 80 percent, with or without the Infield Fly Rule. By contrast, trailing Team H's win expectancy without the Rule drops by 23 percent in the seventh, more than 28 percent in the eighth, and almost 40 percent in the ninth.

The last point is worth exploring in-depth. Imagine Team H loads the bases with none out, trailing by one run, in the bottom of the ninth.[15] Team H's win expectancy is 68.55 percent. The batter hits a fair fly ball playable by an infielder with ordinary effort. With the Infield Fly Rule, the batter is out, the runners remain, and the next batter hits with bases-loaded/one-out, his team holding a win expectancy of 54.91 percent. That is, Team H wins more than half the time when it loads the bases with one out in the bottom of the ninth trailing by one. With the defense turning the double play on the lead runners without the Infield Fly Rule, the next batter hits with first-and-second/two-outs, his team now holding a win expectancy of just over 16 percent. That is, the absence of the Infield Fly Rule and the uncaught-fly-ball double play drops Team H's win expectancy by 38 percent.

Team V experiences a similar effect when trailing by one run in the top of the ninth (Table 5.6). With bases-loaded/one-out (the situation following an Infield Fly Rule call), its win expectancy is 47 percent, meaning it wins close to (although slightly less than) half the time. With first-and-second/two outs (the situation following the double play without the Rule), its win expectancy tumbles to 13 percent, a drop of 34 percent to a small likelihood of victory.

As with run expectancy, measuring change in win expectancy on the one-out infield-fly is more challenging, where the double play without the Infield Fly Rule ends the team's at-bat and the next batter does not appear at the plate in that inning. The comparator must be where the team stands at the end of that at-bat, meaning the beginning of the opposing team's at-bat.

Imagine a double play on an uncaught infield fly with bases-loaded/one-out in the top of the seventh of a tie game (top situation row in Table 5.4). That double play ends the at-bat for Team V and brings Team H to the plate. Team V's win expectancy is the flip of Team H's win expectancy when batting in the bottom of the seventh of a tie game, with none-on/none-out. Looking at the last column in that row of Table 5.4: 47.84 percent represents Team V's win expectancy with the Infield Fly Rule, still batting in the top of the seventh, with bases-loaded/two-outs, while the 39.19 percent figure represents Team V's win expectancy without the Rule (and is the flip side of Team H's win expectancy when batting with none-on/none-out in the bottom of the seventh, with a win expectancy of 60.81 percent).

An alternative approach to this situation might use the team's win expectancy at the beginning of its next turn at bat—when the next batter for Team V (who did not bat in the top of the seventh because of the inning-ending double play) leads-off the top of the eighth. But this does not allow a clean measure of the Infield Fly Rule's effect, because events in the bottom of the seventh (when Team H bats) affect Team V's win expectancy. If Team H scores in the bottom of the seventh, Team V's win expectancy is lower than it would have been, but only because of what its pitching and defense did (or failed to do). If Team H does not score in the bottom of the seventh, on the other hand, Team V's win expectancy actually increases by its next turn at-bat, because it is later in the game and Team V needs fewer outs to win. But Team V cannot be better off for having hit into an inning-ending, fly-ball double play.

Take another example. Team V leads by one in the top of the seventh, with first-and-second/one-out, when the batter hits an infield fly ball. With the Infield Fly Rule, Team V's win expectancy (with the next batter hitting with first-and-second/two-out and a one-run lead in the top of the seventh) is 68.37 percent. Without the Infield Fly Rule, the defense completes an inning-ending double play on the uncaught fly ball, bringing Team H to bat in the bottom of the seventh. If Team H does not score, Team V's win expectancy at the beginning of the top of the eighth increases to 75.42 percent. If Team H scores one run in the bottom of the seventh to tie the game, Team V's win expectancy at the beginning of the eighth inning is 47.81 percent. If Team H scores two runs to take a one-run lead, Team V's win expectancy drops to 22.46 percent.

These figures do not reflect how repealing the Infield Fly Rule implicates team preferences, because the change in win expectancy came from the performance of Team V's pitching and defense. Purely as a matter of win expectancy, Team V is better off in the top of the eighth than at the time of the infield fly in the top of the seventh. So long, that is, as Team V can prevent Team H from scoring in the bottom of the seventh. But Team V could not know in the top of the seventh whether Team H would score in the bottom and would not have wanted to incur the risk. Team V would prefer the greater run-scoring opportunity in the seventh (with two men on base) than leading off the eighth with no one on base. The preference for Team V (and every batting team) must be to continue batting (and continue being able to score runs) as long as possible. Any uncaught-fly-ball double play absent the Rule undermines those preferences.

The 2013 Twins-Angels non-call illustrates the likely effect of repealing the Infield Fly Rule. The visiting Twins were batting in the top of ninth, trailing by one run, with the fly ball coming with first-and-second/none-out. Had infield fly been invoked, the Twins would have been left with first-and-second/one-out, a win expectancy of 28.14 percent. While not great, it is substantially better than the 9.92 percent the Twins were left with following the double play (runner-on-third/two-outs) or the 6.42 percent the Twins would have faced had the Angels turned the expected force-out double play on the two lead baserunners and allowed the batter to reach first base.

Runs Lost

A final measure of the effect of the Infield Fly Rule (or the effect of its repeal) considers the runs that might have been lost during these eight seasons were there no Infield Fly Rule and were infielders free to turn double plays by intentionally not catching those 1,900 easily playable fair fly balls.

Table 5.7 shows each of the infield-fly situations across the top and each season down the left side. Each situation in each season contains three rows.

The first row shows the number of infield-fly calls, imported from the corresponding rows in Table 5.1.

The second row shows the number of runs scored in the same inning as, but subsequent to, an Infield Fly call. Without the Infield Fly Rule and

TABLE 5.7 RUNS LOST

Runs Scored		1st & 2d-0	1st & 2d-1	Bases Loaded-0	Bases Loaded-1	Totals
2010	IFR	65	132	21	42	260
	Runs	27	25	10	14	76
	Effect	8	4	2	5	19
2011	IFR	58	106	24	59	247
	Runs	17	21	12	15	65
	Effect	3	4	4	7	18
2012	IFR	52	106	19	57	234
	Runs	25	27	13	18	83
	Effect	5	9	6	6	26
2013	IFR	51	115	17	51	234
	Runs	25	20	11	20	76
	Effect	7	6	3	5	21
2014	IFR	59	121	20	53	253
	Runs	24	22	16	13	75
	Effect	4	9	6	4	23
2015	IFR	63	105	17	40	225
	Runs	26	24	12	15	77
	Effect	6	4	1	5	16
2016	IFR	53	117	18	45	233
	Runs	18	20	8	12	58
	Effect	12	10	2	2	26
2017	IFR	57	116	18	35	226
	Runs	21	22	13	15	71
	Effect	5	3	1	6	15
Totals	IFR	458	918	154	382	1912
	Runs	183	181	95	122	581
	Affect	50	49	25	40	164

assuming the double play on the lead runners, the double play eliminates some or all baserunners who scored later that inning. If the double play occurs with none out, at least some of those runners do not score, because the offense is left with one fewer baserunner. If the double play occurs with one out and ends the inning and the batting team's opportunity to score, none of those later runs scores, at least not in that inning. In other words, were infielders free to turn double plays on forced baserunners on intentionally uncaught fair fly balls, it is certain that some number of these runs would not have scored in the inning.

The third row shows how often those lost runs would have "affected" the outcome of the game. I define an outcome as having been affected where the runs scored in an inning subsequent to an Infield Fly call provided the margin of victory in a game. This includes games in which, without the post-call runs, the winning team loses or the game becomes tied, but does not include games in which subtracting those runs means the same team wins by a larger or smaller margin. I also included games that went to extra innings, even if the margin was greater than the number of post-infield-fly runs.

The lower-right-hand box of Table 5.7 shows that teams scored runs subsequent to 581 of the 1,912 infield-fly calls (excluding the might-have-been called plays), representing 30.5 percent of calls in the sample. This includes 303 one-out calls (first-and-second and bases-loaded), in which none of the subsequent runs would have scored in that inning. Lost runs affected the outcome on 164 of those calls, including 79 balls hit with one out.

Simply subtracting runs from the final score is an admittedly imprecise measure of the effect of repealing the Infield Fly Rule. Even allowing for a double play on each of 1,912 uncaught fly balls, it is impossible to know whether and how the double play affects the outcome, how a game might have played out under different rules allowing different strategies, or what changes in score or outcome might have followed.

Some post-double-play runs might have scored in the inning, since some runners remain on base, sometimes in scoring position, and the inning may not be over. Imagine an uncaught-fly-ball double play with bases-loaded/none-out. The next batter hits with first-and-second/two-outs, far from an impossible scoring situation (the batting team would have a run expectancy of approximately 0.4 runs). Even if the rest of the inning went as it did, the batting team might have scored some subsequent runs, although fewer than it did in the actual game. Alternatively, the batting team might have scored those same runs later in the game. And even if subtracting post-call runs produces a tie game, it says nothing about how the rest of the game would have proceeded or who would have won.

A double play at one point in the game may alter subsequent plate appearances and innings, as players and teams adopt different strategies and approaches in changed circumstances. Teams in a different game might have used different pitchers or batters or employed different strategies in later innings, producing different scoring opportunities and results. Perhaps they get the game to the same end, perhaps the game changes in unknown ways.

Give that uncertainty, repealing the Infield Fly Rule may do more than these numbers suggest, affecting games even where subtracted runs alone do not alter the winner. Imagine Team H won the game 8–4, with three runs scoring in the fifth-inning subsequent to an infield-fly call. Subtracting those three runs gives Team H a 5–4 win, so I did not code this as an "affected" game. But subtracting three runs makes this a closer game, one that both teams would approach differently as the game progressed. Those different strategies might have yielded more runs for either or both teams, altering the game and the outcome from what happened in the game as played. These unknowns return to the starting problem—the impossibility of testing the counterfactual of how a Major-League Baseball game would be played without the Infield Fly Rule, something that has not happened since the 1890s.

Finally, and as with all the other quantitative measures introduced in this chapter, this data does not resolve the normative debate about the Rule. Even accepting that those 164 infield fly balls might have produced double plays and different game outcomes, it does not answer which of those distinct outcomes is better or preferable. Nor does it answer whether an effect on approximately 20 games per year, spread among all infield-fly situations in all games over eight seasons, is significant enough to justify retaining the Infield Fly Rule to prevent these altered outcomes. As always, the answer depends on pre-existing normative preferences about the Rule itself.

*　*　*

This final chapter shares the virtue and defect of being descriptively interesting, but not normatively conclusive. The numbers presented here offer a picture of the role that the Infield Fly Rule plays in baseball, as well as a speculative sense of how baseball might change without the Rule. That is a worthwhile exercise, even if the numbers do not resolve the debate or convince anyone beyond their pre-existing value judgments about the wisdom of the Infield Fly Rule.

Afterword

I set out to make the case that the Infield Fly Rule is a necessary, proper, and successful part of baseball. Regardless of the outdated sportsmanship-and-amateurism intentions or goals of its drafters more than a century ago, the Rule continues to make sense as a way of avoiding uniquely inequitable cost-benefit disparities and perverse incentives within the game. That policy goal of eliminating disparities and perverse incentives survives more than a century after the Rule's genesis and early evolution. And that goal pervades any system of sports rules, not only for baseball, but for all sports.

The final question is what, if anything, comes next for baseball and the Infield Fly Rule. The likely answer is nothing, despite the best efforts of Judge Guilford in University of Pennsylvania Law Review and the occasional fan or commentator. No one with power or influence in baseball—players, coaches, executives, or umpires—speaks publicly or seriously about repealing the Rule. Many people no doubt adhere to Brent Rice's view—the Rule has been part of baseball for more than a century and should remain as a matter of tradition. Players, coaches, fans, and umpires are accustomed to the Rule (even if many in the first three groups do not understand it) and conform their behavior to account for it. For many, nostalgia is sufficient to retain it, at least absent some other cost or harm that most in the game do not recognize.

The Infield Fly Rule is here to stay. I believe this is and remains a good thing. Most in baseball appear to agree.

But it has been a fun ride exploring why that is, why it should be, and why it should remain so.

Chapter Notes

Preface

1. Rich Marazzi, The Rules and Lore of Baseball 22–23 (1980).

2. *Protests Mar Game*, Evening Star, June 30, 1911, at 5.

3. Andrew J. Guilford and Joel Mallord, *A Step Aside: Time to Drop the Infield Fly Rule and End a Common Law Anomaly*, 164 U. Pa. L. Rev. 281 (2015); *Repeal the IFR* (defunct web site).

4. John Dickerson, *Wait, Am I That Baseball Dad?*, Slate (June 19, 2013).

5. Marty Appel, Pinstripe Empire: The New York Yankees from Before the Babe to After the Boss 411–51 (2012).

6. *Protests Mar Game*, at 5.

7. *A Comparison of Three Rules*, NWUmpires.com.

8. Paul Dickson, The Unwritten Rules of Baseball: The Etiquette, Conventional Wisdom, and Aximatic Codes of Our National Pastime 6 (2009) (hereinafter Dickson, Unwritten).

9. Marazzi, at xiii; Mitchell N. Berman, *Replay*, 99 Cal. L. Rev. 1683, 1687 (2011) (hereinafter Berman, *Replay*).

10. Mitchell N. Berman, *"Let 'Em Play": A Study in the Jurisprudence of Sport*, 99 Geo. L.J. 1325, 1329 (2011) (hereinafter Berman, *Play*).

11. International Football Association Board, Laws of the Game (2016/17); Laws of Cricket 2000 Code (5th ed. 2013); World Rugby, Laws of the Game: Rugby Union (2016).

12. Berman, *Replay*, at 1699.

13. Mitchell N. Berman and Richard D. Friedman, Rules of Play: Sports as Legal Systems (forthcoming).

14. Richard A. Primus, *Bolling Alone*, 104 Colum. L. Rev. 975, 1010 (2004).

15. Dickson, Unwritten, at 43–46; Jason Turbow with Michael Duca, The Baseball Codes: Beanballs, Sign Stealing, & Bench-Clearing Brawls: The Unwritten Rules of America's Pastime 127 (2010).

16. Spencer Weber Waller, Neil B. Cohen, and Paul Finkelman, *Introduction, in* Baseball and the American Legal Mind, at x (Spencer Weber Waller, Neil B. Cohen, and Paul Finkelman, eds. 1995).

17. Charles Yablon, *On the Contribution of Baseball to American Legal Theory*, 104 Yale L.J. 227, 233 (1994).

18. Hunt's Generator Cmte v. Babcock & Wilcox Co., 863 F. Supp. 879 (E.D. Wis. 1994) (Terrence Evans, J.).

19. Waller, Cohen, and Finkelman, at ix.

20. Marazzi, at xiii.

21. Waller, Cohen, and Finkelman, at ix.

22. Douglas O. Linder, *Strict Constructionism and the Strike Zone, in* Waller, Cohen, and Finkelman in Baseball and the American Legal Mind, at 477.

23. *In re* Brett: *The Sticky Problem of Statutory Interpretation, in* Waller, Cohen, and Finkelman in Baseball and the American Legal Mind, at 34.

24. Yablon, at 233–34.

25. *Confirmation Hearings of John G. Roberts, Jr., to Be Chief Justice of the United States, Before the Senate Committee on the Judiciary*, 109th Cong. 55–56 (2005).

26. Erwin Chemerinsky, *Seeing the Emperor's Clothes: Recognizing the Reality of Constitutional Decision Making*, 86 B.U. L. Rev. 1069 (2006); Richard A. Posner, *The Role of the Judge*, 86 B.U. L. Rev. 1049 (2006); Neil S. Siegel, *Umpires at Bat: On Integration and Legitimation*, 24 Const. Comment. 701 (2006).

27. Berman, *Play*, at 1327, 1333–34.

28. Laws of the Game 11 (Offside).

29. *Aside: The Common Law Origins of the Infield Fly Rule*, 123 U. Pa. L. Rev. 1474 (1975) (hereinafter *Aside*).

30. William Grimes, *William S. Stevens, 60, Dies; Wrote Infield Fly Note*, N.Y. Times (Dec. 11, 2008).

31. Neil B. Cohen and Spencer Weber Waller, *Taking Pop-Ups Seriously: The Jurisprudence of the Infield Fly Rule*, 82 Wash. U. L.Q. 453 (2004);

Anthony D'Amato, *The Contribution of the Infield Fly Rule to Western Civilization (and Vice Versa)*, 100 Nw. U. L. Rev. 189 (2006); John J. Flynn, *Further Aside: A Comment on "The Common Law Origins of the Infield Fly Rule,"* in Waller, Cohen, and Finkelman, at 13.

32. Cohen and Waller, at 454.

33. Mark W. Cochran, *The Infield Fly Rule and the Internal Revenue Code: An Even Further Aside,* in Waller, Cohen, and Finkelman in Baseball and the American Legal Mind, at 21.

34. Hinton v. Trans Union LLC, 654 F. Supp. 2d 440, 452 n.26 (E.D. Va. 2009); Mann v. Lima, 290 F. Supp. 2d 190, 194 (D. R.I. 2003); *see* Chad M. Oldfather, *The Hidden Ball: A Substantive Critique of Baseball Metaphors in Judicial Opinions*, 27 Conn. L. Rev. 17 (1994).

35. Guilford and Mallord; *but see* Howard M. Wasserman, *Just a Bit Aside: Perverse Incentives, Cost-Benefit Imbalances, and the Infield Fly Rule*, 164 U. Pa. L. Rev. Online 145 (2016) (published response to Guilford and Mallord).

36. Marazzi, at 23.

37. Bull Durham (Orion Pictures 1988).

38. *Aside*, at 1476.

Introduction

1. Official Baseball Rules (Definitions of Terms: Infield Fly) (2015 ed.) (previously Rule 2.00 (Infield Fly)). Major League Baseball recodified and reorganized its rules in December 2014. Official Baseball Rules, at v (Important Notes 1) (2015 ed.).

2. Official Baseball Rules (Definitions of Terms: Infield Fly).

3. Official Baseball Rules (Definitions of Terms: Infield Fly); Official Baseball Rules § 5.09(a)(5).

4. *Comparison of Three Rules.*

5. Marazzi, at 23.

6. Mark Bowman, *Infield fly ruling draws Braves' ire, sparks disruption*, MLB.com (Oct. 6, 2012).

7. Play-by-Play, National League Wildcard Game, BaseballReference.com (Oct. 5, 2012).

8. Timothy Burke, *Braves Fans Attack Umpires with Garbage After Worst Infield Fly Call Ever*, Deadspin (Oct. 5, 2012); Kevin Kaduk, *Bad infield fly rule call mars Cardinals victory over Braves in NL wild card game*, Yahoo! Sports (Oct. 5, 2012).

9. Official Baseball Rules (Definitions of Terms: Infield Fly) (Comment).

10. Kaduk, Yahoo!Sports.

11. Peter Morris, A Game of Inches: The Stories Behind Innovations that Shaped Baseball, at 167; *Protests Mar Game*, at 5.

12. Howard Wasserman, *In Defense of Baseball's Infield Fly Rule*, Atlantic (Oct. 12, 2012); Howard Wasserman, *The Return of the Infield Fly Rule*, Concurring Opinions (Oct. 6, 2012).

13. Guilford and Mallord, *supra*.

14. Michael Lewis, Moneyball: The Art of Winning an Unfair Game (2003).

15. Bill James, Baseball Abstract (1982); Lewis, at 82; Baseball Prospectus (2017 ed.).

16. Lewis, at 77–78, 82.

17. Rob Archer and Ben Lindbergh, *Yes, the Infield Shift Works. Probably*, FiveThirtyEight (June 30, 2016); Steve Moyer, *Baseball's 'Shift': Does It Work?*, Wall Street J. (Sept. 9, 2014).

18. Michael Baumann, *The End of Baseball as We Know It*, The Ringer (Aug. 3, 2017); Tom Verducci, *Baseball's pressing question: What happens to a sport when nothing happens?*, Sports Illustrated (June 20, 2017).

19. Cliff Corcoran, *New commissioner Rob Manfried's talk of banning shifts makes no sense*, SI.com (Jan. 26, 2015).

20. Official Baseball Rules § 6.01(i).

21. David Adler, *MLB announces pace of play initiatives for '18*, MLB.com (Feb. 19, 2018).

22. *MLB, union agree to use dugout signal for intentional walk*, ESPN.com (Feb. 22, 2017).

23. Official Baseball Rules § 5.04(b)(4).

24. William B. Mead, Two Spectacular Seasons: 1930: The Year the Hitters Ran Wild, 1968: The Year the Pitchers Took Revenge 190–92 (1990).

25. Guilford and Mallord, at 284–85.

26. Morris, at 167; *Aside*, at 1478–79; *Comparison of Three Rules.*

27. Dickson, *Unwritten*, at 3–5; Turbow, at 182; *Aside*, at 1476–79.

28. Turbow, at 182–84; Guilford and Mallord, at 286–87.

29. Turbow, at 184.

30. Berman, *Play*, at 1348–49.

Chapter 1

1. Morris, at 164–65.

2. *Id.*, at 165.

3. Daniel Okrent and Steve Wulf, Baseball Anecdotes 8–9 (1989); *The Red Stockings Defeated*, N.Y. Times, June 15, 1870, at 2.

4. Okrent and Wulf, at 8–9.

5. *Id.*

6. Morris, at 166.

7. *Id.* at 166; *Aside*, at 1477.

8. Morris, at 166.

9. Id., at 167.

10. *Aside*, at 1477.

11. Paul Dickson, Dickson Baseball Dictionary 445 (3d ed. 2011) (hereinafter, Dickson, Dictionary ("ice wagon").

12. *Aside*, at 1477.
13. Barry Di Salvatore, A Clever Baseball-ist: The Life and Times of John Montgomery Ward 183–84 (1999).
14. Harold Seymour, Baseball: The Early Years 286–87, 289–90 (1960).
15. Morris, at 167 (citing source).
16. *Id.*, Dickson, Dictionary, at 889, 140 ("trap ball rule"; "Brush and Von der Ahe's rule").
17. Dickson, Dictionary, at 889 ("trap ball rule"); The Baseball Encyclopedia 2239 (Joseph L. Reichler, ed.) (4th ed. 1979).
18. *Comparison of Three Rules.*
19. Official Baseball Rules (Definitions of Terms: Infield Fly).
20. *Aside*, at 1478.
21. Morris, at 167.
22. *Id.*
23. *Id.*
24. *Id.*
25. *Id.*
26. Seymour, at 276.
27. Seymour, at 275; *Aside*, at 1478.
28. *Aside*, at 1476.
29. Dickson, Unwritten, at 5.
30. Seymour, at 275–76; Morris, at 165.
31. Official Baseball Rules § 5.05(a)(1).
32. Official Baseball Rules §§ 5.05, 5.06(b) (2).
33. Official Baseball Rules § 5.09(a)(1); § 5.09(a)(1) (Catch Comment); § 5.09(c)(1) (Comment).
34. *Protests Mar Game*, at 5.
35. Morris, at 165.
36. *Id.* 167.
37. Official Baseball Rules § 5.09(b)(6).
38. *Wasps Lose a Sensational Ball Game*, San Francisco Call, Apr. 13, 1901.
39. Morris, at 167.
40. *Protests Mar Game*, at 5.
41. Official Baseball Rules (Definitions of Terms: Infield Fly).
42. Official Baseball Rules § 5.09(a)(5).
43. Official Baseball Rules (Definitions of Terms: Infield Fly) (Comment).
44. Official Baseball Rules (Definitions of Terms: Infield Fly).
45. Official Baseball Rules (Definitions of Terms: Infield Fly) (Comment).
46. Dickerson, Slate.
47. Seymour, at 276.
48. Dickson, Dictionary, at 443 ("humpback liner").
49. Bowman, MLB.com.
50. Official Baseball Rules § 5.09(a)(1).
51. Official Baseball Rules § 9.09(c)(1).
52. Marazzi, at 23.
53. Official Baseball Rules §§ 5.05, 5.06(b) (2).
54. Morris, at 167.
55. *Protests Mar Game*, at 5.
56. Mike Berardino, *Minnesota Twins: Um-* *pire's discretion contributes to loss*, Pioneer Press TwinCities.com (July 23, 2013).
57. Marazzi, at 22–26.
58. *Pete Kozma*, BaseballReference.com.
59. Andrew S. Gold, *Absurd Results, Scrivener's Errors, and Statutory Interpretation*, 75 U. Cin. L. Rev. 25, 30–31 (2006).
60. Richard H. Fallon, Jr., *Three Symmetries Between Textualist and Purposivist Theories of Statutory Interpretation—And the Irreducible Roles of Values and Judgment Within Both*, 99 Cornell L. Rev. 685, 704–05 (2014).
61. Lexmark Int'l, Inc. v. Static Control Components, Inc., 134 S. Ct. 1377 (2014).
62. *Twins-Angels*, BaseballReference.com (July 24, 2013).
63. Matthew Pouliot, *Isn't This Why We Have an Infield Fly Rule?*, Hardball Talk/ NBCSports (July 24, 2013).
64. Berardino, Pioneer Press TwinCities. com.
65. Adrian Garro, *The Orioles 6–4–3 triple play has an odd historical parallel-they did the exact same thing in 2000*, MLB.com (May 2, 2017).
66. Garro, MLB.com.
67. Morris, at 167.
68. Marazzi, at 23–26.
69. Dickson, Dictionary, at 919–20 ("walk off").
70. Dickson, Unwritten, at 1; Turbow, at 8–9.
71. Marazzi, at 23–25.
72. Official Baseball Rules § 5.09(a)(12); *Comparison of Three Rules.*
73. Official Baseball Rules § 5.09(a)(12) (Approved Ruling).
74. Guilford & Mallord, at 287.n29.
75. Tim Cato, *Ian Kinsler intentionally dropped a ball instead of catching it, and it was brilliant*, SB Nation (Apr. 18, 2016).
76. *Aside*, at 1476.
77. Morris, at 167.
78. David Schoenfield, *Five worst umpiring calls in history*, ESPN.com (June 13, 2012).

Chapter 2

1. Morris, at 167; *Aside*, at 1476, 1478.
2. Guilford and Mallord, at 283; *Aside*, at 1477.
3. Dickson, Unwritten, at 5.
4. Turbow, at 184.
5. *Id.* at 182.
6. Guilford and Mallord, at 283–84, 286.
7. Turbow, at 182.
8. Dickson, Unwritten, at 24–25; Turbow, at 182.
9. Guilford and Mallord, at 286–87.

10. DICKSON, DICTIONARY, at 408 ("hidden ball trick").

11. *Id.* 175–76 ("changeup")

12. *Id.* 408 ("hidden ball trick") (third definition).

13. Official Baseball Rules § 6.02(a)(2) (3); § 6.02(a)(3)(Official Comment); Guilford and Mallord, at 287 n.27.

14. DICKSON, UNWRITTEN, at 80–81 (R. 1.18.0); TURBOW, at 159.

15. DICKSON, UNWRITTEN, AT 83 (R. 1.18.2.3); TURBOW, at 179; JOSHUA PRAGER, ECHOING GREEN: THE UNTOLD STORY OF BOBBY THOMPSON, RALPH BRANCA, AND THE SHOT HEARD ROUND THE WORLD 31–32 (2006).

16. DICKSON, UNWRITTEN, at 4–6.

17. Guilford and Mallord, at 287 n.27.

18. TURBOW, at 182.

19. Guilford and Mallord, at 286.

20. Oona Hathaway, *Path Dependence in the Law: The Course and Pattern of Legal Change in a Common Law System*, 86 IOWA L. REV. 601, 604, 609 (2001).

21. Guilford and Mallord, at 289.

22. *Aside*, at 1476.

23. *Protests Mar Game*, at 5.

24. MORRIS, at 165, 167; SEYMOUR, at 275–76.

25. MORRIS, at 167.

26. Berman, *Play*, at 1348–49.

27. Cato, SBNation, *Ian Kinsler intentionally dropped a ball instead of catching it, and it was brilliant*, SB NATION (Apr. 18, 2016).

28. *Twins-Angels*, BASEBALLREFERENCE.COM (July 24, 2013).

29. Guilford and Mallord, at 284–85.

30. *Id.*

31. Official Baseball Rules § 6.02(a)(2) (3); § 6.02(a)(3)(Official Comment).

32. For 2016, fielding percentage for all Major League first basemen was .994 percent, second basemen was .984 percent, shortstops was .975 percent, and third basemen was .957 percent. *Team and League Fielding*, BASEBALL-REFERENCE.COM.

33. MORRIS, at 167.

34. Guilford and Mallord, at 284–85.

35. *Id.* 287–88.

36. *Win Expectancy (WE) and Run Expectancy (RE) Stats*, BASEBALLREFERENCE.COM.

37. All calculations were made through the Custom Statistics Report feature at Baseball Prospectus. *Baseball Prospectus*, http://www.baseballprospectus.com/sortable/index.php?cid=975409.

38. *Rickey Henderson*, BASEBALLREFERENCE.COM.

39. *Prince Fielder*, BASEBALLREFERENCE.COM.

40. LEWIS, at 77–78, 129.

41. Cato, SB NATION.

42. *Aside*, at 1477.

43. OKRENT AND WULF, at 8–9.

44. Official Baseball Rules § 5.09(a)(12) and (Official Ruling).

45. DICKSON, DICTIONARY, at 443 ("humpback liner").

46. *Protests Mar Game*, at 5.

47. DICKSON, DICTIONARY, at 733 ("sacrifice bunt").

48. *Id.* 927–28 ("wheel").

49. MARAZZI, at 25 (describing similar bunt triple play in a 1972 Minor League game).

50. Official Baseball Rules § 5.06(c)(5).

51. Official Baseball Rules (Definitions of Terms: Infield Fly).

52. Official Baseball Rules (Definitions of Terms: Infield Fly) (Comment).

53. Guilford and Mallord, at 284–85.

54. MORRIS, at 167.

55. *Infra* Chapter 5.

56. *Aside*, at 1476.

57. Adam F. Scales, *Against Settlement Factoring? The Market in Tort Claims Has Arrived*, 2002 WIS. L. REV. 839, 926; Mark Tushnet, *New Forms of Judicial Review and the Persistence of Rights-and Democracy-Based Worries*, 38 WAKE FOREST L. REV. 813, 835 (2003).

58. Richard A. Posner, *A Theory of Negligence*, 1 J. LEGAL STUD. 29, 32–33 (1972).

59. Kevin M. Clermont, *Jurisdictional Fact*, 91 CORNELL L. REV. 873, 1000 (2006); David Freeman Engstrom, *Agencies as Litigation Gatekeepers*, 123 YALE L.J. 616, 683 n.22 (2013); Alan A. Fisher and Robert H. Lande, *Efficiency Considerations in Merger Enforcement*, 71 CAL. L. REV. 1582, 1586, 1669, 1671 (1983).

60. Fisher and Lande, at 1586.

61. Official Baseball Rules § 5.06(b)(4)(F).

62. Official Baseball Rules § 5.09(a)(12).

63. Official Baseball Rules § 5.09(a)(12) (Approved Ruling).

64. *See supra* n.32.

Chapter 3

1. Official Baseball Rules § 5.09(a)(2), (3); § 5.09(a)(2) (Comment).

2. Official Baseball Rules § 5.05(a)(2); § 5.05(a)(2) (Comment).

3. JACK NORWORTH AND ALBERT VON TILZER, TAKE ME OUT TO THE BALLGAME (York Music Co. 1908).

4. *Comparison of Three Rules*; David Wade, *Inside the Rules: It's Not a Dropped Third Strike*, HARDBALL TIMES (Nov. 16, 2010).

5. MARAZZI, at 129; Richard Goldstein, *Mickey Owen Dies at 89; Allowed Fateful Passed Ball*, N.Y. TIMES, July 15, 2005.

6. MORRIS, at 167.

7. Guilford and Mallord, at 284. Judge Guilford elaborated on this point in several email exchanges.

8. Guilford and Mallord, at 290.

9. Judge Guilford made this point in our email exchanges.

10. Official Baseball Rules § 9.15(a)(3).

11. Official Baseball Rules (Definitions of Terms: Catch); (Definitions of Terms: Catch) (Comment).

12. Dave Cameron, *Baseball's New Strategy: Drop the Ball on Purpose*, FANGRAPHS (Apr. 14, 2014); *New 2014 Rule Interpretation: Catch/ Transfer Explained*, CLOSECALLSPORTS (Apr. 9, 2014).

13. Cameron, FANGRAPHS.

14. Press Release, *Playing Rules Committee reviews interpretation of transfer play*, MLB.COM (Apr. 25, 2014).

15. DICKSON, DICTIONARY, at 643 ("pitcher's Best Friend"), 898 ("twin killing").

16. Franklin Pierce Adams, *Baseball's Sad Lexicon*, NEW YORK EVENING MAIL, July 10, 1910.

17. John Walsh, *The worst thing a batter can do*, HARDBALL TIMES (Mar. 20, 2009).

18. *Custom Statistics Report: Run Expectancy*, BASEBALL PROSPECTUS.

19. Official Baseball Rules § 5.06(c)(5).

20. Official Baseball Rules § 5.08(a).

21. Sam Miller, *'Skunk in the Outfield': How the most epic trick play in history broke baseball*, ESPN.COM (Aug. 17, 2017).

22. Official Baseball Rules § 5.02(a); DICKSON, DICTIONARY, at 457 ("intentional base on balls").

23. Adam Kilgore, *Bryce Harper's walks mean unique pressure for Ryan Zimmerman*, WASH. POST, May 9, 2016.

24. Jay Jaffe, *Despite Hall of Fame's Wishes, Barry Bonds is Trending Towards Induction*, SI.COM, Dec. 12, 2017.

25. *Barry Bonds*, BASEBALLREFERENCE.COM.

26. LEWIS, at 77.

27. Harold Friend, *Baseball History: Dick Williams Embarrassed Johnny Bench*, BLEACHER REPORT (Aug. 19, 2010).

28. *MLB, union agree to use dugout signal for intentional walk*, ESPN.COM (Feb. 22, 2017).

29. Official Baseball Rules § 9.08(d); DICKSON, DICTIONARY, at 733 ("sacrifice fly").

30. DICKSON, DICTIONARY, at 735 ("safety squeeze"), 818 ("squeeze play"), 840 ("suicide squeeze").

31. *Id.* 733 ("sacrifice bunt").

32. *Id* 414 ("hit-and-run play").

33. *Id* 647 ("pitchout").

34. Cohen and Waller, at 458.

35. BULL DURHAM (Orion Pictures 1988).

36. Official Baseball Rules § 7.01(c)(1)-(3).

37. LAWS OF CRICKET Law 14 (5th ed. 2013).

Chapter 4

1. Adler, MLB.COM.

2. Official Playing Rules of the National Football League Rule 4–4(c) (f).

3. NFL Rules R. 4–5–1–1.

4. Official Rules of the National Basketball Association R.12B-I-Penalties (3) (4) (5).

5. NBA Rules R.7-IV(d)(1); R.12B-I-Penalties (2).

6. *That stubborn final minute of regulation*, INPREDICTABLE (Apr. 19, 2014); *How long is each minute of NBA game time?*, INPREDICTABLE (Apr. 13, 2014).

7. The problem is worse in high-school basketball, which is played without a shot clock. Team W could hold the ball without shooting for the remainder of the game.

8. Ray Glier, *Does the Ending Need Rewriting?*, N.Y. TIMES, Mar. 23, 2010.

9. NCAA Men's Basketball Rulebook R. 8, § 2, art. 1–2 (2013–15); Glier, N.Y. TIMES.

10. Zach Lowe, *NBA watching the Basketball Tournament's innovative approach to crunch time*, ESPN.COM (Apr. 5, 2017).

11. Barry Patchesky, *Here's a Perfectly Executed "Miss the Free Throw, Score the Putback" to Send a Game to 3 OT*, DEADSPIN (Feb. 13, 2013).

12. John Ezekowitz, *Up Three, Time Running Out: The First Comprehensive CBB Analysis*, HARVARD SPORTS ANALYSIS COLLECTIVE (Aug. 24, 2010); Adrian Lawhorn, *"3-D": Late-Game Defensive Strategy with a 3-Point Lead*, 82GAMES.COM; Ken Pomeroy, *Yet another study about fouling when up 3*, KENPOM.COM (Feb. 12, 2013).

13. *Shaquille O'Neal*, BASKETBALLREFERENCE.COM.

14. Matt Femrite, *Examining the state of Hack-a-Shaq*, NYLONCALCULUS (Apr. 26, 2016).

15. John Ezekowitz, *Intentionally Fouling DeAndre Jordan Is Futile*, FIVETHIRYEIGHT (Apr. 29, 2104).

16. NBA Rules R.12B-X-a(1).

17. NBA Rules R.12B-VIII.

18. Femrite, NYLON CALCULUS.

19. *Detroit Pistons at Houston Rockets Play-by-Play*, BASKETBALL-REFERENCE.COM (Jan. 20, 2016).

20. NBA Rules R.12B-V-a(1) (2).

21. Ezekowitz, FIVETHIRTYEIGHT.

22. *Aside*, at 1476.

23. J.A. Adande, *Who wins from 'Hack-a-Shaq' strategy?*, ESPN.COM (Feb. 20, 2015).

24. Nick Friedell, *Gregg Popovich hates foul strategy*, ESPN.com (Jan. 30, 2014).

25. Jerry Brown, *Shaq Gets Last Laugh on Spurs' Joke of Early Foul*, NBA.com (Oct. 28, 2008).

26. NBA Rules R.12B-X-a.

27. Kevin Draper, *The NBA Is Finally Getting Rid of Hack-a-Player*, DEADSPIN (July 13, 2016); Ohm Youngmisuk, *NBA tries to curb 'hack a' strategy by tweaking away-from-play rules*, ESPN.com (July 13, 2016); *NBA announces rule changes to 'Hack-a' fouls*, SI.com (July 13, 2016);

28. Draper, DEADSPIN.

29. NBA Rules R. R.4-III-g; R.12B-X-c-1; R.12B-IV.

30. NFL Rules R.3-9.

31. Jason Scheib, *Never Punting*, FOOTBALL OUTSIDERS (Aug. 10, 2006).

32. Adam Kilgore, *The highly successful high school coach who never punts has another radical idea*, WASH. POST, Aug. 13, 2015.

33. NFL Rules R. 7-4-2.

34. NFL Rules R. 12-1-3(c).

35. NFL Rules R. 8-5.

36. NFL Rules R.5-1-1.

37. *Super Bowl XLVI-New York Giants vs. New England Patriots*, PROFOOTBALLREFERENCE.COM (Feb. 5, 2012).

38. RICH COHEN, MONSTERS: THE 1985 CHICAGO BEARS AND THE WILD HEART OF FOOTBALL (2013).

39. NFL Rules R.14-2-1.

40. Consentino; *Buddy Ryan's Polish Goalline tactic*, SMART FOOTBALL (Oct. 19, 2011).

41. NFL Rules R.5-1-1.

42. NFL Rules R.4-3-2(e).

43. NFL Rules R.4-3-2(e)(1) (2).

44. NFL Rules R.4-7-1; 4-7-1(8) (Penalty).

45. NRL Rules R. 7-4-3.

46. NFL Rules R. 7-4-2.

47. NFL Rules R. 8-4-6.

48. NFL Rules R.12-1-6.

49. *New Orleans Saints at Atlanta Falcons*, PROFOOTBALLREFERENCE.COM (Nov. 21, 2013).

50. Bill Pennington, *Untangling Pileup of Miscues in Giants' Loss*, N.Y. TIMES, Sept. 14, 2015.

51. *New York Giants at Dallas Cowboys*, PROFOOTBALLREFERENCE.COM (Sept. 13, 2015).

52. NFL Rules R. 8-4-6 (Penalty).

53. ADVANCED NFL STATS, http://www.advancednflstats.com (last visited Jan. 6, 2014); FOOTBALL OUTSIDERS, http://www.footballoutsiders.com/.

54. Conor McGovern, *A Closer Look at Touchdowns in the Red Zone*, FOOTBALL OUTSIDERS (Apr. 19, 2013).

55. *Sortable Stats*, YAHOO! SPORTS.

56. *The Super Bowl, Bill Belichick, and Letting Your Opponent Score*, HARV. SPORTS ANALYSIS COLLECTIVE (Feb. 6, 2012).

57. Tim Keown, *Unworthy End to Super Bowl XLVI*, ESPN.com (Feb. 7, 2012).

58. NFL Rules R.3-29; R.11-5-1.

59. NFL Rules R.3-18-5-12; R.11-5-1.

60. NFL Rules R.10-2-4(b).

61. NFL Rules R.10-2-4(a), 11-4-3.

62. Barry Petchesky, *The Rarest Play in the NFL*, SLATE (Feb. 4, 2013).

63. NFL Rules R.11-5-1(a).

64. NFL Rules R.14-8-2(f).

65. Louis Bien, *Ravens intentionally committed egregious holding penalties to beat the Bengals*, SB NATION (Nov. 27, 2016); Steven Ruiz, *The Ravens masterfully run out the clock with ingenious holding tactic*, USA TODAY, Nov. 27, 2016.

66. NFL Rules R.4-8-2(c).

67. NFL Rules R.12-3-4.

68. NFL Rules R.4-8-2(b)(3).

69. Brian Tinsman, *Ravens' Take Safety Play Wasn't a 'Palpably Unfair Act,'* CBSDC (Nov. 27, 2016).

70. NFL Rules R.12-3-3.

71. Doug Farrar, *Joe Flacco told teammates to tackle Ted Ginn from the sideline during Super Bowl free kick return*, YAHOO! SPORTS (Feb. 7, 2013); Mike Florio, *Flacco urged teammates on sideline to tackle Ted Ginn*, PROFOOTBALLTALK (Feb. 7, 2013).

72. NFL Rules R.4-8-2(a).

73. Emma Carmichael, *Jeff Foster and the Brutal Art of the NBA's Playoff Foul*, DEADSPIN (Apr. 6, 2011).

74. Laws of the Game, Law 14 (Offside).

75. *World Cup 2010: Luis Suarez handball against Ghana 'instinctive,' says Uruguay coach*, TELEGRAPH (July 3, 2010).

76. Laws of the Game, Law 11.

77. *Id.*

78. FINA Swimming Rules SWH.4 (Federation Internationale de Natation 2015–2017).

79. IAAF Competition Rules R.162.6 (2016–2017).

80. FINA Swimming Rules SWH.4.

81. *IAAF Athletics Forum*, IAAF News No. 40, at 10–12 (Apr. 2000) (debating whether IAAF should change false start rule).

82. USATF Competition Rules R.162.12 (2009).

83. IAAF Competition Rules R.162.6 (2016–17).

84. Jeff Eisenberg, *The Cruelest Rule in Sports: Track and Field's Zero-Tolerance False Start Policy*, YAHOO! SPORTS (July 19, 2012); Alex Thomas, *Is it time to change false-start rules?*, CNN WORLD SPORT (Aug. 29, 2011).

85. Thomas, CNN WORLD SPORT.

86. IAAF Rules R.162.6 (Note (i)).

Chapter 5

1. *Infield Fly? Easy!*, Little League Online. To the extent fewer balls are presumptively catchable by 11-year-olds, the Rule defines ordinary effort to account for the "league or classification of leagues" involved. Official Baseball Rules (Definitions: Ordinary Effort).

2. *Infield Fly Controversy Mars Tension Filled Baseball Grudge Match*, Rocket News 24 (July 16, 2012).

3. Richard J. Evans, Altered Pasts: Counterfactuals In History (2013); Cass R. Sunstein, *What if Counterfactuals Never Existed?*, New Republic (Sept. 20, 2014).

4. Official Baseball Rules § 9.09(c)(1).

5. *Cardinals-Braves Play-by-Play*, ESPN.com (Oct. 5, 2012).

6. *2012 National League Wild Card Game*, BaseballReference.com (Oct. 5, 2012).

7. *St. Louis Cardinals 6, Atlanta Braves 3*, RetroSheet (Oct. 5, 2012).

8. *Id.*

9. http://mlb.mlb.com/mediacenter/index.jsp?c_id=mlb.

10. Guilford and Mallord, at 284–85.

11. I gathered this information from the web site BaseballReference.com, using the Play Index/Batting Events tool, narrowing the search to first-and-second/none out.

12. Guilford & Mallord, at 284.

13. *Win Expectancy (WE) and Run Expectancy (RE) Stats*, Baseball-Reference.com.

14. *Win Expectancy (WE) and Run Expectancy (RE) Stats*, Baseball-Reference.com.

15. Guilford and Mallord begin their article critiquing the Infield Fly Rule with this base-out-inning situation, in Game 7 of the World Series. Guilford and Mallord, at 281–83.

Bibliography

Books

Appel, Marty. Pinstripe Empire: The New York Yankees from Before the Babe to After the Boss (New York: Bloomsbury 2012).

Cohen, Rich. Monsters: The 1985 Chicago Bears and the Wild Heart of Football (New York: Farrar, Strauss, and Giroux 2013).

Di Salvatore, Barry. A Clever Baseball-ist: The Life and Times of John Montgomery Ward (Baltimore: Johns Hopkins University Press 1999).

Dickson, Paul. Dickson Baseball Dictionary (New York: W.W. Norton 3d ed. 2011).

Dickson, Paul. The Unwritten Rules of Baseball: The Etiquette, Conventional Wisdom, and Axiomatic Codes of Our National Pastime (New York: Harper 2009).

Evans, Richard J. Altered Pasts: Counterfactuals in History (Waltham: Brandeis University Press 2013).

James, Bill. Baseball Abstract (New York: Ballantine 1982).

Lewis, Michael. Moneyball: The Art of Winning an Unfair Game (New York: Norton 2003).

Marazzi, Rich. The Rules and Lore of Baseball (New York: Stein and Day 1980).

Mead, William B. Two Spectacular Seasons: 1930: The Year the Hitters Ran Wild, 1968: The Year the Pitchers Took Revenge (1990).

Morris, Peter. A Game of Inches: The Stories Behind the Innovations that Shaped Baseball (Chicago: Ivan R. Dee 2010).

Okrent, Daniel, and Steve Wulf. Baseball Anecdotes (New York: Oxford University Press 1989).

Prager, Joshua. Echoing Green: The Untold Story of Bobby Thompson, Ralph Branca, and the Shot Heard Round the World (New York: Simon & Schuster 2006).

Reichler, Joseph L., ed. The Baseball Encyclopedia (London: Macmillan 1979) (4th ed.).

Seymour, Harold. Baseball: The Early Years (New York: Oxford University Press 1960).

Turbow, Jason, with Michael Duca. The Baseball Codes: Beanballs, Sign Stealing, & Bench-Clearing Brawls: The Unwritten Rules of America's Pastime (New York: Anchor Books 2010).

Waller, Spencer Weber, Neil B. Cohen, and Paul Finkelman, eds. Baseball and the American Legal Mind (New York: Garland 1995).

Articles

Aside: *The Common Law Origins of the Infield Fly Rule*, 123 U. Pa. L. Rev. 1474 (1975).

Berman, Mitchell N. *"Let 'Em Play": A Study in the Jurisprudence of Sport*, 99 Geo. L.J. 1325 (2011).

Berman, Mitchell N. *Replay*, 99 Cal. L. Rev. 1683 (2011).

Chemerinsky, Erwin. *Seeing the Emperor's Clothes: Recognizing the Reality of Constitutional Decision Making*, 86 B.U. L. Rev. 1069 (2006).

Clermont, Kevin M. *Jurisdictional Fact*, 91 Cornell L. Rev. 873 (2006).

Cohen, Neil B., and Spencer Weber Waller. *Taking Pop-Ups Seriously: The Jurisprudence of the Infield Fly Rule*, 82 Wash. U. L.Q. 453 (2004).

D'Amato, Anthony. *The Contribution of the Infield Fly Rule to Western Civilization (and Vice Versa)*, 100 Nw. U. L. Rev. 189 (2006).

Engstrom, David Freeman. *Agencies as Litigation Gatekeepers*, 123 Yale L.J. 616 (2013).

Fallon, Richard H., Jr., *Three Symmetries Between Textualist and Purposivist Theories of Statutory Interpretation—And The Irreducible Roles of Values and Judgment Within Both*, 99 Cornell L. Rev. 685 (2014).

Fisher, Alan A., and Robert H. Lande. *Efficiency Considerations in Merger Enforcement*, 71 Cal. L. Rev. 1582 (1983).

Gold, Andrew S. *Absurd Results, Scrivener's Errors, and Statutory Interpretation*, 75 U. Cin. L. Rev. 25 (2006).

Guilford, Andrew J., and Joel Mallord. *A Step Aside: Time to Drop the Infield Fly Rule and End a Common Law Anomaly*, 164 U. Pa. L. Rev. 281 (2015).

Hathaway, Oona. *Path Dependence in the Law: The Course and Pattern of Legal Change in a Common Law System*, 86 Iowa L. Rev. 601 (2001).

Posner, Richard A. *The Role of the Judge*, 86 B.U. L. Rev. 1049 (2006).

Posner, Richard A. *A Theory of Negligence*, 1 J. Legal Stud. 29 (1972).

Primus, Richard A. Bolling *Alone*, 104 Colum. L. Rev. 975 (2004).

Scales, Adam F. *Against Settlement Factoring? The Market in Tort Claims Has Arrived*, 2002 Wis. L. Rev. 839 (2002).

Siegel, Neil S. *Umpires at Bat: On Integration and Legitimation*, 24 Const. Comment. 701 (2006).

Sunstein, Cass R. *What If Counterfactuals Never Existed?*, New Republic (Sept. 20, 2014).

Tushnet, Mark. *New Forms of Judicial Review and the Persistence of Rights-and Democracy-Based Worries*, 38 Wake Forest L. Rev. 813 (2003).

Wasserman, Howard M. *Just a Bit Aside: Perverse Incentives, Cost-Benefit Imbalances, and the Infield Fly Rule*, 164 U. Pa. L. Rev. Online 145 (2016).

Yablon, Charles. *On the Contribution of Baseball to American Legal Theory*, 104 Yale L.J. 227 (1994).

www.ingramcontent.com/pod-product-compliance
Ingram Content Group UK Ltd.
Pitfield, Milton Keynes, MK11 3LW, UK
UKHW041355190726
13851UKWH00014B/120